THE VARMINT

By Owen Johnson

Lawrenceville Stories

THE PRODIGIOUS HICKEY
THE VARMINT
THE TENNESSEE SHAD
SKIPPY BEDELLE

STOVER AT YALE
THE WASTED GENERATION
BLUE BLOOD
CHILDREN OF DIVORCE

"LIKE MY JIBS?" SAID STOVER

THE VARMINT

A LAWRENCEVILLE STORY

BY

OWEN JOHNSON

AUTHOR OF "THE TENNESSEE SHAD," "STOVER AT YALE," ETC.

WITH ILLUSTRATIONS BY

F. R. GRUGER

WILDSIDE PRESS

TO
Alexander Lambert, M.D.
IN FRIENDSHIP, IN GRATITUDE,
AND IN MEMORY OF MY WIFE.

LIST OF ILLUSTRATIONS.

	OPPOSITE PAGE
"LIKE MY JIBS?" SAID STOVER	*Frontispiece*
"WHY, SOME OF 'EM ARE SO SLICK .... I LOCK UP THE CASH DRAWER"	54
"CRACKY, WHAT A PRIZE! SAY, I'D LIKE TO MAKE A BID MYSELF"	70
"BEHIND HIM, PELLMELL, SHRIEKING AND MURDEROUS .... CAME THE VANQUISHED"	86
"EACH MEMBER OF THE OUTRAGED NINE CLIMBED TO THE TRANSOM"	88
"NOTHING IN YOUR CAREER HAS INDICATED TO ME YOUR FITNESS FOR SUCH A RESPONSIBILITY"	344

THE VARMINT

THE VARMINT

I

When young Stover disembarked at the Trenton station on the fourth day after the opening of the spring term he had acquired in his brief journey so much of the Pennsylvania rolling stock as could be detached and concealed. Inserted between his nether and outer shirts were two gilt "Directions to Travelers" which clung like mustard plasters to his back, while a jagged tin sign, wrenched from the home terminal, embraced his stomach with the painful tenacity of the historic Spartan fox. In his pockets were objects—small objects but precious and dangerous to unscrew and acquire.

Being forced to wait, he sat now, preternaturally stiff, perched on a heap of trunks, clutching a broken dress-suit case which had been re-enforced with particolored strings.

There was about young Stover, when properly washed, a certain air of cherubim that instantly struck the observer; his tousled tow hair had a cathedral tone, his cheek was guileless and his big blue eyes had an upward cast toward the angels which, as in the present moment when he

THE VARMINT

was industriously exchanging a check labeled Baltimore to a trunk bound for Jersey City, was absolutely convincing. But from the limit whence the cherub continueth not the imp began. His collar was crumpled and smutty with the descent of many signs, a salmon-pink necktie had quarreled with a lavender shirt and retreated toward one ear, one cuff had broken loose and one sulked up the sleeve. His green serge pockets bulged in every direction, while the striped blue-and-white trousers, already outgrown, stuck to the knees and halted short of a pair of white socks that in turn disappeared into a pair of razor-pointed patent-leathers.

Young Stover's career at Miss Wandell's Select Academy for boys and girls had been a tremendous success, for it had ended in a frank confession on Miss Wandell's part that her limited curriculum was inadequate for the abnormal activities of dangerous criminals.

As Stover completed the transfer of the last trunk-checks the stage for Lawrenceville plodded cumbrously up, and from the box Jimmy hailed him.

"Eh, there, young Sporting Life, bound for Lawrenceville? Step lively."

Stover swung up, gingerly pushing ahead of him the battered bag.

THE VARMINT

"Lawrenceville?" said the driver, looking at it suspiciously.

"Right the first time."

"What house?"

"Oh, the Green will be good enough for me."

"Well, tuck in above."

"Thanks, I'll cuddle here," said Stover, slipping into the seat next to him, "just to look over the way you handle the ribbons and see if I approve."

Jimmy, connoisseur of new arrivals, glanced behind at the only other passenger, a man of consular mould, and then looked at Stover in sardonic amusement.

"Don't look at me like that, old Sport," said Stover impressively; "I've driven real coaches, sixteen horses, rip-snorters, and all that sort of thing."

Jimmy, having guided the placid animals through the labyrinths of Trenton, gave them the rein on the long highway that leads to Lawrenceville and turned to examine Stover with new relish.

"Say, Bub," he said at length, "you're goin' to have a great time at this little backwoods school—you're going to enjoy yourself."

"Think I'm fresh, eh?"

"Fresh?" said Jimmy thoughtfully. "Why, fresh ain't at all the word."

THE VARMINT

"Well, I can take care of myself."

"What did they fire you for?" said Jimmy, touching up the horses.

"Who said they fired me?" said Stover, surprised.

"Well, what was it?" said Jimmy, disdaining an explanation.

"They fired me," said Stover, hesitating a moment—"they fired me for trying to kill a man."

"You don't say so!"

"I drew a knife on him," said Stover rapidly. "I'd 'a' done for him, too, the coward, if they hadn't hauled me off."

At this there was a chuckle from the passenger behind who said with great solemnity:

"Dear me, dear me, a dreadful state of affairs—quite thrilling."

"I saw red, everything—everything red," said Stover, breathing hard.

"What had he done to you?" said Jimmy, winking at Mr. Hopkins, alias Lucius Cassius, alias The Roman, master of the Latin line and distinguished flunker of boys.

"He insulted my—my mother."

"Your mother?"

"She—she's dead," said Stover in a stage voice he remembered.

THE VARMINT

At this Jimmy and Mr. Hopkins stopped, genuinely perplexed, and looked hard at Stover.

"You don't mean it! Dear me," said The Roman, hesitating before a possible blunder.

"It was long ago," said Stover, thrilling with the delight of authorship. "She died in a shipwreck to save me."

The Roman was nonplussed. There was always the possibility that the story might be true.

"Ah, she gave her life to save yours, eh?" he said encouragingly.

"Held my head above water, breeches buoy and all that sort of thing," said Stover, remembering something in Dickens. "I was the only one saved, me and the ship's cat."

"Well, well," said The Roman, with a return of confidence; "and your father—is he alive?"

"Yes," said Stover, considering the distant woods; "but—but we don't speak of him."

"Ah, pardon me," said The Roman, gazing on him with wonder. "Painful memories—of course, of course. And what happened to your brother?"

Stover, perceiving the note of skepticism, turned and looked The Roman haughtily in the face, then, turning to Jimmy, he said in a half whisper:

"Who's the old buck, anyhow?"

THE VARMINT

Jimmy stiffened on the box as though he had received an electric shock; then, biting his lips, he answered with a vicious lunge at the horses:

"Oh, he comes back and forth every now and then."

They were now in the open country, rolling steadily past fields of sprouting things, with the warm scent of new-plowed earth borne to them on the gentle April breeze.

All of a sudden Stover seemed to dive sideways from the coach and remained suspended by his razor-tipped patent-leathers.

"Hi, there!" cried Jimmy, bringing the coach to a stop with a jerk, "what are you trying to do?"

Stover reappeared.

"Seeing if there are any females inside."

"What's that to you?" said Jimmy indignantly.

"Keep your eye peeled and I'll show you," said the urchin, standing up, freeing his belt and unbuttoning his vest. In a moment, by a series of contortions, he drew forth the three signs and proudly displayed them.

"See these gilt ones," he said confidentially to the astounded Roman, "got 'em in the open car; stood right up and unscrewed them— penal offense, my boy. The tin one was easier, but it's a beaut. 'No loitering on these premises.' Cast your eye over that," he added, passing it to The Roman, who, as he gravely received it, gave Jimmy a dig that cut short a fit of coughing.

"Pretty fine, eh?" said Stover.

"Em, yes, quite extraordinary—quite so."

"And what do you think of these?" continued Stover, producing two silver nickel-plated knobs ravished from the washbasin. "'Pull and Push'—that's my motto. Say, Bill, how does that strike you?"

The Roman examined them and handed them back.

"You'll find it rather—rather slow at the school, won't you?"

"Oh, I'll put ginger into it."

"Indeed."

"What's your line of goods, old Sport?" said Stover, examining Mr. Hopkins with a knowing eye.

"Books," said The Roman with a slight jerk of his thin lips.

"I see!"

Jimmy stopped the horses and went behind, ostensibly to see if the door was swinging.

"Let me drive?" said Stover, fidgeting after a moment's contemplation of Jimmy's method. "I'll show you a thing or two."

"Oh, you will, will you?"

THE VARMINT

"Let's have 'em."

Jimmy looked inquiringly at Mr. Hopkins and, receiving a nod, transferred the reins and whip to Stover, who immediately assumed a Wild West attitude and said patronizingly:

"Say, you don't get the speed out of 'em."

"I don't, eh?"

"Naw."

They were at that moment reaching the brink of a hill, with a sharp though short descent below.

"In my country," said Stover professionally, "we call a man who uses a brake a candy dude. The trick is to gallop 'em down the hills. Hang on!"

Before he could be stopped he sprang up with an ear-splitting war-whoop and brought the whip down with a stinging blow over the ears of the indignant horses, who plunged forward with a frightened leap. The coach rose and rocked, narrowly missing overturning in its sudden headlong course. Jimmy clamped on the brakes, snatched the reins and brought the plunging team to a stop after narrowly missing the gutter. Stover, saved from a headlong journey only by the iron grip of The Roman, had a moment of horrible fear. But immediately recovering his self-possession he said gruffly:

"All right, let go of me."

THE VARMINT

"What in blazes were you trying to do, you young anarchist?" cried Jimmy, turning on him wrathfully.

"Gee! Why don't you drive a couple of cows?" said Stover in disgust. "Why, in my parts we alway drive on two wheels."

"Two wheels!" said Jimmy scornfully. "Guess you never drove anything that did have four wheels but a baby-buggy."

But Stover, as though discouraged, disdained to reply, and sat in moody silence.

The Roman, who was still interested in a possible brother or two, strove in vain to draw him out. Stover wrapped himself in a majestic silence. Despite himself, the mystery of the discoverer was upon him. His glance fastened itself on the swelling horizon for the school that suddenly was to appear.

"How many fellows have you got here?" he said all at once to Jimmy.

"About four hundred."

"As much as that?"

"Sure."

"Big fellows?"

"Sizable."

"How big?"

"Two-hundred-pounders."

"When do we see the school?"

"Top of next hill."

THE VARMINT

The Roman watched him from the corner of his eye, interested in his sudden shift of mood.

"What kind of a football team did they have?" said Stover.

"Scored on the Princeton 'Varsity."

"Jemima! You don't say so!"

"Eight to four."

"Great Heavens!"

"Only game they lost."

"The Princeton championship team, too," said Stover, who was not deficient in historical athletics. "Say, how's the nine shaping up?"

"It's a winner."

All at once Jimmy extended his whip. "There it is, over there—you'll get the water tower first."

Stover stood up reverentially. Across the dip and swell of the hills a cluster of slated roofs, a glimpse of red brick through the trees, a touch of brownstone, a water tower in sharp outline against the sky, suddenly rose from the horizon. A continent had been discovered, the land of possible dreams.

"It's ripping—ripping, isn't it?" he said, still standing eagerly.

The Roman, gazing on it for the thousandth time, shook his head in musing agreement.

Across the fields came the stolid ringing of the school bell, ringing a hundred laggards

THE VARMINT

across the budding campus to hard seats and blackboarded walls, ringing with its lengthened, slow-dying, never-varying note.

"That the bell?" said Stover, rebelling already at its summons.

"That's it," said Jimmy.

Stover sat down, his chin in his hands, his elbows on his knees, gazing eagerly forward, asking questions.

"I say, where's the Green House?"

"Ahead on your left—directly."

"That old, stone, block-house affair?"

"You win."

"Why, it's not on the campus."

"No, it ain't," said Jimmy, flicking the flies off the near horse; "but they've got a warm bunch of Indians all the same." Then, remembering the Wild-Western methods of driving, he added: "Don't forget about the ginger. Sock it to them. Fare, please."

"I'll sock it," said Stover with a knowing air. "I may be tender, but I'm not green."

He slapped a coin into the outstretched hand and reached back for the battle-scarred valise, to perceive the keen eye of Mr. Hopkins set on him with amusement.

"Well, Sport, ta-ta, and good luck," said Stover, who had mentally ticketed him as a commercial traveler. "Hope you sell out."

THE VARMINT

"Thanks," said Mr. Hopkins, with a twitch to his lip. "Now just one word to the wise."

"What's that?"

"Don't get discouraged."

"Discouraged!" said Stover disdainfully. "Why, old Cocky-wax, put this in your pipe and smoke it—I'm going to own this house. In a week I'll have 'em feeding from my hand."

He sprang down eagerly. Before him, at the end of a flagged walk, under the heavy boughs of evergreens, was a two-story building of stone, and under the Colonial portico a group curiously watching the new arrival.

The coach groaned and pulled heavily away. He was alone at the end of the interminable stone walk, clutching a broken-down bag ridiculously mended with strings, face to face with the task of approaching with dignity and ease these suddenly discovered critics of his existence.

II

In all his fifteen years Stover had never been accused of standing in awe of anything or anybody; but at the present moment, as he balanced from foot to foot, calculating the unending distance of the stone flags, he was suddenly seized with an overpowering impulse to bolt. And yet the group at the steps were only mildly interested. An urchin pillowed on the knees of a Goliath had shifted so as languidly to command the approach; a baseball, traveling back and forth in lazy flight, had stopped only a moment, and then continued from hand to hand.

Stover had thought of his future associates without much trepidation, as he had thought of the Faculty as Miss Wandell in trousers—being inferior to him in mental agility and resourcefulness who, he confidently intended, should shortly follow his desires.

All at once, before he had spoken a word, before he had even seen the look on their countenances, he realized that he stood on the threshold of a new world, a system of society of which he was ignorant and by whose undivined laws he was suddenly to be judged.

THE VARMINT

Everything was wrong and strangely uncomfortable. His derby hat was too small—as it was—and must look ridiculous; his trousers were short and his arms seemed to rush from his sleeves. He tried desperately to thrust back the cuff that had broken loose and stooped for his bag. It would have been wiser to have embraced it bodily, but he breathed a prayer and grasped the handle. Then he started up the walk; half way, the handle tore out and the bag went down with a crash.

He dove at it desperately, poking back the threatened avalanche of linen, and clutching it in his arms as a bachelor carries a baby, started blindly for the house.

A roar of laughter had gone up at his discomfiture, succeeded by a sudden, solemn silence. Then the White Mountain Canary pillowed against the knees of Cheyenne Baxter, spoke:

"No old clothes, Moses; nothing to sell to-day."

At this Butsey White's lathery face suddenly appeared at the second-story window.

"He doesn't want to buy—he wants to sell us something," he said. "Patent underwear and all that sort of thing."

Stover, red to the ears, advanced to the steps and stopped.

THE VARMINT

"Well?" said the Coffee-colored Angel as the guardian of the steps.

"I'm the new boy," said Stover in a gentle voice.

"The what?"

"The new boy."

"Impossible!"

"He's not!"

"New boys always say 'sir,' and take off their hats politely."

The White Mountain Canary looked at Tough McCarty, who solemnly interrogated the Coffee-colored Angel, who shook his head in utter disbelief and said:

"I don't believe it. It's a blind. I wouldn't let him in the house."

"Please, sir," said Stover hastily, doffing his derby, "I am."

"Prove it," said a voice behind him.

"Say, I'm not as green as all that."

Stover smiled a sickly smile, shifted from foot to foot and glanced hopefully at his fellow-imps to surprise a look of amusement. But as every face remained blank, serious and extremely critical, the smile disappeared in a twinkling and his glance went abruptly to his toes.

"He certainly should prove it," said the Coffee-colored Angel anxiously. "Can you prove it?"

THE VARMINT

Stover gingerly placed the gaping valise on the top step and fumbled in his pockets.

"Please, sir, I have a letter from—from the Doctor," he blurted out, finally extracting a crumpled envelope and tendering it to the Coffee-colored Angel, who looked it over with well-simulated surprise and solemnly announced:

"My goodness gracious! Why, it *is* the new boy!"

Instantly there was a change.

"Freshman, what's your name?" said little Susie Satterly in his deepest tones.

"Stover."

"Sir."

"Sir."

"What's your full name?"

"John Humperdink Stover, sir."

"Humper—what?"

"Dink."

"Say it again."

"Humperdink."

"Say it for me," said the Coffee-colored Angel, with his hand to his ear.

"Humperdink."

"Accent the last syllable."

"Humper—DINK!"

"Are you trying to bluff us, Freshman?" said Cheyenne Baxter severely.

"No, sir; that's my real name."

"Humperdink?"

"Yes, sir."

"Well, Rinky Dink, you've got a rotten name."

"Yes, sir," said Stover, who never before had felt such a longing to agree.

"How old?"

"Fifteen, sir."

"Weight?"

"One hundred and thirty, sir."

"Ever been in love?"

"No, sir."

"Ever served a penal sentence?"

"No, sir."

"Then where did you get these clothes?"

The group slowly circulated about the embarrassed Stover, scanning the amazing costume. Cheyenne Baxter took up the inquisition.

"Say, Dink, honest, are these your *own* clothes?" he said with a knowing look.

"Yes, sir."

"Now, honest," continued Cheyenne in a whisper, bending forward and putting his hand to his ear as though inviting a confidence.

Stover felt suddenly as though his own ears were swelling to alarming proportions—swelling and perceptibly reddening.

"What do they feed you on, Rinky Dink?" said the White Mountain Canary softly.

THE VARMINT

"Feed?" said Stover unwarily, not perceiving the intent of the question.

"Do they give you many green vegetables?"

Stover tried to laugh appreciatively, but the sound fizzled dolefully out.

"Because, Dink," said the White Mountain Canary earnestly, "you must not eat green vegetables, really you must not. You're green enough already."

"Why did they fire you?" said Tough McCarty.

Stover raised his eyes instinctively. There was a new accent to the inquisition, different from all the other questions he had run. He looked at Tough McCarty's stocky frame and battling eyes, and suddenly knew that he was face to face with a human being between whom and himself there could never be a question of compromise or quarter.

"Well, Freshman," said McCarty impatiently.

"What did you ask me?" said Dink purposely.

"Sir."

"Sir."

"What did they fire you for?"

"They fired me," began Stover slowly, and then stopped to reconsider. The story he had told on the coach, somehow, did not seem quite in place here. The role of firebrand and hothead, drawing villainous knives on frightened

THE VARMINT

boys, would not quite convince his present audience. To tell the truth was impossible—to admit himself the product of Miss Wandell's and coeducation would be fatal—and likewise the truth was, in his philosophy (and be this remembered), only a lazy expedient to a man of imagination. So he said slowly:

"They fired me for bringing in a couple of rattlesnakes and—and assaulting a teacher."

"My! You are a bad man, aren't you?" said Tough McCarty seriously. "I'm afraid you're too dangerous for the Green, Dink. Really I do."

"He does look devilishly wicked, Tough."

"Assaulting a teacher—how broo-tal."

"Why, Rinky Dink," said the Coffee-colored Angel sadly, "don't you know that was very wicked of you? You should love your teachers."

Stover suddenly perceived that his audience was unsympathetic.

"Don't you know you should love your teachers?"

Stover essayed a grin, then looked at the ground and stirred up a stone with his foot.

"So you're fond of rattlesnakes?" said McCarty, persisting.

"Ye-es, sir."

"Very fond?"

THE VARMINT

"I was brought up with them," said Stover, trying to fortify his position.

"You don't mean it," said McCarty, looking hard at Baxter. "Cheyenne, he's just the man to train up that little pet rattler of yours."

"Just the thing," said Cheyenne instantly; "we'll let him take out the fangs."

Stover smiled a superior smile; he was not to be caught on such tales.

"What are you smiling at, Freshman?" said McCarty immediately.

"Nothing, sir."

Butsey White, at the second-story window, scanning the road, perceived Mr. Jenkins approaching, and announced the fact, adding:

"Send him up; he belongs to me."

"Make a nice bow, Freshman," said McCarty. "Take your hat off, keep your heels together. Oh, that wasn't a very nice bow. Try again."

At this moment Jimmy, returning on the stage, reined in with a sudden interest. Stover hastily executed a series of grotesque inclinations and, grasping the clumsy valise, disappeared behind the door, hearing, as he struggled up the stairs, the roar from without that greeted his departure.

"The freshest of the fresh."

"Green all over."

"Will we tame him?"

THE VARMINT

"Oh, no!"

"And Butsey's got him."

"Humper—DINK!"

"Wow!"

As Stover reached the head of the stairs a door was thrown open and Butsey White appeared in undress uniform. The next moment Stover found himself in a large double room gorgeously decorated with flags, pennants, sporting prints and souvenirs, while through the open window came a grateful feeling of quiet and repose.

Butsey White, a roly-poly, comical fellow of sixteen or seventeen, with a shaving-brush in one hand, held out the other with an expression of lathery solicitude.

"Well, Stover, how are you? How did you leave mother and the chickens? My name's White. Mr. White, please. I'm most particular."

"How do you do, Mr. White?" said Stover, recovering some of his composure.

"There's your kennel," said Butsey White, indicating the bed. "The washtrough's over here. Bath's down the corridor. Do you snore?"

"What?" said Stover, taken back.

"Oh, never mind. If you do I'll cure you," said White encouragingly. "What did they fire you for?"

THE VARMINT

Stover, smarting at his humiliation below, seized the opportunity for revenge.

"They fired me for drinking the alcohol out of the lamps," he said with his most convincing smile.

Butsey White, who had returned to the painful task of shaving, suddenly straightened up and extended the deadly razor in angry rebuke.

"There's a little too much persiflage around here," he said sternly. "We don't like it. We prefer to see young, unripe freshmen come in on their tiptoes and answer when they're spoken to. Young Stover, you've got in wrong. You're just about the freshest cargo we've ever had. You've got a lot to learn, and I'm going to start right in educating you. Savez?"

"It was only a joke," said Stover, looking down.

"A joke! I'll attend to any joking around here," said Butsey, with a reckless wave of his razor. "There may be a few patent, nickel-plated jokes roaming around here, soon, you hadn't thought of. Now, what did they fire you for?"

"They fired me for kissing a teacher."

"A teacher?"

"The drawing teacher," said Stover hastily, perceiving the danger of the new assertion.

The old boy looked at him hard, gave a sort

THE VARMINT

of grunt and, turning his back, took up again the interrupted task of shaving. Stover, a little dismayed at his own audacity, sought to conciliate his future roommate.

"Mister White, I say, where'll I stow my duds?"

No answer.

"I'm sorry—I didn't mean to be fresh. Which is my bureau?"

The razor, suddenly extended, pointed between the windows. Stover, crestfallen, hastily sorted out the contents of his bag and silently ranged collars and neckties, waiting hopefully for a word. Suddenly he remembered the properties of the Pennsylvania Railroad and, sorting out the signs, he advanced on Butsey White, saying:

"I brought these along—thought they might help decorate the room, Mr. White."

Butsey White gazed at the three stolen signs and grunted a somewhat mollified approval.

"Got anything else?"

"A couple of sporting prints coming in the trunk, sir."

"You want to get everything you can lay your hands on when you go home. Now run on down and report to Fuzzy-Wuzzy—Mr. Jenkins. He'll be waiting for you. After lunch I'll take you up to the village and fit you out."

THE VARMINT

"I say, that's awfully good of you."

"Oh, that's all right."

"Say, I didn't mean to be fresh."

"Well, you were."

White, having carefully noted the ravages of the razor, turned from the looking-glass and surveyed the penitent Stover.

"Well, what *did* they fire you for?" he said point-blank.

"They fired me——" began Stover slowly, and stopped.

"Out with it," said Butsey militantly.

But at that moment the voice of Mr. Jenkins summoned Stover below, and left the great question unanswered.

III

The interview with the house master was not trying. Mr. Jenkins was a short, fuzzy little man, who looked him over with nervous concern, calculating what new strain on his temper had arrived; introduced him to Mrs. Jenkins, and seized the occasion of the luncheon-bell to cut short the conversation.

At lunch Stover committed an unpardonable error which only those who have suffered can understand—he sent his plate up for a second helping of prunes.

"What in the name of peanuts did you do that for?" said Butsey in a whisper, while the Coffee-colored Angel jabbed him with his elbow and trod on his toes. "Now you *have* put your foot in it!"

Stover looked up to behold every countenance grim and outraged.

"What's wrong?" he said in a whisper.

"Wrong? Didn't you ever have prunes and skimmed milk before, thousands and thousands of times?"

"Yes, but——"

"You don't like 'em, do you?"

"Why, I don't know."

THE VARMINT

"Do you want to have them five times a week—in springtime?"

The plate, bountifully helped, returned from hand to hand down the table, laden with prunes and maledictions.

"I didn't know," Stover said apologetically.

"Well, now you know," said the Coffee-colored Angel vindictively, "don't you so much as stir 'em with your spoon. Don't you dare!"

Stover, being thus forbidden, calmly, wickedly, chuckling inwardly, emptied his plate, smacked his lips and exclaimed:

"My! those are delicious. Pass my plate up for some more, will you, Mr. White?"

"Now, why did you do that?" said Butsey White when they were alone in their room.

"I couldn't help it. I just couldn't help it," said Stover ruthfully. "It was such a joke!"

"Not from you," said Butsey White with Roman dignity. "You've got the whole darn house down on you already, and the Coffee-colored Angel will never forgive you."

"Just for that?"

Butsey White disdained an answer. Instead, he scanned Stover's clothes with critical disfavor.

"Say, if I'm going to lead you around by the hand you've got to come down on that color scheme of yours, or it's no go."

THE VARMINT

Stover, surprised, surveyed himself in the mirror.

"Why, I thought that pretty fine."

"Say, have you got a pair of trousers that's related to a coat?"

Stover dove into the trunk and produced a blue suit that passed the censor, who had in the meanwhile confiscated the razor-tipped patent-leathers and the red-visored cap, saying:

"Now you'll sink into the landscape and won't annoy the cows. Stick on this cap of mine and hoof it; you're due at the Doctor's in half an hour, and I promised old Fuzzy-Wuzzy to show you the lay of the land and give you some pointers."

Outside, Cheyenne Baxter, who was pitching curves to Tough McCarty, stopped them:

"Hello, there, Rinky Dink: turn up here sharp at four o'clock."

"What for—sir" said Stover, surprised.

"We've got a game on with the Cleve. Play baseball?"

"I—I'm a little out of practice," said Stover, who loathed the game.

"Can't help it; you're it. You play in the field. Four o'clock sharp."

"You're the ninth man in the house," Butsey explained as they started for the school. "Every one has to play. Are you any good?"

THE VARMINT

Stover was tempted to let his imagination run, but the thought of the afternoon curbed it.

"Oh, I used to be pretty fair," he said half-heartedly, plunging into the distant past.

But Stover had no desire to talk; he felt the thrill of strange sensations. Scarcely did he heed the chatter of his guide that rattled on.

The road lay straight and cool under the mingled foliage of the trees. Ahead, groups of boys crossed and recrossed in lazy saunterings.

"There's the village," said Butsey, extending his hand to the left. "First bungalow is Mister Laloo's, buggies and hot dogs. There's Bill Appleby's—say, he's a character, rolling in money—we'll drop in to see him. Firmin's store's next and the Jigger Shop's at the end."

"The Jigger Shop!" said Stover, mystified. "What's that?"

"Where they make Jiggers, of course."

"Jiggers?"

"Oh, my beautiful stars, think of eating your first Jigger!" said Butsey White, the man of the world. "What wouldn't I give to be in your shoes! I say, though, you've got some tin?"

"Sure," said Stover, sounding the coins in his change pocket.

Butsey's face brightened.

"You see, Al has no confidence in me just at

present. It's a case of the regular table d'hôte for me until the first of the month. Say, we'll have a regular gorge. It'll be fresh strawberry Jiggers, too."

They began to pass other fellows in flannels and jerseys, who exchanged greetings.

"Hello, you, Butsey!"

"Why, Egghead, howdy-do?"

"Ah, there, Butsey White!"

"Ta-ta, Saphead."

"See you later, old Sport."

"Four o'clock sharp, Texas."

Under the trees, curled in the grass, a group of three were languidly working out a Greek translation.

"Skin your eyes, Dink," said Butsey White, waving a greeting as they passed. "See the fellow this side? That's Flash Condit."

"The fellow who scored on the Princeton 'Varsity?"

"Oh, you knew, did you?"

"Sure," said Stover with pride. "Gee, what a peach of a build!"

"Turn to your left," said Butsey suddenly. "Here's Foundation House, where the Doctor lives. Just look at that doorway. Wouldn't it give you the chills?"

They were in front of a red-brick house, hidden under dark trees and overgrown with vines that congregated darkly over the porte-cochère and gave the entrance a mysterious gloom that still lives in the memory of the generations.

"It swallows you up, doesn't it?" said Dink, awed.

"You bet it does, and it's worse inside," said Butsey comfortingly. "Come on; now I'll show you the real thing."

They passed the surrounding trees and suddenly halted. Before them the campus burst upon them.

"Well, Dink, what do you think of that?" said Butsey proudly.

Stover plunged his hands in his trousers pockets and gazed awed. Before him extended an immense circle of greensward, dotted on the edge with apple trees in blossom, under which groups of boys were lolling, or tumbling over one another in joyous cublike romping. To the left, across the circle, half a dozen red-coated, slate-topped, portly houses, overgrown with ivy, were noisy with urchins hanging out of myriad windows, grouped on steps, chasing one another in twisting spirals over the lawns. Ahead, a massive brownstone chapel with pointed tower rose up, and to its right, in mathematical bulk, was the abode of Greek and Latin roots, syntax and dates, of blackboards, hard seats and the despotism of the Faculty. To the right, close at hand,

THE VARMINT

was a large three-storied building with wonderful dormer windows tucked under the slanted slate roof, and below was a long stone esplanade, black with the grouped figures of giants. At the windows, propped on sofa cushions, chin in hand some few conned the approaching lesson, softening the task by moments of dreamy contemplation of the scuffle below or stopping to catch a tennis ball that traveled from the esplanade to the window. Meanwhile, a constant buzz of inquiry and exclamation continued:

"Say, Bill, how far's the advance?"

"Middle page ninety-two."

"Gee, what a lesson!"

"You bet—it's tough!"

"Hi, there, give me a catch."

"Look out! Biff!"

"Oh, you, Jack Rabbit, come up and give me the advance!"

"Can't. I'm taking my chances. Get hold of Skinny."

"What time's practice?"

"That's the Upper House, House of Lords, Abode of the Blessed," said Butsey with envious eyes. "That's where we'll land when we're fifth-formers—govern yourself, no lights, go to the village any time, and all that sort of thing. Say!" He swept the circle comprehensively with his arm. "What do you think of it? Pretty fine, eh—what?"

"Gee!" said Stover with difficulty, then after a moment he blurted out: "It's—it's terrific!"

"Oh, that's not all; there's the Hammil House in the village and the Davis and Rouse up the street. The baseball fields are past the chapel."

"Why, it's like a small college," said Stover, whose gaze returned to the giants on the esplanade.

"Huh!" said Butsey in sovereign contempt. "We'll wipe up anything in the shape of a small college that comes around here! Do you want to toddle around the circle?"

"Oh, Lord, no!" said Stover, cold at the thought of running the inspection of hundreds of eyes. "Besides, I've got to see the Doctor."

"All right. Stand right up to him now. Don't get scared," said Butsey, choosing the one method to arouse all latent fears.

"What's he like?" said Stover, biting his nails.

"There's nothing like him," said Butsey reminiscently. "He's got an eye that gives you the creeps. He knows everything that goes on—everything."

Stover began to whistle, keeping an eye on the windows as they approached.

"Well, ta-ta! I'll hang out at Laloo's for

THE VARMINT

you," said Butsey, loping off. "Say, by the way, look out—he's a crackerjack boxer."

Stover, like Æneas at the gates of Avernus, stood under the awful portals, ruminating uneasily on Butsey's last remark. There certainly was something dark and terrifying about the place, that cast cold shadows over the cheery April day. Then the door opened, he gave his name in blundering accents to the butler, and found himself in the parlor sitting bolt-upright on the edge of a gilded chair. The butler returned, picking up his steps and, after whispering that the Doctor would see him presently, departed, stealing noiselessly away. Abandoned to the classic stillness, nothing in the room reassured him. The carpets were soft, drowning out the sounds of human feet; the walls and corridors seemed horribly stilled, as if through them no human cry might reach the outer air. All about were photographs of broken columns —cold, rigid, ruined columns, faintly discerned in the curtained light of the room. The Doctor's study was beyond, through the door by which the butler had passed. Stover's glance was riveted on it, trying to remember whether the American Constitution prohibited head masters from the brutal English practice of caning and birching; and,—listening to the lagging tick of the mantel clock, he solemnly vowed to lead that upright, impeccable life that would keep him from such another soul-racking visit.

The door opened and the Doctor appeared, holding out his hand.

Stover hastily sprang up, found himself actually shaking hands and mumbling something futile and idiotic. Then he was drawn to the horror of horrors, and the door shut out all retreat.

"Well, John, how do you like the school?"

Stover, more terrified by this mild beginning than if the Doctor had produced a bludgeon from behind his back, stammered out that he thought the buildings were handsome, very handsome.

"It's a pretty big place," said the Doctor, throwing his nervous little body back in an easy chair and studying the four-hundred-and-second problem of the year. "You'll find a good deal in it—a great many interests."

"He certainly has a wicked eye," thought Stover, watching with fascination the glance that confronted him like a brace of pistols suddenly extended from under shaggy bushes. "Now he's sizing me up—wonder if he knows all?"

"Well, John, what was the trouble?" said the Doctor from his easy, reclining position.

"The trouble, sir? Oh," said Stover, sitting

THE VARMINT

bolt-upright with every sinew stiffened. "You mean why they fired—why they expelled me, sir?"

"Yes, why did they fire you?" said the Doctor, trying to descend.

"For getting caught, sir."

The Doctor gazed at him sharply, seeking to determine whether the answer was from impertinence or fright or a precocious judgment of the morals of the nation. Then he smiled and said:

"Well, what was it?"

"Please, sir, I put asafetida in the furnace," said Stover in frightened tones.

"You put asafetida down the furnace?"

"Yes, sir."

"That was a very brilliant idea, wasn't it?"

"No, sir," said Stover, drawing a long breath and wondering if he could possibly stay after such a confession.

"Why did you do it?"

Stover hesitated, and suddenly, yielding to an unaccountable impulse toward the truth that occasionally surprised him, blurted out:

"I did it to make trouble, sir."

"You didn't like the school?"

"I hated it! There were a lot of girls around."

"Well, John," said the Doctor with heroic seriousness, "it may be that you didn't have enough to do. You have evidently an active brain—perhaps imagination would be a fitter word. As I said, you'll find this a pretty big place, just the sort of opening an ambitious boy should delight in. You'll find here all sorts of boys—boys that count, boys you respect and want to respect you, and then there are other boys who will put asafetida in the furnace if you choose to teach them chemistry."

"Oh, no, sir," said Stover, all in a gasp.

"Your parents think you are hard to manage," said the Doctor, with the wisp of a smile. "I don't. Go out; make some organization; represent us; make us proud of you; count for something! And remember one thing: if you want to set fire to Memorial Hall or to dynamite this study do it because *you* want to, and not because some other fellow puts it into your head. Stand on your own legs." The Doctor rose and extended his hand cordially. "Of course, I shall have my eye on you."

Stover, dumbfounded, rose as though on springs. The Doctor, noticing his amazement, said:

"Well, what is it?"

"Please, sir—is that all?"

"That's all," said the Doctor seriously.

Stover drew a long breath, shook hands precipitately and escaped.

IV

The spell was still on him as he stumbled over the resounding steps. But, twenty feet from the door, the spirit of irreverence overtook him. Then, at the thought of the waiting Butsey, he began to pipe forth voluminously the martial strains of Sherman's March to the Sea, kicking enormous pebbles victoriously before him.

Butsey White, sitting on the doorstep of Laloo's, gazed at him from the depths of a steaming frankfurter sandwich.

"Well, you look cheerful," he said in surprise.

"Why not?"

"How was he?"

"Gentle as a kitten."

"Come off! Were you scared?"

"Scared! Lord, no! I enjoyed myself."

"You're a cheerful liar, you are. What did he say to you?"

"Hoped I'd enjoy the place and all that sort of thing. And—oh, yes, he spoke about you."

"He did, did he?" said Butsey, precipitately leaving the frankfurter sandwich.

"He hoped I'd have a good influence on you,"

THE VARMINT

said Stover, whose imagination had been too long confined.

Butsey rose wrathfully, but the answer he intended could not be made, for, reckoning on his host, he was already in his third frankfurter, and there was the Jigger Shop yet to be visited.

"Dink, if you ever have to tell the truth," he said, "it'll kill you. Come in and meet Mr. Laloo."

Mr. Laloo was leaning gratefully on the counter—as, indeed, he was always leaning against something—his legs crossed, lazily plying the afternoon toothpick.

"Laloo, shake hands with my friend, Mr. Stover," said Butsey White professionally. "Mr. Stover's heard about your hot dogs, way out in California."

Laloo transferred the toothpick and gave Stover his hand in a tired, unenthusiastic way.

"Well, now, they do be pretty good hot dogs," he drawled out. "Suppose you want one?" He looked at Stover in sleepy reproachfulness, and then slid around the counter in the shortest parabola possible.

"Pick him out a nice, young Pomeranian," said Butsey, peering into the steaming tin.

Laloo forked a frankfurter, selected a roll and looked expectantly at Stover.

"What's the matter?" said Dink, mystified.

THE VARMINT

"Mustard or no mustard?" Butsey said in explanation. "He likes to talk, but the doctor won't let him."

"I'll have all that's coming to me," said Dink loudly.

A second later his teeth had sunk into the odorous mass. He shut his eyes, gazed seraphically at the smooty ceiling and winked at Butsey.

"Umm?" said Butsey.

"Umm! Umm!"

"Isn't he the fancy young dog-catcher?"

"Well, I should rather!" said Dink, lost in the vapors. "I say, have another?"

"Thanks, old chap, but I had a couple while you were chucking the Doctor under the chin," said Butsey glibly. "Save up now; we've got a couple more places to visit."

"How much?" said Dink.

Laloo, who was reclining against the nearest wall, elevated four fingers and gazed out the window.

"Four!" said Stover.

"One and three."

"Three!" said Butsey in feigned surprise. "Oh, come, I didn't eat three—well, I never; what do you think of that?"

Dink rubbed his ear thoughtfully, looked hard at Butsey and paid. Laloo followed them to the door, leaned against the jamb and gazed down the road.

"Now for Bill Appleby's," said Butsey cheerily. "He's rolling—rolling in wealth. We'll go in later for lamps and crockery and all that sort of thing. I thought we might sort of wash down the hot dogs before we go up to the Jigger Shop—eh, what?"

In Appleby's general merchandise store Stover gravely shook hands with a quick, businesslike little man with a Western mustache, a Down-East twang and a general air of being on the trigger.

"Well, Bill, how's business?" said Butsey affably, nudging Stover.

"It's bad, boys, it's bad," said Bill mournfully.

"Bad, you old robber," said Butsey; "why, that little iron safe of yours is just cracking open with coin. How's the rootbeer to-day?"

"It's very nice, Mr. White. Just come in this morning."

"Yes, it did! Bet it came in with the Ark," said Butsey, to Stover's great admiration. "Well, are you going to set us up to a couple of bottles, or have we got to pay for them?"

"We've got some very fine Turkish paste, Mr. White," said Bill, producing the rootbeer.

"Well?" said Butsey, looking at Stover.

"Sure!"

THE VARMINT

"I'd like to show you some of our new crockery sets, Mr. Stover," said Appleby softly. "Just come in this morning. Want a student's lamp?"

"No time now, Bill," said Butsey, hastily consulting the clock. "See you later."

Other groups came in; Appleby moved away. Stover, quenching the hot dogs in rootbeer, heard again the opening salutations:

"Well, Bill, how's business?"

"It's bad, Mr. Parsons. It's bad."

"Well, Bill, ta-ta," said Butsey, as they moved off. "Seen Doc Macnooder this morning?"

"No, Mr. White, I haven't saw him to-day."

"Always make him answer that," said Butsey chuckling, "and always ask him about business. We all do. It's e-tiquette. There's Firmin's," he said, with a wave of his hand—"post-office, country store, boots and shoes and all that sort of thing. And here's the Jigger Shop!"

Stover had no need of the explanation. Before a one-story, glass-fronted structure a swarm of boys of all ages, sizes and colors were clustered on steps and railings, or perched on posts and backs of chairs, all ravenously attacking the jigger to the hungry clink of the spoon against the glass. They elbowed their way in through the joyous, buzzing mass to where

THE VARMINT

by the counter, Al, watchdog of the jigger, scooped out the fresh strawberry ice cream and gathered in the nickels that went before. At the moment of their arrival Al was in what might be termed a defensive formation. One elbow was leaning on the counter, one hand caressed the heavy, drooping mustache, one ear listened to the promises of a ravenous, impecunious group, but the long, pointer nose and the financial eyes were dreamily plunged on the group without.

"Gee, did you ever see such an eye?" said Butsey, who had reasons of his own for quailing before it. "It's almost up to the Doctor's. You can't fool him—not for a minute. Talk about Pierpont Morgan! Why, he knows the whole blooming lot of us, just what we're worth. Why, that eye of his could put a hole right through any pocket. Watch him when he spots me." Pushing forward he exclaimed: "Hello, Al; glad to see me?"

Al turned slowly, fastening his glance on him with stony intentness.

"Don't bother me, you Butsey," he said shortly.

"Al, I've sort of set my sweet tooth on these here strawberry jiggers of yours."

The Guardian of the Jigger made a half motion in the air, as though to brush away an imaginary fly.

THE VARMINT

"Two nice, creamy, double strawberry jiggers, Al."

Al's eyes drooped wearily.

"My friend, Mr. Vanastorbilt Stover, here's setting up," said Butsey in conciliating accents.

The eyes opened and fastened on Stover, who advanced saying:

"That goes."

"Ring a couple of dimes down, Astorbilt," said Butsey. "Al's very fond of music."

"Give me change for that," said Stover, rising to the occasion with a five-dollar bill.

"And, for the love of Mike, hustle 'em," said Butsey White. "I've only got a second."

The shop began to empty rapidly as the hour of the two o'clock recitation neared. Stover gazed into the pink, fruity depths of his first strawberry jigger, inserted his spoon gingerly and took a nibble. Then he drew a long, contented breath, gazed into the land of dreams, and gave himself up to the delights of a new, of an incomparable sensation.

Butsey White, gobbling against time, flung out occasional, full-mouthed phrases:

"Got to run—'xcuse us—jemima! Isn't it the stuff—see you at three—better bring some back in box—don't tell any one, though—especially the Coffee-colored Angel."

Across the fields the bell suddenly, impatiently, brutally clanged out. With a last convulsive gulp Butsey White finished his glass, and burst from the shop in the helter-skelter company of the last laggards. Stover, left alone, looked inquiringly at Al.

"Recitation," said Al. "They've got a two-twenty sprint before the bell stops. We're out of hours, now, except for the Upper House."

"Meaning me?" said Stover, rising.

"Sit where you are," said Al. "You're all right for to-day. Where do you hang out?"

"Green House," said Dink, who, beginning to feel hungry, ordered another jigger and selected a chocolate éclair.

"You're not rooming with Butsey White?"

"The same."

"You are?" said Al pityingly. "Well, just let me give you one word of advice, young fellow. Sew your shirt to your back, or he'll have it off while you're getting into your coat."

"I wasn't born yesterday," said Dink impudently, gesturing with his spoon. "And I rather fancy I'm a pretty cute little proposition myself."

"So!"

"If any of these smart Alecs can get the best of me," said Dink grandiloquently, egged on by the other's tone of disbelief, "he'll have to get up with the chickens!"

"WHY, SOME OF 'EM ARE SO SLICK THAT WHEN THEY COME IN I LOCK THE CASH DRAWER AND STUFF COTTON IN MY EARS"

THE VARMINT

"You're pretty slick?"

"As slick as they make 'em."

"Say, bub," said Al, with his dreamy drawl, "is this the line of talk you've been putting out to that bunch of Indians down in the Green?"

"Oh, I'll put it out."

"Say, you're going to have a wonderful time here!"

"Watch me," said Dink, cocking his head; but with less confidence than when he had announced his intentions on the stage-coach.

"Young fellow," said Al, leaning back and looking at him from under his eyelids, "you're in wrong. You don't know what you've come to. Why, there's a bunch of young stock jobbers around here that would make a Wall Street bunco-steerer take to raising chickens! Slick? Why, some of 'em are so slick that when they come in I lock the cash drawer and stuff cotton in my ears."

"Bring 'em on," said Dink disdainfully.

At this moment there was a loud flop by the window in the rear, and the Tennessee Shad rose slowly from the floor. At the same moment Doc Macnooder, ambling innocently by on the farther sidewalk, turned, dashed across the street, bounded into the shop and, returning to the door, carefully surveyed the approaches.

THE VARMINT

"All clear," said the Tennessee Shad from the window.

"All's well on the Rappahannock," returned the scout at the door.

Macnooder, with a well-executed double shuffle, the Tennessee Shad, with a stiff-jointed lope of his bony body, advanced and shook hands.

"Al, we come not to take your hard-earned money, but do you good," said Macnooder as usual, genially shaking an imaginary hand.

The Tennessee Shad camped on the back of a chair, drew up his thin, long legs, laid one bony finger against a bony nose and looked expectantly at Macnooder.

Meanwhile Al, without turning his back, carefully moved over to the glass counter that sheltered appetizing trays of éclairs, plum cakes and cream puffs and, whistling a melancholy note, locked the door, scanned the counter, and placed a foot on the cover of the jigger tub.

Doc Macnooder, whose round, bullet head and little rhinoceros eyes had followed the hostile preparation, said sorrowfully:

"Al-bert, your conduct grieves us."

"Go ahead, now," said Al in a tired voice.

"Go ahead?" said Macnooder, looking in surprise at the equally impassive Tennessee Shad.

"What's the flimflam to-day?"

"Al," said Macnooder, in his most persuasive

tones, "you wrong me. My motives are honorable. At four o'clock this very afternoon Turkey Reiter will proceed to cash a check and settle for a fountain pen, a pair of suspenders and a safety razor I sold him. Just trust me till then—will you?"

"Nothing doing," said Al.

"Honor bright, Al!"

"No use."

"You *must* trust me till then."

Al, producing a patent clipper, began to pare his nails.

"Al?"

"What?"

"Won't you trust me?"

"Don't make me laugh!"

"Al's right, Doc," said the Tennessee Shad, entering the discussion. "You ought to put up some guarantee."

Al slowly turned his gaze on the Tennessee Shad and waited hopefully for the real attack.

"Well, what?" said Macnooder.

"How about your watch?"

"It's loaned."

"You haven't got a stickpin on you?"

"Left 'em at home—never thought Al would go back on me."

Al smiled.

"That's a very nice spring coat you've got on,"

THE VARMINT

said the Tennessee Shad, as though struck by an inspiration. "Why don't you put that up for a couple of hours?"

"Not on your life," said Macnooder indignantly. "This coat's brand new, worth thirty dollars."

Al, suddenly shifting, leaned forward, both elbows on the counter, and studied the coat with a reminiscent air.

"Oh, put it up," said the Tennessee Shad.

"Never. I've got associations about this coat and, besides, I've got to make a swell call in Princeton to-morrow."

"What's the diff?" said the Tennessee Shad, yawning. "It's only a couple of hours; and you know you said you were going to clean off the whole slate with Al, sure as Turkey boned up."

Macnooder seemed to hesitate.

"It's idiotic to put up a real, high-life coat for a couple of jiggers."

"Hurry up; I'm hungry."

"Stop," said Al, drawing back satisfied. "I wouldn't bother about that coat if I were you."

"Why not?" exclaimed the two partners.

"'Cause I remember that coat gag now," said Al with a far-off look. "I bit once—way back in '89. It's a good game, specially when the real owner comes ramping in the next day."

"What do you mean?" said Doc Macnooder indignantly.

"I mean that it don't button, you young pirate," said Al scornfully, but without malice. "When you try anything as slick as that again you want to be sure the real owner ain't been around. That coat belongs to Lovely Mead."

Doc Macnooder looked at the Tennessee Shad.

"Have we really got to pay for them?" he said mournfully.

"Looks that way."

"Oh, well," said Doc, slapping down a quarter, "fill 'em up."

Al heaped up the glasses, adding an appreciative extra dab with the magnanimity of the victor, and said:

"Say, you boys want to rub up a little. Here's Stover, over there, just come. He's about your size."

The Tennessee Shad and Doc Macnooder about faced and stared at Stover, who all the while had remained in quiet obscurity, dangling his legs over the counter.

"Just come, Stover?" said Macnooder at last.

"Yes, sir."

"On the noon stage?"

"Yes, sir."

"What form?"

THE VARMINT

"Second, sir."

"Why, shake, then, brother," said the Tennessee Shad, offering his hand. "Shake hands with Doc Macnooder."

Doc Macnooder grasped his hand with extra cordiality, saying:

"What house?"

"Green House, sir," said Stover, awed by the sight of a 'varsity jersey. "I'm rooming with—with Mr. White."

"What'll you have?"

"I beg pardon."

"What'll you have?"

"Why," said Stover, quite taken back by the offer, "I think it's up to me, sir."

"Rats!" said Macnooder. "If you've been in tow of Butsey, I'll bet you've been paying out all day. Butsey White's a low-down, white-livered cuss, who'd take advantage of a freshman. Step up."

"I'll have another one of these," said Stover gratefully, feeling his heart warm toward the unexpected friends.

"Bet Butsey's stuck you pretty hard," said the Tennessee Shad, nodding wisely. "He's just loaded with the spondulix, too."

"Well, he did sort of impose on me," said Stover, thinking of the frankfurters at Laloo's.

"It's a shame," said Macnooder indignantly.

THE VARMINT

"Here, Al, make that a triple. Don't think we're all like that, though."

Al, listening, was sorely puzzled at this sudden cordiality, knowing of old the firm of Doc Macnooder and the Tennessee Shad.

"I say, let me set up for éclairs, or something," said Stover, exceedingly moved.

"Not a cent," said Macnooder firmly.

"I hope Butsey hasn't been steering you around to Firmin's and Appleby's for crockery and all that sort of thing," said the Tennessee Shad, with a look that at once convinced Stover of his roommate's criminal complicity.

"Why, he was going to do that after this recitation."

"He was, was he?" said Doc. "Think of that! He's going to stick you for everything first hand."

"What can I do?"

"Do? Save half your chink, get everything second hand, the way we do."

Al, comprehending, leaned back and smiled.

"I'll bet he get's a rake off," said Stover indignantly.

"I don't say that," said Macnooder, with the air of insinuating as much.

"I wish I knew the ropes."

"That's easy enough. Any one can tell you."

"I wish you fellows'd put me on."

THE VARMINT

"Glad to do it," said Macnooder, without enthusiasm. "Finish up and we'll fit you out in a jiffy."

When the three went shuffling down the street Al did an unusual, an unprecedented thing. He actually made the turn of the counter and stationed himself at the door, watching the group depart—Macnooder with his arm on Stover's shoulder, the Tennessee Shad guarding the other side.

When they disappeared beyond Bill Orum's, the cobbler's, in the direction of the Dickinson, he said slowly, in profound admiration:

"Well, I'll be jiggered! If those body-snatchers don't get electrocuted, they'll own Fifth Avenue!"

V

"Come up to my room and we'll see what's on hand," said Doc, entering the Dickinson. "Too bad you're stuck down in the Green—no house spirit there—you must get in with us next year."

"Doc's a great fellow," said the Tennessee Shad, as Macnooder went quickly ahead, "a great business man. He's a sort of clearing house for the whole school. Say, he's taken a regular fancy to you."

"What did he get his 'L' for?" said Stover, as the Tennessee Shad, to gain time, showed him the lower floor.

"Quarter on the eleven last fall. Here's the Triumphant Egghead's room. Isn't it a peach? They've got a good crowd here; you must be with them or us next year. Here's Turkey Reiter's and Butcher Stevens' quarters. They're crackerjacks, too; on the eleven and the nine. Come on, now. We'll strike Doc. You know he studies medicine and all that sort of thing. Wait till I give the countersign. Doc's most particular."

Stover found himself in a den, a combination of drug-store, taxidermist's shop and general warehouse. All about the room were ranged an extraordinary array of bottles—green bottles that lurked under the bed, red, blue and white bottles that climbed the walls and crowded the mantelpiece, tops of bottles that peered out of half-opened boxes, all ticketed and mustered in regiments. From the ceiling a baby alligator swung on a wire, blinking at them horribly with shining glass eyes; a stuffed owl sat in one corner; while opposite, a muskrat peered into a crow's nest. The closet and all available floor space were heaped high with paper boxes and wooden cases, while over all were innumerable catalogues.

"Pretty fine, isn't it?" said the Tennessee Shad.

"It's wonderful," said Stover, not quite at ease.

"It's not bad," said Doc. "I'd like to have a nice, white skeleton over there in that corner; but they're hard to get, nowadays. Now let's get down to business. Sit down."

Stover took the only chair; the Tennessee Shad curled up languidly on the bed, after brushing aside the débris; while Macnooder, perched on a drygoods box, poised a pencil over a pad of paper.

"You want a crockery set, first; a student lamp, and an oil can to keep your oil in."

"Especially the can," said the Tennessee Shad

gravely. "Better get a padlock with it, or the whole Green House will be stealing from you."

"I don't know whether I have a can on hand," said Macnooder anxiously. "But here's a lamp."

He placed a rather battered affair in the middle of the floor, saying:

"It's a little squee-geed, but you don't care about looks. They ask you all kinds of prices for them when they're new; but you can have this for two-twenty-five. There's a bite out of the shade, but you can turn that side to the wall. They're rather hard to get second hand."

"All right," said Stover.

"Better light it up first," said the Tennessee Shad professionally.

"That's businesslike," said Macnooder, who lit a match and, after an unsuccessful attempt, said: "There's no oil in it. Still, if Stover wants——"

"Never mind that," said Stover loudly, to show his confidence.

"Now for the toilet set."

"Say, how about the can?"

"Oh, the can. Let me look," said Macnooder, disappearing among the packing boxes in the closet.

"You want that." said the Tennessee Shad confidentially.

"Hope he's got one," said Stover.

THE VARMINT

Macnooder reappeared with an ordinary kerosene can and a padlock, announcing:

"This is the only one I've got on hand. It's my own."

"Let him have it," said the Tennessee Shad. "No one can get in here; you're always locked and bolted."

Macnooder hesitated.

"How does it work?" said Stover, interested.

"The spigot is plugged up and the top cover is padlocked to the side. See? Now no one can get it. I don't particularly care about selling it, but if you want it take it at one-twenty-five."

"That's too much," said the Tennessee Shad. "One plunk's enough."

"You're paying cash?" said Macnooder, considering.

"Sure!" said Stover.

"Well, call it one bone, then."

Stover looked gratefully at the Tennessee Shad, who winked at him to show him he was his friend.

"Now, about a crockery set," said Macnooder, scratching his head. "I've got two, plain and fancy, what we call a souvenir set—but you wouldn't understand that. I'll show you the regular kind."

"What's a souvenir set?" said Dink, mystified.

THE VARMINT

"Oh, it's a sort of school fad," said the Tennessee Shad, as Doc disappeared. "Every piece is different, collected from all sorts of places—swap 'em around like postage stamps, don't you know. We've got rather tired of the ordinary thing, you know."

"Say, that's a bully idea," said Dink, whose imagination was appealed to.

"Some of the fellows have perfect beauts," said the Tennessee Shad, yawning; "got at hotels, and house parties, and all that sort of thing."

"Why, that beats hooking signs all hollow," said Dink, growing enthusiastic.

"I didn't know you'd be interested," said the Tennessee Shad carelessly. "Like to see one?"

"You bet I would."

"I say, Doc, old boy," said the Tennessee Shad; "bring out the souvenir set, too, will you, like a good fellow?"

"Wait till I get this out," said Macnooder, who, after much rummaging, puffed back with a blue-and-white set which he ranged on the floor.

"How's that appeal to you?" he said with a flourish of his hand. "Good condition, too; only the soap dish has a nick. You can have it for two-fifty."

But Dink had no eyes for the commonplace.

THE VARMINT

"Could I see the other," he said, "before I decide?"

Macnooder appeared loth to exert himself to no purpose.

"You wouldn't cotton to it, bub," he said, with a shake of his head.

"I'm not so sure about that," said the Tennessee Shad. "This chap's no bottle baby; he's more of a sport than you think. I'll bet you he's got a few swagger trophies, in the line of signs, himself."

"I've got two or three might strike your fancy," said Dink with a reckless look.

"Come on, Doc, don't be so infernally lazy. You're the deuce of a salesman. Out with the crockery."

"What's the use?" said Doc half heartedly, moving back into the litter of the closet.

"Don't get it unless you can afford it," said the Tennessee Shad in a friendly whisper.

When at length the souvenir set had been carefully displayed on the top of a box, cleared for the occasion, Stover beheld a green and white pitcher, rising like a pond lily from the depths of a red and white basin, while a lavender tooth mug, a blue cup and a pink soap dish gave the whole somewhat the effect of an aurora-borealis.

The Tennessee Shad sprang up and examined each piece with a connoisseur's enthusiasm.

THE VARMINT

The lavender tooth mug, especially, attracted his curiosity. He looked it over, handled it gingerly, holding it to the light.

"Don't think this is up to the rest," he said finally, looking at Doc. "It's cracked."

"Suppose it is!" said Doc scornfully. "Do you know whose that is? That was swiped out of the set of Brother Baldwin."

"No?"

"Fact. Last day of spring term, when he was giving a math exam."

"You don't say so!"

"What are the rest?" said Stover, wondering what sum could possibly compensate for such treasures.

"The rest are not so much; from the other houses, but they're good pieces. The water pitcher was traded by Cap Kiefer, catcher of the nine, you know. But there's one article," said Doc, pointing melodramatically, "that's worth the whole lot. Only I'll have to put you under oath—both of you."

The Tennessee Shad, puzzled, looked hard at Macnooder and raised his right hand. Stover, blushing, followed suit.

"That," said Macnooder, "came *di*rect from Foundation House. That belonged to his Nibs himself!"

"Come off!" said the Tennessee Shad, not daring to look at Macnooder. "That's a bunco game."

"I didn't say it was swiped," said Macnooder indignantly. "Just give me a chance, will you? It was smashed up at the fire scare and thrown away with a lot of other things. Tough McCarty, down at the Green, I think, has got the slop jar."

"Excuses!" said the Tennessee Shad. "I did think for a moment you were trying to impose on my young confidence. Gee! Just think, of it! Cracky, what a prize! The Doctor himself—well—well! Say, I'd like to make a bid myself."

"It goes with the set," said Macnooder. "It ain't mine; I'm only getting the commission."

Stover, having caressed each article, drew a long breath and said falteringly:

"I suppose it comes pretty high!"

"Of course it's worth more than the other set."

"Oh, of course."

"The price set on it was four flat."

"That's a good deal of money," said the Tennessee Shad. "Specially when you've got to fit yourself out."

"Well, the other's cheaper at two-fifty," said Macnooder.

"Stover's sort of set his heart on this," said the Tennessee Shad. "Haven't you, Sport?"

"CRACKY, WHAT A PRIZE! SAY, I'D LIKE TO MAKE A BID MYSELF."

THE VARMINT

Stover confessed that he had.

"Come on; make him a better price, Doc."

"I'd have to consult my client."

"Well, consult your old client."

Macnooder disappeared.

"Stand firm now," said the Tennessee Shad, "you can beat him down. Doc wants to make his commish. I tell you what I'd do if I were you."

"What?"

"If I were looking for a real trophy I'd make him a bid on this. This is the best thing in the whole caboodle. Come over here. Say, just cast your eyes on this!"

Stover gazed in awe. On the wall, suspended on the red and black flag of the school, were a pair of battered and torn football shoes, while underneath was a photograph of Flash Condit and the score—Princeton 'Varsity, 8; Lawrenceville, 4.

"Gee!" said Stover. "He wouldn't sell those!"

"He might," said the Tennessee Shad. "Between you and me and the lamppost, Doc is devilishly hard up. Offer him a couple of dollars and see."

"The shoes that made the touchdown," said Dink reverentially. The Tennessee Shad did not contradict him.

Half an hour later Dink Stover sallied forth

THE VARMINT

with the ecstasy of a collector who has just discovered an old master. Klondike Jackson, who shook up the beds at the Dickinson, preceded him, drawing in an express wagon the lamp, the padlocked kerosene can and the souvenir set, slightly reduced. Wrapped in tissue paper, tucked under Stover's arm, were the precious shoes, which he had purchased on the distinct understanding that Macnooder should have the right to redeem them at any time before the end of the term, on the payment of costs and fifty-per-cent interest. In Stover's pocket was a new fountain pen, a box of elastics, a pair of Boston garters and a patent nail clipper. Only the limits of his exchequer had prohibited his availing himself of the opportunity to purchase, at a tremendous bargain, a pair of snow-shoes, a tobogganing cap and a pair of corduroy trousers, slightly spotted.

Luckily for Dink, marching warily behind the vanguard, the three o'clock recitation had begun, and but a scattering of his schoolmates were abroad to witness his progress.

He arrived thus, virtually unnoticed, at the Green and, with the help of Klondike, arranged his possessions so as to make the greatest display.

He was standing in the middle of the floor, clutching the historic shoes and searching the

THE VARMINT

walls for the proper place of honor, when Butsey White blew in.

"Where in thunder have you been?" he exclaimed, and then stopped at the sight of the twisted lamp. He looked at Dink, gave a grunt and examined the new purchase.

"Broken-winded, spavined, has the rickets— bet it leaks and won't burn. Where in——"

All at once he perceived the kerosene can, with its attached padlock.

"What's this thing?" he said, in genuine surprise, picking it up with two fingers and regarding it with a look of blank incomprehension.

"That's the safety can," said Stover, yielding to a vague feeling of uneasiness.

"What's this?"

"That's a padlock."

"What for?"

"Why, for the kerosene."

"What kerosene?"

"The kerosene for the lamp."

"Why, you nincompoop, we don't furnish the kerosene."

"We don't?" said Stover faintly, with a horrible sinking feeling. "Don't furnish the kerosene?"

"Who got hold of you?" said Butsey, too astounded to laugh.

THE VARMINT

"I met Macnooder——"

"And the Tennessee Shad, I'll bet my pants on it," said Butsey.

"Yes, sir."

"What else did they unload on you?"

"Why—why, I bought a souvenir set."

"A what?"

"A souvenir toilet set."

Butsey wheeled to the washstand, uttered a shriek and fell in convulsions on the bed.

Stover stood stockstill, gazing in horror from the variegated crockery to Butsey, who was thrashing to and fro in hysterical flops, holding both the pillows where they would most ease the agony. Then, with a sudden deft movement, Dink dropped the historic shoes, sent them under the bed with a savage kick and, rushing to the window, threw the safety can into the tall grass of the fields beyond. Then he returned solemnly, sat down on the edge of the bed, took his head in his hands and began to do some rapid thinking. Butsey White, prone on the bed, burying his head in the covers, by painful degrees returned, gasping, to self-control.

"Mr. White," said Dink solemnly.

There was a slight commotion opposite and a hand fluttered beseechingly, while Butsey's weak voice managed to say:

"Take it away—take it away."

THE VARMINT

Dink rose and cast a towel over the set of seven colors, and then resumed his seat.

"It's all right; I've hidden it," he said.

Butsey rolled from the bed, tottered over to his own washstand and drank deeply from the water pitcher. Then he turned on the melancholy Stover.

"Say!"

"Go ahead! Soak it to me!"

"I thought you were old enough to go out alone."

"They lied to me," said Stover, kicking a chair.

"Say that again."

"They lied," repeated Dink, but with a more uncertain note.

"This from you!" said Butsey maliciously.

A great ethical light burst over Dink. He scratched his head and then looked at Butsey, grinning a sheepish grin.

"Well, I guess it was coming to me—but they are wonders!" he said, with reluctant admiration. "I'll take my medicine, but I'll get back at them, by jiminy! You see if I don't."

"For the love of Mike, give us the story!"

"You'll keep it twenty-four hours?"

"So help me——"

"I'm a sucker, all right." said Dink ruefully. Then he stopped and blurted out: "Say, White,

THE VARMINT

I guess it was about what I needed. I guess I'm not such a little wonder-worker, after all. I've been fresh—rotten fresh. But, say, from now on I'm holding my ear to the ground; and when it comes to humbly picking up a few crumbs of knowledge you'll find me ready and willing. I'm reformed. Now, here's the tale:"

VI

Dink, under the influence of the new emotion, made a fairly full confession, merely overlooking the shoes that Flash did not carry over the Princeton goal line, and suppressing that detail of the Foundation House's supposed contribution, which had lent such a peculiar value to the souvenir crockery set. By four o'clock Butsey White had sufficiently recovered to remember the afternoon baseball match.

Ten minutes later Dink, lost in a lapping baseball suit lent by Cheyenne Baxter, re-enforced with safety pins, stationed himself in the outfield behind a catcher's mitt, for preliminary practice with little Susie Satterly and Beekstein Hall, who was shortsighted and wore glasses.

The result of five minutes' frantic chasing was that Dink, who surprised every one by catching a fly that somehow stuck in his glove, was promoted to centerfield; Susie Satterly, who had stopped two grounders, took left; while Beekstein was ignominiously escorted to a far position in rightfield and firmly requested to stop whatever he could with his chest.

The Cleve cohorts arrived, thirty strong, like

banditti maching to sack a city, openly voicing their derision for the nine occupants of the Green House. The contest, which at first sight seemed unequal, was not in reality so, Tough McCarty and Cheyenne Baxter being an unusually strong battery, while the infield, with Butsey White at first, the White Mountain Canary at second, Stuffy Brown short-stop and the Coffee-colored Angel at third, quite outclassed the invaders. The trouble was in the outfield—where the trouble in such contests are sure to congregate.

Stover had never been so thoroughly frightened in his life. His imagination, boylike, was aghast at the unknown. A great question was to be decided in a few minutes, when his turn would come to step up to the box and expose himself to the terrific cannonade of Nick Carter, the lengthy pitcher of the Cleve. The curious thing was that on this point Stover himself was quite undecided. Was he a coward, or was he not? Would his legs go back on him, or would he stand his ground, knowing that the stinging ball might strike anywhere—on the tender wrist bones, shattering the point of the elbow, or landing with a deadly thud right over his temple, which he remembered was an absolutely fatal spot?

His first two innings in the field were a com-

THE VARMINT

plete success—not a ball came his way. With his fielding average quite intact he came in to face the crisis.

"Brown to the bat, Stover on deck, Satterly in the hole," came the shrill voice of Fate in the person of Shrimp Davis, the official scorer.

Stover nervously tried one bat after another; each seemed to weigh a ton. Then Cheyenne Baxter joined him, crouching beside him for a word of advice.

"Now, Dink," he said in a whisper, keeping his eye on Stuffy Brown, who, being unable to hit the straightest ball, was pawing the plate and making terrific preparatory swings with his bat. "Now, Dink, listen here. (Pick out an easy one, Stuffy, and bang it on the nose. Hi-yi, good waiting, Stuffy) Nick Carter's wild as a wet hen. All he's got is a fast outcurve. Now, what you want to do is to edge up close to the plate and let him hit you. (Oh, robber! That wasn't a strike! Say, Mr. Umpire, give us a square deal, will you?) Walk right into it, Dink, and if it happens to hit you on the wrist rub above the elbow like the mischief."

"Above the elbow?" said Dink in a hollow voice.

"That's it. You've got a chance to square yourself with the House. Step right into it. What? Three strikes? Say, Mr. Umpire,

THE VARMINT

you're not taking Nick Carter's word for it, are you?"

Amid a storm of execrations Stuffy Brown retired, appealing frantically to the four quarters of the globe for justice and a judge.

Impelled by a resounding whack, Dink approached the plate as a balky horse tries his hoofs in a pool of water. He spread his feet and shouldered his bat, imitating the slightly-crouching position of Cheyenne Baxter. Then he looked out for a favorable opening. The field was thronged with representatives of the Cleve House. He turned to first base—it was miles away. He looked at Nick Carter, savagely preparing to mow him down, and he seemed to loom over him, infringing on the batter's box.

"Why the devil don't they stick the pitcher back and give a fellow a chance?" he thought, eying uneasily the quick, jerky preparations. "Why, at this distance a ball could go right through you."

"Come on, Nick, old boy," said a voice issuing from the iron mask at his elbow. "We've got an umpire that can't be bluffed. This is nothing but a Statue of Liberty. Chop him right down."

Dink shivered from the ground up, Carter's

THE VARMINT

long arms gyrated spasmodically, and the ball, like the sweep of a swallow from the ground, sprang directly at him. Stover, with a yell, flung himself back, landing all in a heap.

"Ball one," said the umpire.

A chorus of taunts rose from the Green House nine.

"Trying to put him out, are you?"

"Mucker trick!"

"Put him out!"

"Good eye, Dinky!"

"That's the boy."

Stover rose, found his bat and ruthfully forced himself back to his position.

"I should have let it hit me," he said angrily, perceiving Baxter's frantic signals. "It might have broken a rib, but I'd have showed my nerve."

Clenching his bat fiercely he waited, resolved on a martyr's death. But the next ball coming straight for his head, he ducked horribly.

"Ball two—too high," said the umpire.

Stover tightened his belt, rapped the plate twice with his bat, as Butsey had done, and resumed his position. But the memory of the sound the ball had made when it had whistled by his ears had unnerved him. Before he could summon back his heroic resolves Carter, with a sudden jerk, delivered the ball. Involuntarily

THE VARMINT

Stover stepped back, the ball easily and slowly passed him and cut the corner of the plate.

"Ball three," said the umpire hesitatingly.

The Cleve catcher hurled his mask to the ground, Carter cast down his glove and trod on it, while the second baseman fell on his bag and wept.

When order was restored Stover dodged the fourth wild ball and went in a daze to first, where to his amazement he was greeted with jubilant cheers.

"You're the boy, Dinky."

"You've got an eye like Charlie De Soto."

"They can't fool Rinky Dink."

"Why, he's a wonder."

"Watch him steal second."

Stover slapped his foot on first base with the joy of unhoped-for victory. He glowered about his own possessions. The perspective had suddenly changed; the field was open, all his, the Cleve House representatives were a lot of dubs, butterfingers and fumblers, anyhow! Under Cheyenne Baxter's directions he went plunging down to second, slid, all arms and legs, safely on to the bag, thanks to a wild pitch, and rose triumphantly, blowing the dust from his mouth.

There he remained, as Susie Satterly and Beekstein methodically struck out.

But the joy of that double voyage was still

THE VARMINT

on him as he went back to centerfield, ready to master the hottest liner or retrieve the sky-scraping fly. It was a great game. He felt a special aptitude for it and wondered why he had never discovered the talent before. He began to dream of sizzling two-baggers and long home-runs over the fence.

"I wish I'd get a chance," he said, prancing about digging vicious holes in the glove, that looked like a chest protector. "I'd show 'em what I can do out here."

But no chance came. The battle was between pitchers, and to the surprise of every one the Green House came up to the last inning with the score of 2 to 1 in their favor, the solitary run of the Cleve being due to a fly that Beekstein had failed to notice.

The Green House nine went jubilantly out into the field for the last half of the ninth inning, determined to shut out the Cleve and end the season with at least one victory.

Dink ran out on his tiptoes, encased himself in his mitt and turned, tense and alert. He had gone through his first ordeal triumphantly. No chances had come to him in the field, but at bat he had accidently succeeded in being hit, and though he had struck out the next time he had hit a foul and knew the jubilant feeling that came with the crack of the bat.

"Give me a week and I'll soak 'em out," he said, moving restlessly, and he added to himself: "Strike 'em out, Cheyenne, old man! They're easy."

But the Cleves suddenly woke up and began to fight. One man beat out a grounder, and one struck out; another error of the temperamental White Mountain Canary put a man on third and one on second. Then Cheyenne, pulling himself together, made his second strike-out.

"Two out, play for the batter," came Cheyenne Baxter's warning hallo.

"Two out," said Dink to his fellow-fielders. "One more and we spink 'em. Come on, now!"

Both sides settled for the final play, the man on second leading well up toward third.

"Steady!" said Cheyenne.

Stover drew in his breath and rose to his toes, as he had done thirty times already.

Suddenly there was a sharp crack, and the ball meeting the bat, floated fair and free, out toward centerfield.

Dink did not have to move a step; in fact, the ball rose and fell straight for the massive mitt as though it had chosen his glove from all the other gloves in the field. It came slowly, endlessly, the easiest, gentlest, most perfect fly imaginable, directly for the large brown mitt that looked like a chest protector.

THE VARMINT

Stover, turned to stone, saw it strike fair in the middle, and then, irresistibly, slowly, while, horribly fascinated, he stood powerless, slowly trickle over the side of the mitt and drop to the ground.

Dink did not stop for a look, for a second thought, to hesitate or to deliberate. He knew! He gave a howl and broke for the House, and behind him, pell-mell, shrieking and murderous, like a pack of hounds in full cry, came the vanquished, thirsting body of the Green.

He cleared the fence with one hand, took the road with two bounds, fled up the walk, burst through the door, jumped the stairs, broke into his room, slammed the door, locked it, backed the bed against it and seized a chair.

Then the Green House struck the door like a salvo of grapeshot.

"Open up, you robber!"

"Open the door, you traitor!"

"You Benedict Arnold!"

"Open up, you white-livered pup!"

"You quitter!"

"You chickenheart!"

"You coward!"

Stover, his hair rising, seized the wooden chair convulsively, waiting for the door to burst in.

All at once the transom swung violently and

THE VARMINT

the wolfish faces of Tough McCarty, the White Mountain Canary, Cheyenne and the Coffee-colored Angel crowded the opening.

"Get back or I'll kill you," said Dink in frantic fear, and, advancing, he swung the chair murderously. In a twinkling the transom was emptied.

The storm of voices rose again.
"The freshest yet!"
"The nerve of him!"
"Let's break in the door!"
"Come out!"
"Come out, Freshman!"
"He did it on purpose!"
"He chucked the game!"
"Wait till I get my hands on him!"
"I'll skin him!"

All at once the face of Butsey White appeared at the transom.

"Dink, you let me right in, you hear?"

No answer.

"You let me in right off!"

Still no answer.

"It's my room; you let me in to my room, do you hear?"

Stover continued silent.

"Dink," said Butsey in his loudest tones, "I'm coming right over the transom. Don't you dare to touch me!"

BEHIND HIM, PELLMELL, SHRIEKING AND MURDEROUS .. CAME THE VANQUISHED.

THE VARMINT

Stover again seized the chair.

Butsey White, supported from behind, carefully drew up one foot, and then convulsively disappeared as Stover charged with the chair.

There was a whispered consultation and then the battling face of Tough McCarty appeared with a new threat:

"You lay a hand on me and I'll rip the hide off you!"

"Keep back!" said Stover hoarsely.

"Put down that chair, you little varmint; do you hear me?"

"Don't you come over!"

"Yes, I'm coming over, and you don't dare to touch me. You don't——"

Stover was neither a coward nor a hero; he was simply in a panic and he was cornered. He rushed wildly to the breach and delivered the chair with a crash, Tough McCarty barely saving himself.

This open defiance of the champion angered the attacking party.

"He ought to be lynched!"

"The booby!"

"Wait till to-morrow!"

Tough McCarty reappeared for a brief second.

"I'll get you yet," he said, pointing a finger at the embattled Stover. "You're a muff, a low-down muff, in every sense of the word!"

THE VARMINT

Then succeeded the Coffee-colored Angel:
"Wait till I catch you, you Rinky Dink!"
Followed the White Mountain Canary:
"You'll reckon with *me* for this!"

Down to Beekstein Hall, with his black-rimmed spectacles, each member of the outraged nine climbed to the transom and expressed his unflattering opinion.

Stover sat down, his chin in his hands, his eyes on the great, lumbering mitt that lay dishonored on the floor.

"I'm disgraced," he said slowly, "disgraced. It's all over—all over. I'm queered—queered forever!"

EACH MEMBER OF THE OUTRAGED NINE CLIMBED TO THE TRANSOM AND EXPRESSED HIS UNFLATTERING OPINION

VII

Until dusk, like Gilliatt in Victor Hugo's Toilers of the Sea, waiting for the tide to swallow him up, Stover sat motionless, brooding. There was only one thing to do—to run away. His whole career had been ruined in a twinkling. He knew. There could be no future for him in the school. What he had done was so awful that it could never be forgiven or forgotten. Why had he run? If only he had made a quick dive at the ball as it had trickled off the glove and caught it before it reached the ground, instead of standing there, horrified, hypnotized. Yes, he would escape, run off to sea somewhere—anywhere! But he wouldn't go home; no, never that! He would ship around the Horn, like the hero in that dreadful book, Two Years Before the Mast. He would run away that night, before the story spread over the whole school. He would never face them. He hated the school, he hated the Green, he hated every one connected with it!

A tap came on the door, and the voice of Butsey White said coldly:

"Open up! Fuzzy-Wuzzy's in the House;

you're safe. Open up. I've got to get ready for supper."

Stover drew back the bed, unlocked the door and waited with clenched fists for Butsey to spring at him. Butsey White, whose tempestuous rage had long since spent itself in hilarious laughter, as, indeed, had been the case with the rest, thought it best, however, for the purposes of authority, still to preserve a grave face.

"You're a fine specimen!" he said curtly. "You've had a beautiful day of it."

"Yes, I have," said Dink miserably, "a beautiful day!"

Butsey, to whom the tragedy of the century was nothing but an incident, had not the slightest suspicion of Stover's absolute, overwhelming despair. Yet Butsey, too, had suffered, and profited by the suffering.

"You better square up with Tough McCarty," he said, failing to read the anguish in Stover's eyes. "You certainly were the limit."

"I hate him!" said Dink bitterly.

"Why?"

"He's a bully."

"Tough McCarty? Not a bit of it."

"He tried to bully me."

"Why didn't you let them in?" said Butsey, putting the part in the middle of his hair with a dripping comb.

THE VARMINT

"Let them in!"

"Why, what do you think they'd have done to you?"

Stover had never thought of that. After all, what could they have done to him?

"I didn't think——"

"Rats!" said Butsey. "They might have pied you on the bed; but that's nothing if you lie face down and keep your elbows in. That's all you'd have got. Then it would have been over; now you've got to square yourself. Well, brush up and come down to supper, and for the love of Mike smile a little."

Butsey White's sentiments neither consoled nor convinced. Stover was too firmly persuaded of the enormity of his offense and the depth of his ignominy.

In all his life he had never done a more difficult thing than to follow Butsey into the dining-room and face the disdainful glances of those from whom he had so lately fled.

He sat in abject mental and physical suffering, his eyes on his plate, tasting nothing of what went into his mouth, chewing mechanically.

Mr. Jenkins, to be affable, asked him how he had enjoyed the day. He mumbled some reply, he never knew what, hearing only the dreadful snicker that ran the table. He refused the des-

THE VARMINT

sert and left the table. It had been a nightmare.

He stayed in his room, watching from behind the curtains his fellow-beings romping and shrieking over a game of baby-in-the-hat. The bottom had, indeed, dropped out of things—the universe was topsy-turvy. More keenly than in the afternoon he felt the utter hopelessness of his disgrace. If he could only get away—escape from it all. If he only had had five dollars in his pocket he could have reached Trenton and worked his way to some seaport town. He looked at the now ridiculous souvenir toilet set and bitterly thought where the precious dollars had gone—that story, too, would be abroad by the morrow. The whole school would probably rise and jeer at him when he entered chapel the next morning. That night he crept into his bed to the stillness of the black room, to suffer a long hour that first overwhelming anguish that can only be suffered once, that no other suffering can compare to, that is complete, because the knowledge of other suffering has not yet come, and he who suffers suffers alone. Then the imagination came to the rescue. He fell into blissful unconsciousness by a process of consoling half dreams in which he vindicated himself by feats of extraordinary valor, carrying the suffocating Tough McCarty and the Coffee-colored

THE VARMINT

Angel out of burnng houses at the risk of his own life, and earning the plaudits of the whole school.

Suddenly a peal of thunder shook the building; he landed all in a heap in the midst of the sunlit floor, rubbing his eyes. Outside, the morning came in with warm embrace; green things stirred against the window-panes; the flash of a robin's wing cut a swift shadow on the floor and was gone. Below, the horrid clanging of the gong rattled the walls and called on the dead to rise.

Dink gazed at the opposite bed. Butsey, with the covers wound around him, with his knees under his chin, was actually asleep. In great alarm he went over and shook him gently. One eye opened and reproachfully fastened on him.

"I say, the gong—the gong's rung, Mr. White," said Dink.

"The rising gong?"

"Yes, sir."

"Well, when the breakfast gong explodes wake me up."

The eyes shut, but presently reopened and a muffled voice added:

"Pour out water—washbasin—stick my shoes over here."

Dink obeyed, mystified. Then, going to the window, he drank in all the zest and glory of

THE VARMINT

green fields and blue skies with woolly clouds drifting over the tingling air. Joyfully he turned for a plunge in cold water and the unspeakable crockery set met his eye. Then he remembered. A shadow fell across the room; the day went into eclipse. Mechanically, heavily, he dressed, and the fever of yesterday sprang up anew.

Meanwhile, not a sound in the House except down the hall a snore—a glorious, triumphant note. A second time the gong took up its discordant march. Then from the cocoon on the bed a flash of legs and arms sprang out and into the waiting garments. There was a splash in the basin that spattered the water far and near, and Butsey, enveloped in a towel, rushed into his upper garments, flung back his hair with a masterful swooping stroke of the comb, and bolted out of the door, buckling his belt and struggling into a sweater. Down the stairs they went in the midst of floating coats, collars to be buttoned and neckties to be tied; and when the last note of the gong had ended not a place was vacant, though every eye still drooped with drowsiness.

Breakfast over, Dink followed Butsey to their room and, after the more permanent preparations had been attended to, they left for chapel.

The much-dreaded breakfast had passed with

but one incident; the Coffee-colored Angel, in passing him the sugar, had said in a terrific whisper:

"I'll get you to-day. I'll tame you!"

But, being still in a nodding state, his anger was contented with this slight expression. Tough McCarty had given him just one look, but somehow he remembered nothing else. The instinctive hostility he had felt at the first meeting of their eyes rose anew. The Coffee-colored Angel and the White Mountain Canary were but incidents; the enemy, *le sacré* Albion, was Tough McCarty.

He went in the current of boyhood past Foundation House and around the circle toward chapel. For the first time the immensity of the school was before him in the hundreds that, streaming across the campus in thin, dotted lines, swelled into a compact, moving mass at the chapel steps. It was more than an institution; it was a world, the complex, marvelously ordered World of Youth.

Somehow, he did not attract the attention he had expected. His entrance into the pew was attended by no hilarious uprising *en masse*. He found his place in the gallery, between Pebble Stone and Duke Straus, who sleepily asked his name and went off for a supplementary nap on the shoulder of D. Tanner. Stone evidently had

THE VARMINT

heard nothing of his disgrace, or else was too absorbed in a hurried conning of the Latin lesson to make remarks.

Dink lifted his head a little and stole a glance—strange, no one seemed to be paying the slightest attention to him. Somewhat astonished and unutterably relieved he gazed down at the body of the school marshaled below, at the enormous fifth-formers who seemed—and never was that illusion to fade—the most terrifically immense and awesome representatives of manhood he had ever seen. The benches were hard, decidedly so; but he lost himself pleasantly in the vaulted roof, and gazed with respect at the distant pulpit.

The Doctor ascended and swept the school with that glance peculiar to head masters which convinces each separate boy it is directed at him. Stover felt the impact on his own forehead and dropped his eyes uneasily. When the hymn began he looked curiously among his classmates, located Doc Macnooder and caught the eye of the Tennessee Shad, who winked at him to show him he was still his friend.

Somehow, his awful disgrace seemed to slip from him—the Green House was but a grain in the sand. There were friends, undiscovered friends, in the mass before him, to be won and held. An easier feeling came to him. When

THE VARMINT

the school shuffled out he sought the Tennessee Shad and, holding out his hand said:

"Say, you are wonders; and I'm the only living sucker!"

"Dink, you're a real sport," said the Tennessee Shad, pleased; "but we did come it pretty strong. Now, if you want to turn in those shoes——"

"Not on your life!" said Dink. "I deserved it, but—but look out for next year!"

"All right," said the Tennessee Shad with an approving look. "If you do us we'll take you into the firm. Tack on to me, and I'll pilot you to The Roman's."

Following his lanky guide Stover went in the churning, lagging mass across to Memorial Hall, rubbing elbows with the heroes, who stalked majestically in their voluminous bulk, with the coveted 'Varsity caps riding on the backs of their cropped heads, or being jostled by the freckled imps who ran zigzag, shrieking chases past him.

At the steps they divided, some surging upward and others crowding into the lower corridor.

"Below for us," said the Tennessee Shad, pushing his way forward.

Dink found himself outside of one of the dozen classrooms in a throng that waited hopefully, as other classes waited hopefully every hour of every day in the hopes of an improbable cut.

"The Roman," said the Tennessee Shad wisely, "is the one master you want to stand in with. Study like the devil the first two weeks; and say, get up on the gerund and the gerundive—they're his pets."

"I will," said Dink.

"You can't bluff him and you can't beat his system," continued the Tennessee Shad. "If you guess don't hesitate; jump at it. The only thing you can do is to wait for his jokes, and then grab the desk and weep for salvation—it's his one weak spot."

"I will," said Dink.

A cry of dismay went up from the sentinels at the window.

"Oh, rats! Here he comes."

"Oh, peanuts!"

"Oh, melancholy!"

"All in!"

Dink modestly took a seat in the back, at the end of the row of S's where he must sit. On four sides, like prison walls that no convict might hope to scale, the slippery blackboards rose up and bound them in. On a raised stand was the master's pulpit where presently The Roman would come and sit, like the watcher of the galley slaves in Ben Hur, with his eagle glance sweeping the desks that, in regimental file, ran back from him.

Outside, through two open windows, was the warm, forbidden month of April, and the gateway to syntax-defying dreams. At this moment Dink's copy of Cæsar's Gallic Wars slid on to the floor. He bent down, laboriously collecting the scattered pages and straightened up. Then he glanced at the pulpit. Directly in front of him, his eyes on his eyes, sat the big consular frame of his stage companion of the day before.

Dink gasped in horror; twice his hand went instinctively toward his lip, stopped half-way and dropped. Then his mouth opened, set, and galvanically he rose to his feet, while the room seemed to tip up.

He grasped the desk to keep from slipping, never taking his eyes from the Ciceronian countenance and the twinkling orbits above the slightly twitching lips.

"Dear me," said a low, mocking voice with a curious rising and falling infection, "who's here? Another delegate to this congress of scintillating intelligences?"

"Yes, sir," said Dink in a whisper.

"Quite a valuable addition, I hope. Yes? What is the name?"

"John."

"Well—well?"

THE VARMINT

"John Humperdink Stover," said Dink with difficulty.

"Ah, yes, Stover: the name is familiar—very familiar," said The Roman, with a twitch to his lip and a sudden jump of the eyebrow. "Haven't we met before?"

Dink, suffocating, nodded. The class, at a loss, turned from one to the other, watching for the cue.

"Well, Stover, come a little nearer. Take the seat between Stone and Straus. Straus will be better able to take his little morning nap. A little embarrassed, Stover? Dear me! I shouldn't have thought that of you. Sit down now and—try to put a little ginger into the class, Stover."

Dink looked down and blushed until it seemed as though his hair would catch on fire. The class, perceiving only that there was a point for laughter, burst into roars.

"There—there," said The Roman, stilling the storm with one finger. "Just a little joke between us two; just a little confidential joke. Now for a bee-ootiful recitation. Splendid spring weather—yesterday was a cut; of course you all took the hour to study conscientiously—eager for knowledge. Fifth and sixth rows go to the board."

While The Roman's modulated accents doled

THE VARMINT

out conjugations and declensions Stover sat, without a thought in his head, his hands locked, staring out at the green and yellow necktie that rose on Pebble Stone's collar.

"Oh, Lord! Oh, Lord!" he said at last. "Dished! Spinked! He'll flunk me every day. I certainly am in wrong!"

He raised his eyes at the enthroned Natural Enemy and mentally threw down the gage of battle with a hopeless, despairing feeling of the three years' daily conflict that was to come. For, of course, now there could be no question of The Roman's mortal and unsparing enmity. But after the first paralyzing shock Dink recovered himself. It was war, but the war he loved—the war of wits.

The Roman, having flunked a dozen by this time, had Channing, the Coffee-colored Angel, on his feet, on delicate matters of syntax.

"Top of page, third word, Channing—gerund or gerundive?" said The Roman.

"Gerund, sir."

"Too bad!" said The Roman musically, and on a lower octave repeated: "Too bad! Third line, fifth word—gerund or gerundive?"

"Gerund, sir," said the Coffee-colored Angel with more conviction.

"No luck, Channing, no luck. Tenth line, last word—gerund, Channing, or gerundive?"

THE VARMINT

"Gerund-ive," said the Coffee-colored Angel hesitatingly.

"Poor Channing, he didn't stick to his system. The laws of probability, Channing——"

"I meant gerund," said the Coffee-colored Angel hastily.

"Dear me! Really, Channing?"

"Yes, sir."

"Positive?"

"Absolutely, sir."

"It *was* the gerundive, Channing."

The Coffee-colored Angel abruptly sat down.

"Don't want to speculate any more, Channing?"

"No, sir."

"No feeling of confidence—no luck to-day? Try the gerundive to-morrow."

The discouraged began to return from the boards, having writ in water. The Roman, without malice, passed over the rows and, from flunking them individually, mowed them down in sections.

"Anything from the Davis House to-day? No, no? Anything from the Rouse House combination? Nothing at all? Anything from the Jackson twins? Alas! How about the D's this morning? Davis, Dark, Denton, Deer, Dickson, nothing from the D's. Let's try the F's. Farr, Fenton, Foster, Francis, Finch? Nothing from

THE VARMINT

the F's—nothing from the D F's! Nothing at all?"

Dink burst into laughter, and laughed alone. The Roman stopped. Every one looked surprised.

"Ah, Stover has been coached—well coached," said The Roman. "But, Stover, this is not the place to laugh. The D F's are not a joke; they are painful, every day facts. Well, well, it has been a beautiful recitation in the review—not exceptional, not exceptional at all. Has any one the advance? Don't all rise at once. Strange what trying weather it is—too sunny, not enough rain—every one rises exhausted. Will Macnooder kindly lead the massacre?"

Macnooder disdained to rise; one or two faltered and tripped along for brief spaces, and then sat down. The Roman, counting his dead, hesitated and called:

"Stover."

"Me, sir?" said Dink, too astonished to rise. "Why, I'm unprepared, sir."

"Unprepared?" said The Roman with a wicked smile. "I never thought you would be unprepared, Stover."

The smile decided Stover.

"I'll try, sir," he said.

"Very kind of you, Stover."

Dink rose slowly, put the book on his desk.

tightened his belt, buttoned his coat and took up the prosy records of Cæsar. Pebble Stone showed him the place. He straightened up and, glancing at the first line, saw:

"*Ubi eo ventum est, Cæsar initio orationis . . .*"

"Cæsar," began Dink in a firm voice.

"Excellent!" said The Roman.

"Cæsar, wherever the wind blew him, initiated the orators . . ." Dink continued smoothly, after a rapid glance.

The Roman, from a listless attitude, gripped the desk, pivoted clear on one leg of his chair, staring at the familiar text as though it had suddenly taken on life and begun to crawl about the page.

Dink, resolved not to be bested, gravely and fluently continued to glide on, without pause or hitch, turning syllables into words, building sentences wherever he met an acquaintance. On and on he went, glib and eloquent, weaving out of the tangled text a picture that gradually, freeing itself from the early restraints, painted in vivid detail a spirited conference between Cæsar and the German envoys. The class, amazed, resorted to their books; many of the unprepared, quite convinced, stared at him as though a new rival to the high markers had suddenly appeared.

The Roman, fascinated, never quitted the text,

THE VARMINT

marveling as the tale ran on, leaping adverbs and conjunctions, avoiding whole phrases, undismayed by the rise of sudden, hostile nouns, impressing into service whatever suited it, corrupting or beating down all obstacles.

Once or twice he twitched spasmodically, twice he switched the leg of his chair, murmuring all the while to himself. Finally he rose and, slowly approaching to where Stover stood, glanced incredulously at his book.

"Shall I stop, sir?" said Stover.

"Heaven forbid!"

Stover completed the page with a graphic, rushing account of the athletic exercises of the ancient Germans, and sat down without a smile.

The Roman, back at his post, wiped his eyes with his handkerchief and spoke:

"Very well run, indeed, Stover; excellently well run. Take your breath. Very fluent, very vivid, very persuasive—a trifle free, a trifle—but, on the whole, a very creditable performance. Very! I was sure, whatever you did, Stover, you wouldn't bore us. Now, let us see how the same passage will appeal to a more prosaic, less richly-endowed mind."

Then Red Dog rose and, unfeelingly, brought the scene back to Rome and the deliberations of the Senate.

But this was a detail that did not interest Dink in the least. He had clashed with The Roman and not retreated. He had his first moment of triumph, attested by the admiring glances of the class and the muffled whisper of Straus, saying:

"Gee, you're a peach!"

The session ended with a solemn warning from The Roman.

"One word," he said in his deepest tones, "just one word to the wise. We have journeyed together for two whole terms; there is only one more between you and reassignment. Candor compels me to say that you have acquired not even a flunking knowledge." He turned and raked the awed ranks with the sweep of a pivot gun, and then took up again in cutting, chilling, spaced syllables: "I have, in the course of my experience as a teacher, had to deal with imbeciles, had to deal with mere idiots; but for sheer, determined, *monumental* asininity I have never met the equal of this aggregation. I trust this morning's painful, disgraceful, disheartening experience may never, never be repeated. You may go."

And Stover, who had brazenly planned to remain and converse, went swiftly out with the rest, little imagining that he whom he had ranked as a deadly, unforgiving foe sat a long while chuckling over the marvelous route Dink had gone, murmuring gratefully to himself:

"Wherever the wind blew him, Cæsar initiated the orators."

VIII

In the hallway the Coffee-colored Angel jabbed him with his elbow, muttering:

"You laughed at me, you miserable Rinky Dink. I'll fix you for that."

He disappeared swiftly. Before Dink could frame a reply he was surrounded by an admiring chorus. The Tennessee Shad and Macnooder shook hands with ceremony.

"You'll do," said the Tennessee Shad.

"You certainly will!" said Doc Macnooder.

"You've made a hit with Lucius Cassius," said the Tennessee Shad.

Dink shook his head; he knew better.

"You must always recite—always," said Doc Macnooder, from his great knowledge of the nature of masters. "Whether you're prepared or not—recite."

"I will," said Dink.

"And say, Dink," said Macnooder, "keep that outfit we sold you. There'll be more hayseeds in the fall."

Dink had thought of that; he had thought of something else, too, which he craftily hid in his own memory.

THE VARMINT

"Next fall I'll show them a thing or two," he said gleefully. "I'll make souvenir crockery sets the rage."

The Coffee-colored Angel and the petty annoyances of the Green House forgot, he went with a hitch and a kick, loping along, while his delicately-balanced imagination, now soaring above the gloomy descents of the morning, swam joyfully in the realms of future triumphs.

In this abstracted mood he passed Foundation's gloomy portals and Laloo standing in his door gazing down the road, and took the leafy path that led to the Green.

All at once he heard a battle cry and, turning, beheld the Coffee-colored Angel and the White Mountain Canary spring from their concealment and bear down upon him with unmistakable intent. Now, whether in a former existence Dink had been parent to the fox, or whether the purely human instinct was quicker than the reason, before he knew what he had done he had bounded forward and burst for home in full flight, with his heart pumping at his ribs. Easily distancing his pursuers, he arrived at the Green House before it dawned upon him that he had been challenged and run away.

He stopped abruptly with clenched fists, breathing deep.

"Now let them come," he said, turning.

THE VARMINT

But the Coffee-colored Angel and the White Mountain Canary, having abandoned the hopeless chase, had gone another way.

Angry and ashamed, Dink went to his room, vowing terrific vengeance. He planted himself before the mirror and, doubling up either arm, felt the well-hardened muscles.

"There were two of them, and I didn't have time to think," he said. "I'll fight 'em—any of 'em."

Reassured by the scowling ferocity of his reflected countenance, he turned away. But, passing near the window, he saw the Coffee-colored Angel and the White Mountain Canary come militantly up the stone walk. A moment later their steps sounded on the stairs. He went hastily to the door and shot the key. An instant later the door was tried, and then the contemptuous face of the Coffee-colored Angel loomed through the transom.

"I knew you were yellow the moment I looked at you," he said scornfully. "Pah!"

Dink did not answer. He was all in a whirl. His action in locking the door, so contrary to his heroic resolutions, left him in confusion.

"I wonder if I really am afraid," he said, sitting down all in a heap. The look in the Coffee-colored Angel's eye had brought him an unpleasant creeping sensation in the region of the back.

And yet the Coffee-colored Angel, bone for bone and inch for inch, was just what he was—only he had fled from him, inadvertently, instinctively, it is true, yet feeling the running menace at his back.

"I'm a coward!" he said, staring at the opposite wall. "I must be a coward! If I weren't I would have opened that door."

Now, Dink had never fought a real fight. He had had a few rough-and-tumble skirmishes, but a fight where you stood up and looked a man in the whites of the eyes, a deliberate, planned-out fight, was outside his knowledge, in the mists of the unknown. And so his imagination—which later should be his strength—recoiled before that unknown as it had recoiled the moment he stepped from the stage to face his new judges; as it had recoiled in the hushed parlor before the closed door of the head master's den, and again at the thought of stepping into the batter's box and risking his head against the deadly shoots of Nick Carter, of the Cleve. He had never fought, therefore he was aghast at the fear of being afraid.

"Well, I won't run again," he said desperately. "I'll have it over with—he can only lick me."

THE VARMINT

But he did run again, and often, despite all his resolves, impelled always by the psychological precedent that he had run before.

The Coffee-colored Angel and the White Mountain Canary made a regular ceremony of it, raising a hue and cry at the sight of him and bursting into derisive laughter after short chases.

Dink was miserable and now thoroughly frightened. He slunk into the solitude of his own company, avoiding the disdainful looks of his House mates. He knew now he was a coward and should never be anything else. He did not blame Butsey, who scarcely spoke to him. All he thought of was, by roundabout ways, to put off the dreadful hour when either the Coffee-colored Angel or the White Mountain Canary should catch him and beat him to a quivering, senseless pulp.

Then the unexpected happened. One day, cutting across fields to avoid his persecutors, he was suddenly shut off by the White Mountain Canary, who rose from ambush, jeering horribly. Cut off from the Green, Dink returned posthaste up the village, when all at once the Coffee-colored Angel closed in on him. Only one way of escape was open to him, down an alley between two houses. With the Coffee-colored Angel at his heels he dashed ahead, turned the cor-

THE VARMINT

ner of the house and found himself caught in a blind area.

Whereupon he turned on the Coffee-colored Angel and slathered him, drove him hither and thither with terrific blows, knocked him head over heels, caught him by the throat and beat him against a wall, rolled him on the ground and rubbed him in the dust, tore his clothes, blacked his eyes and left him beaten and supinely, passively wallowing.

He walked out on his tiptoes, like a terrier, head erect, his chest out, fists still filed, tears in his eyes—tears of pride and relief. He had fought a fight, he had received terrific blows and minded them not. He had thrashed the Coffee-colored Angel: he could thrash or take a thrashing from any one. He had his first thrill, the thrill of conscious rage, comparable only to first love and first sorrow. He had licked the Coffee-colored Angel—he was not a coward!

At this highly-auspicious moment the unsuspecting White Mountain Canary perceived the despised object of his chase and, raising a shout, triumphantly bore down upon him. With a rush he cleared the intervening space and then, catching sight of the new Dink, stopped as though he had been jerked in by a rope.

. . . . .

A few moments later the group on the Green

THE VARMINT

House steps were lazily working out a French translation, which Beekstein, the Secretary of the Department of Education, was reading to them, when suddenly, in the fields opposite, two figures appeared, zigzagging wildly.

"Here comes the Dink again," said Stuffy Brown. "They'll get him this time."

"Who's after him?" said Tough McCarty. "He's a disgrace to the House."

"It's the White Mountain Canary," said Susie Satterly.

"Hello!" said Cheyenne.

"What?"

"I'll be darned—no—yes—dinged if it isn't the Dink chasing the Canary!"

As they sprang up, amazed, Stover dove at the fleeing tormentor, caught him, and the two went down in a heap, thrashing to and fro.

"Well, I'll be jig-swiggered!" said Cheyenne.

"I'll eat my pants!"

"The Dink!"

At this moment the awful wreck of the Coffee-colored Angel limped up. A chorus broke out:

"The Coffee-colored Angel!"

"Shot to pieces!"

"Massacred!"

"Kicked by a horse!"

"What hit you?"

"Dink," said the Coffee-colored Angel, taking

THE VARMINT

a tooth out of his muddy mouth. "I caught him."

Presently they saw Stover arise and loose the battered White Mountain Canary, who broke wildly for shelter.

"Well, anyhow," said the Coffee-colored Angel, "Dink's swallowed the Canary."

"What's he up to now?" said Cheyenne.

They watched him approach the fence, deliberately take off his coat, remove his collar and necktie, tighten his belt and methodically, slowly roll up his sleeves.

"Here he comes," said the Coffee-colored Angel, moving swiftly away. "Why, he's crying!"

Dink came up the path, choking with rage and the knowledge of his own tears, and in front of them all threw down his coat.

"You thought I was afraid, did you? You thought I was a coward!" he sobbed. "Well, I'll show you whether I'm afraid of you, any of you, you big bullies! You big stuff, you, come on!"

And suddenly advancing, he squared off and struck Tough McCarty a wild blow, crash on the nose.

IX

They adjourned to a sheltered spot back of the stump willows and chose a bare space of soft, green turf. At their sides the brook ran splashing over the cool stones.

"Who'll be Dink's second?" said Cheyenne Baxter, the referee.

There was an embarrassed pause.

"Go on, any of you," said Tough McCarty generously.

"I'll be," said the Coffee-colored Angel. "He licked me square."

He stepped over and held out his hand.

"I don't want you—I don't want your hand!" said Dink with a scream. "I don't want any second; I won't have any! I hate you—I hate the whole lot of you!"

Cheyenne Baxter consulted with Tough McCarty and came over.

"Say, Dink," he said kindly, "Tough doesn't want to fight you now; it isn't fair. He'll give you a fight any time you want—when you're fresh."

"I don't want to wait," cried Stover, blubbering despite himself. "I'll fight him now. I'll show him if I'm afraid, the big bully!"

THE VARMINT

"What rounds do you want?" said Cheyenne, seeing it was wisest not to interfere.

"I don't want any rounds," cried Dink wildly. "I want to get at him, the great, big mucker!"

Cheyenne went over to Tough, who stood apart, looking very uncomfortable.

"Better go on, Tough. Don't hurt the little varmint any more than you have to."

It was a strange fight. They stood around in silence, rather frightened at Stover's frenzy. Tough McCarty, overtopping his antagonist by four good inches, stood on the defensive, seeking only to ward off the storm of frantic blows that rained on him. For Dink cared not a whit what happened to him or how he exposed himself.

Blinded by rage, crying from sheer excess of emotion, shrieking out inarticulate denunciations, he flung himself on McCarty with the recklessness of a mad dervish, crying:

"You thought I was a coward,—darn you! You great, fat slob! You thought I was afraid of a licking, did you? I'll show you. Lick me now if you can, you big brute! Lick me every day! I'm not afraid of you!"

"Confound the lunatic!" said Tough McCarty, receiving a solid thump in the ribs. "I can't stand here, getting pummeled all day. Got to hit him—ouch!"

THE VARMINT

Dink, in his frantic rush, throwing himself under his enemy's guard, almost bore him to the ground by the shock of his onslaught. McCarty, angrily brushing the blood from his already outraged nose with the cuff of his sleeve, shook himself like an angry bear and, catching Stover with a straight-arm blow, sent him rolling on the turf.

Back again and again came Stover, hurling himself wildly onto the scientific fists that sent him reeling back. The green arms of the trees, the gray faces of the onlookers, the blue of the tilting sky rushed into the reeling earth, confounded together. He no longer saw the being he was fighting, a white film slipped over everything and then all went out in blank unconsciousness.

When he opened his eyes again he was on his back, looking up through the willows at a puffy cloud that turned against the blue. At his side the brook went softly, singing in whispers the note that stirred the leaves.

Something wet fell on his face and trickled uncomfortably down his neck. Some one was applying a dripping cloth.

"Coming to?" said Cheyenne Baxter.

Then Dink remembered.

"Where is he?" he cried, trying to spring up. "Fight him,—fight him to the end!"

THE VARMINT

A strong hand pressed him down.

"There, there, you fire-eater!" said Cheyenne. "Go easy. You've had enough blood for one afternoon. Lie back. Shut your eyes."

He heard whispering and the sound of voices going, and lost consciousness again.

When he saw the face of the day once more he was alone with Cheyenne, who was kneeling by his side, smiling as he watched him.

"Better now?"

"I'm all right."

"Let me carry you."

"I can stand."

Cheyenne's good right arm caught him as he tottered and held him.

"I'm all right," said Dink gruffly.

Aided by Cheyenne, he went weakly back to the Green. At the steps Tough McCarty sprang up and advanced with outstretched hand, saying:

"Put her here, Dink; you're dead game!"

Stover put his hand behind his back.

"I don't want to shake hands," he said, flushing and gazing at Tough McCarty until the pupils of his eyes seemed to dwindle, "with you or any of you. I hate you all; you're a gang of muckers. I'll fight you now: I'll fight you tomorrow. You're too big for me now, but I'll lick you—I'll lick you next year—you, Tough

THE VARMINT

McCarty—or the year after that; you see if I don't!"

Tough McCarty stood back, rightfully offended. Cheyenne led Dink up to his room and lectured him.

"Now, young bantam, listen to me. You've shown your colors and we respect you for it. But you can't fight your way into being liked—put that in your pipe and smoke it. You've got to keep a civil tongue in your head and quit thinking this place was built for your special benefit. Savez? You've got to win your way if you want to be one of us. Now, when you get your head clear, go down and apologize to Tough McCarty and the Angel, like a man."

The advice, which a day later would have been gratefully received, came inopportunely for Dink's overwrought nerves. He gave an angry answer—he did not want to be friends—he hated them all—he would never apologize—never.

When Butsey White came with friendly offers he cut him short.

"Don't *you* come rubbering around now," he said scornfully. "You went back on me. You thought I was afraid. I'll do without your friendship now."

When a calmer view had come to him he regretted what he had done. He eliminated Tough McCarty—that was a feud of the instincts—

THE VARMINT

but it certainly had been white of the Coffee-colored Angel to offer to be his second; Cheyenne was every inch a leader, and Butsey really had been justified. Unfortunately, his repentance came too late; the damage had been done. Only one thing could right him—an apology to the assembled House; but as the courage to apologize is the last virtue to be acquired—if it ever is acquired—Dink in his pride would rather have chopped off his hand than admit his error. They had misjudged him; they would have to come to him. The breach, once made, widened rapidly—due, principally, to Dink's own morbid pride. Some of the things he did were simply ridiculous and some were flagrantly impudent.

He was one against eight—but one who had learned his strength, who feared no longer the experiences he knew. He stood ready to back his acts of belligerency with his fists against any one—except, of course, Butsey White; for roommates do not fight unless they love one another.

He had always in him the spirit of the rebel. To be forbid a thing, with him, was to do it instantly. He refused all the service a Freshman should do. At table he took a malignant delight in demanding loudly second and third helps of the abhorrent prunes—long after he had come to feel the universal antagonism. He would not

THE VARMINT

wake Butsey in the morning, fill his basin or arrange his shoes. He would run no errands. He refused to say sir or doff his hat to his superiors in the morning; and, being better supplied with money, he took particular pleasure in entering the House with boxes of jiggers or tins of potted meats and a bottle of rootbeer, with which he openly gorged himself at night, while Butsey squirmed over the unappetizing pages of the Gallic Wars.

Finally, the blow came. Cheyenne Baxter, as president of the House, appeared one evening and hurled on him the ban of excommunication—from that hour he was to be put in Coventry.

From that moment no one spoke to him or by the slightest look noticed his existence. Dink at first attempted to laugh at this exile.

At every opportunity he joined the group on the steps. No one addressed him. If he spoke no one answered. At table the Coffee-colored Angel no longer asked him to pass his plate, but passed it around the other way. He went out in the evenings and placed his cap in line with the other boys', but the ball never went into his hat. If he stood, hoping to be hit, no one seemed to notice that he was standing there. For several days he sought to brazen it out with a miserable, sinking feeling, and then he gave it up. He had thought he cared nothing for the company of his House mates—he soon discovered his error and recognized his offending. But apology was now out of the question. He was a pariah, a leper, and so must continue—a thing to be shunned.

The awful loneliness of his punishment threw him on his own resources. At night he lay in his bed and heard Butsey steal out to a midnight spread behind closed doors, or to join a band that, risking the sudden creak of a treacherous step, went down the stairs and out to wend their way with other sweltering bands across the moonlit ways, through negro settlements, where frantic dogs bayed at the sticks they rattled over the picket fences, to the banks of the canal for a cooling frolic in the none too fragrant waters.

In the morning he could not join the group that congregated to listen to Beekstein—Secretary of Education—straighten out the involved syntax or track an elusive x to its secret lair. In the afternoon he could not practice on the diamond with them, learning the trick of holding elusive flies or teaching himself to face thunderous outshoots at the plate.

This enforced seclusion had one good result: left to his own devices his recitations improved tremendously, though this was scant consolation.

He kept his own company proudly, reading

long hours into the land of Dumas and Victor Hugo; straying up to the 'Varsity diamond, where he cast himself forlornly on the grass, apart from the groups, to watch Charlie DeSoto dash around the bases, and wonderful Jo Brown on third base scrape up the grounders and shoot them to first.

He was too proud to seek other friends, for that meant confession. Besides, his own classmates were all busy on their own diamonds, working for the success of their own House nines.

Only when there was a 'Varsity game and he was swallowed up in the indiscriminate mass that whooped and cheered back of first, thrilling at a sudden crisis, did he forget himself a little and feel a part of the great system. Once when, in a game with the Princeton Freshmen, Jo Brown cleared the bases with a sizzling three-bagger, a fourth-former he didn't know thumped him ecstatically on the back and he thrilled with gratitude.

But the rest was loneliness, ever recurrent loneliness, day in and day out. His only friends were Charlie DeSoto and Butcher Stevens at first, whom he could watch and understand—feeling, also, the fierce spirit of battle cooped up and forbidden within him.

One night in the second week of June, when

THE VARMINT

Butsey White had gone to a festal spread in Cheyenne Baxter's rooms, Dink sat cheerlessly over the Latin page, seeing neither gerund nor gerundive.

The windows were open to the multiplied chorus of distant frogs and the drone of near-by insects. The lamp was hot, his clothes steamed on his back. He thought of the rootbeer and sarsaparilla being consumed down the hall and, going to the closet, consulted his own store of comforting things.

But to feast alone was no longer a feast at all. He went to the window and sniffed the warm air, trying to penetrate the outer darkness. Then, balancing carefully, he let himself out and, dropping on the yielding earth, went hungrily up to the campus.

He had never been on the Circle before at night, with all the lights about him. It gave him a strange, breathless feeling. He sat down, hugging his knees, in the center of the Circle, where he could command the blazing windows of the Houses and the long, lighted ranks of the Upper, where the fourth-formers were singing on the Esplanade. The chapel at his back was only a shadow; Memorial Hall, a cloud hung lower than the rest.

From his position of vantage he could hear scraps of conversation through the open win-

THE VARMINT

dows, and see dark figures flitting before the mellow lamps. The fellowship in the Houses, the good times, the feeling of home that hung about each room came to him with acute poignancy as he sat there, vastly alone. In the whole school he had made not a friend. He had done nothing; no one knew him. No one cared. He had blundered from the first. He saw his errors now—only too plainly—but they were beyond retrieving.

There was only a week more and then it would be over. He would never come back. What was the use? And yet, as he sat there outside the life and lights of it all, he regretted, bitterly regretted, that it must be so. He felt the tug at his heartstrings. It was something to win a place in such a school, to have the others look up to you, to have the youngsters turn and follow you as you passed, as they did with Charlie DeSoto or Flash Condit or Turkey Reiter or a dozen of others. Instead, he would drop out of the ranks, and who would notice it? A few who would make a good story out of that miserable game of baseball. A few who would speak of him as the freshest of the fresh, the fellow who had to be put in Coventry—if, indeed, any one would remember Dink Stover, the fellow who hadn't made good.

The bell clanged out the summons to bed for

THE VARMINT

the Houses. One by one the windows dropped back into the night; only the Upper remained ablaze.

At this moment he heard somewhere in the dark near him the sound of scampering feet. The next moment a small body tripped over his legs and went sprawling.

"What in the name of Willie Keeler!" said a shrill voice. "Is that a master or a human being?"

"Hello!" said Stover gruffly, to put down the lump that had risen in his throat. "Who are you."

"Me? Shall we tell our real names?" said the voice approaching and at once bursting out into an elfish chant:

Wow, wow! Wow, wow, wow!
  Oh, me father's name was Finnegan,
Me mother's name was Kate,
  Me ninety-nine relations
To you I'll now relate.

"Oh, you're Dennis de Brian de Boru Finnegan, are you?" said Dink, laughing as he dashed his cuff across his eyes. "The kid that wrote the baseball story."

"Sir, you do me honor," said Finnegan. "Who are you?"

"I'm Stover."

THE VARMINT

"The Dink?"

"Yes, the Dink."

"The cuss that translates at sight?"

"You've heard of it?"

"Cracky, yes! They say The Roman was knocked clean off his pins, first time in his life. I say——"

"What?"

"Then you're the fellow down in the Green, aren't you?"

"Yes," said Dink, thinking only of the ban of excommunication.

"Why, you're a regular cross-sawed, triple-hammered, mule-kick, beef-fed, rarin'-tearin' John L. Sullivan, ain't you?" said the exponent of the double adjective in rapid admiration.

"What do you mean?"

"Why, you're the cuss that smeared the Angel, swallowed the Canary, and bumped Tough McCarty, all at once."

"Oh, yes."

"My dear boy, permit me—you're it, you're the real thing."

Dink, with a feeling of wonder, shook hands, saying:

"Well, they don't think so much of it at the Green."

"Anything wrong?"

"Nothing much."

THE VARMINT

Finnegan, perceiving the ground was shaky, switched.

"I say, you want to get into the Kennedy next year; we've got the A No. 1 crowd there. I'm there, the Tennessee Shad, the Gutter Pup—he's the president of the Sporting Club, you know; prize-fights and all that sort of thing—and King Lentz and the Waladoo Bird, the finest guards Lawrenceville ever had. And say, you'n I and the Tennessee Shad could strike up a combine and get out a rip-snorting, muzzle-off, all-the-news, sporting-expert, battle-cry-of-freedom newspaper that would put the *Lawrence* out of biz. I say, you must get in the Kennedy."

"I'm not coming back."

"What!"

"I guess my par-ticular style of talent isn't suited around here."

"What's wrong?"

"Well, everything."

"I say, Dink, confide in me!"

Stover, at that moment, in his loneliness, would have confided in any one, especially the first human being who had given him a thrill of conscious pride.

"It's just this, youngster," he said, wondering how to begin: "they don't like me."

"You like the school, don't you?" said Finnegan in alarm.

THE VARMINT

Dink had never had the question put to him before. He was silent and his look went swiftly over to the coveted House of Lords. He drew a long breath.

"You bet I do. I love it!"

"What then?"

"I started wrong; didn't understand the game, I guess. They've put me in Coventry."

"You must have been pretty fresh."

"What!"

"Oh, don't mind me," said Dennis cheerfully. "I'm fresher than you ever thought of being. I was the freshest bit of verdure, as the poet says, that ever greened the place. I'm the freshest still. But I'm different. I'm under six inches —that's the cinch of it."

"Yes, I was fresh," said Dink, intensely relieved.

"You're always fresh if you're any good, the first term," said Finnegan. "Don't mind that. Next year you'll be an old boy, and then they'll follow you around for sugar."

"I hadn't thought of that," said Dink slowly.

"Keep a-thinking. I'm off now. Ta-ta! Got to slink in Fatty Harris' room before The Roman makes his rounds. Proud to have met you. Au revoir!"

Dink sat a long while thinking, and a lighter mood was on him. After all, he was not a

THE VARMINT

blank. Some one had recognized him; some one had taken his hand in admiration. He rose and slowly made his way toward the singers on the Esplanade, and by the edge of the road camped under the shadows of an apple tree and leaned his back against the trunk.

The groups of the Esplanade stood out in cut outlines against the warm windows of the Reading-room. Above, the open windows were tenanted by boys who pillowed their heads on one another and sent their treble or bass notes down to swell the volume below.

Led by a tenor voice that soared clear and true above the rest came the melody to Stover huddled under the apple tree:

> *At evening, when twilight is falling*
>   *And the birds to their nests are all gone,*
> *We'll gather around in the gloaming,*
>   *And mingle our voices in song.*
>   *Yes, in song.*
> *The bright stars are shining above us,*
>   *Keeping their watch and ward.*
> *We'll sing the old songs that we love, boys.*
>   *Out on the Esplanade.*

Stover listened, pressing his knuckles to his lips, raised out of himself by the accord of voices and the lingering note of melancholy that

THE VARMINT

was in the hour, the note of the dividing of the ways.

Again in deeper accents a song arose:

We sing the campus, green and fair.
 We sing the 'leven and nine
Who battle for the old school there
 And guard the base and line.
No cause for fear when they appear
 And the school flag floats above our head.
When the game begins 'tis Lawrence wins,
 While we cheer the Black and Red.
When the game begins 'tis Lawrence wins,
 While we cheer the Black and Red.

The song ended in lingering accents. Dink shut his eyes, clenching his fists, seeing wonderful days when the school should gather to cheer him, too, and lay its trust in him.

Suddenly near him in the road came the crunching sound of footsteps, and a voice said:

"Is that you, Bill?"

"Yes."

"Bill, I wanted to say a word to you."

"Well?"

"We've only got a few days more in the old place. I don't want to go out with any hard feelings for anybody, do you?"

"No."

THE VARMINT

"Let's call it off! Shake hands."

Stover listened breathless, hearing little more, understanding only that a feud had ceased, that two enemies on the verge of the long parting had held each other's hands, slapped each other's backs with crude, embarrassed emotion, for the sake of the memories that lived in the shadow of a name. And something like a lump rose again in Dink's throat. He no longer thought of his loneliness. He felt in him the longing to live as they had lived through the glorious years, to know the touch of a friend's arm about his shoulders, and to leave a name to stand with the names that were going out.

He raised his fists grotesquely, unconsciously, and swore an oath:

"No, I won't give up; I'll never give up. I'll come back. I'll fight it out!" he said almost aloud. "I'll make 'em like me. I'll make 'em proud of me."

X

My father sent me here to Lawrenceville,
And resolved that for college I'd prepare;
  And so I settled down
  In this ancient little town,
About five miles away from anywhere.

Five miles away from anywhere, my boys,
Where old Lawrenceville evermore shall stand.
For has she not stood since the time of the flood,
About five miles away from anywhere?

The school was returning after the long summer vacation, rollicking back over the dusty, Trenton highway, cheering and singing as they came.

Jimmy, on the stage, was swallowed up in the mass of exultant boyhood that clustered on the top like bees on a comb of honey, and clung to step and strap. Inside, those who had failed of place stuck long legs out of the windows, and from either side beat the time of the choruses.

"Next verse!" shouted Doc Macnooder as leader of the orchestra.

THE VARMINT

The First Form then I gayly entered,
And did so well, I do declare,
  When they looked my record o'er
  All the masters cried "Encore!"
About five miles away from anywhere.

"Chorus!" cried Macnooder. "Here, you legs, keep together! You're spoiling the effect."

Dink Stover sat quietly on the second seat, joining in the singing, but without the rollicking abandon of the others. He had shot up amazingly during the vacation and taken on some weight, but the change was most marked in his face. The roundness was gone and with it the cherubic smile. The oval had lengthened, the mouth was straighter, more determined, and in the quiet set of eyes was something of the mental suffering of the last months. He had returned, wondering a little what would be his greeting. The first person he had met was the Coffee-colored Angel, who shook hands with him, pounded him on the back and called him "Good old Dink." He understood—the ban was lifted. But the lesson had been a rude one; he did not intend to presume. So he sat, an observer rather than a participant, not yet free of that timidity which, once imposed, is so difficult to shake off.

The stage, which was necessarily making slow

THE VARMINT

progress, halted at the first hill, with a sudden rebellion on the part of the long suffering horses.

"All out!" shouted Macnooder.

In a jiffy every boy was on the ground.

"All push!"

The stage, propelled by dozens of vigorous hands, went up the hill on a run.

"Same places!"

"All ready?"

"Let her go!"

Mamie Reilly, being discovered on the roof and selfishly claimed below, was thrust kicking and wriggling over the side and into the ready hands at the window.

"All ready, orchestra?" said Macnooder.

"Aye, aye, sir."

"All legs in the air!"

"Aye, me Lord!"

"One, two, three!"

And then the Second Form received me,
Where I displayed such genius rare,
  That they begged me to refrain,
  It was going to my brain.
About five miles away from anywhere!

Meanwhile, at the approach of the astounding coach, which looked like a drunken centipede,

THE VARMINT

the farmers stopped their plows or came to the thresholds, shading their eyes; while the cattle in the fields put up their tails and bolted, flinging out their heels, amid triumphant cheers from the students.

All the while, the bulk of the school in two seaters, and three seaters, the Fifth Formers, the new Lords of Creation, in buggies specially retained, went swirling by exchanging joyful greetings.

"Oh you, Doc Macnooder!"
"Why, Gutter Pup! You old son-of-a-gun!"
"Look at the Coffee-Colored Angel!"
"Where's Lovely Mead?"
"Coming behind."
"Hello, Skinny."
"Why, you Fat Boy!"
"See you later."
"Meet me at the Jigger Shop."
"There's Stuffy!"
"Hello, Stuffy! Look this way!"
"Look at the Davis House bunch!"
"Whose legs are those?"

> *Hallegenoo, nack, nack!*
> *Hallegenoo, nack, nack!*
> *Hooray! Hooray!*
> *Lawrenceville!*

"Next verse," shouted Doc Macnooder.

THE VARMINT

"Legs at attention. More action there! La-da-da-dee! One, two, three!"

In course of time, I reached the Third Form,
But was caught in examination's snare.
  Reassignment played its part,
  And it almost broke my heart,
About five miles away from anywhere.

"What house are you in?" said the Coffee-Colored Angel to Stover, between breaths.

"Kennedy."

"The Roman, eh?"

"Yes, he reached out and nabbed me," said Stover, who was persuaded that his new assignment was a special mark of malignant interest.

"Who are you rooming with?"

"The Tennessee Shad."

"Well, you'll be a warm bunch!"

A shout burst out from the back of the coach.

"A race, a race!"

"Here come the Tennessee Shad and Brian de Boru."

"Turn out, Jimmy!"

"Give 'em room!"

"Go it, Dennis!"

"Go it, Shad!"

Two runabouts came up at a gallop, neck and neck, four boys in each, the Tennessee Shad standing at the reins in one, Dennis de Brian de Boru Finnegan in the other, each firmly clutched about the waist by the boy on whose knees he jolted and jostled.

"Push on the reins!"
"Home run, Dennis!"
"Swim out, you Shad!"
"Pass him, Dennis! Pass him!"
"Shad wins!"
"Look at his form, will you!"
"Oh, you jockey!"
"Shad wins!"
"Hurrah!"
"Hurray!"
"Hurroo!"

But at this moment, when it seemed as though the race was to go to the Tennessee Shad's nag, which had that superiority which one sacrificial horse in a Spanish bullfight ring has over another, Dennis de Brian de Boru suddenly produced the remnants of a bag of cream puffs and, by means of three well-directed, squashing shots on the rear quarters of his coal-black steed, plunged ahead and won the road, amid terrific cheering.

"Dennis forever!"
"Oh, you, Brian de Boru!"
"Get an éclair, Shad!"
"Get an omelet!"
"Get a tomato!"

THE VARMINT

"Get out and push!"

The racers disappeared in mingled clouds of dust.

Macnooder, whirling around like a dervish on the stage top, conducted the next verse. Suddenly another shout went up.

"Here comes Charlie DeSoto and Flash Condit."

"Three cheers for the football team!"

"How are you, Charlie?"

"Flash, old boy!"

"What do you weigh?"

"Pretty fit?"

"Too bad you can't run, Flash!"

"What'll we do to Andover?"

DeSoto and Condit passed, acknowledging the salutations with joyful yelps.

"Give 'em the Fifty-six to Nothing, boys," shouted Macnooder. "All you tenor legs get into this. Oom-pah! Oom-pah! Oom-pah! One, two, three!"

There is a game called football,
  And that's the game for me.
And Lawrenceville can play it,
  As you will shortly see.
She goes to all the schools about,
  And with them wipes the ground.
For it's fifty-six to nothing, boys,
  When Lawrenceville's around.

THE VARMINT

She has a gallant rush-line
  That wears the Red and Black.
Each man can carry the ball through
  With six men on his back.
They carry it through the middle
  And then they touch it down.
For it's fifty-six to nothing, boys,
  When Lawrenceville's around.

Little by little Stover was drawn into the spirit of the song. He forgot his aloofness, he felt one of them, thrilling with the spirit of the coming football season.

"Gee, it's great to be back," he found himself saying to Butcher Stevens next to him.

"You bet it is!"

"Charlie DeSoto looks fit, doesn't he?"

"He's eight pounds heavier, Doc tells me."

"By George, that's fine!"

They stopped to sing the third verse.

"It won't be any fifty-six to nothing when Andover comes around," said Butcher gruffly.

"We've got to hustle?" asked Stover respectfully of the 'Varsity left tackle.

"We certainly have!"

"What's the prospects?"

"Behind the line, corking. It's the line's the trouble—no weight."

"There may be some new material."

THE VARMINT

"That's so." Stevens looked him over with an appraising eye. "Played the game?"

"No, but I'm going to."

"What do you strip at?"

"Why, about 140—138."

"Light."

"I thought I might try for the second eleven."

"Perhaps. Better learn the game, though, with your House team."

Hearing them talk football the crowd eagerly began to ask questions.

"Who's out for center?"

"Will they move Tough McCarty out to end?"

"Naw, he's too heavy."

"I'd play him at center, and stick the Waladoo Bird in at tackle."

"You would, would you? Shows what you know about it."

"Butcher, you'll be in at tackle, won't you?"

"Hope so," said Stevens laconically.

Stover, who had entered the observant stage of his development, noted the laconic, quiet answer and stored it away for classification and meditation among the many other details that his new attitude of watchful analysis was heaping up.

"There's the water tower! I see the water tower!" cried a voice.

"I see the Cleve!"

THE VARMINT

"All up!"

"Long cheer for the school!"

"All together!"

"Rip her out!"

They gave a cheer and then two more.

"Now, fellows," said Doc Macnooder shrilly, as master of ceremonies, "we want to pull this off in fine shape. We're going to drive around the Circle. And I want this orchestra to keep together. Whose legs are those with the cannon-cracker socks?"

"Beekstein's," cried several voices from inside.

"Well, he's rotten. He gums the whole show. Now, get together, fellows, will you?"

"We will!"

As they turned to enter the campus the voice of the master spoke, clanging its inexorable note from the old Gym. Instantly a shout broke out:

"Hang the old thing!"

"Drown it!"

"Down with the Gym bell!"

"Murder!"

"Oh, Melancholy!"

"Silence!" cried the bandmaster. "Give 'em The Gym Bell—all ready below! La-da-da-dee!"

"Too high!"

THE VARMINT

"La-da-da-*dum*. Slow and melancholy. One, two, three!"

> *When the shades of night are falling*
> *Round our campus, green and fair,*
> *All the drowsy sons of Lawrence*
> *To their couches then repair.*
> *Soon the slumber god has bound them*
> *With his spell of magic power,*
> *And he holds them thus enchanted*
> *Till the early morning hour.*

"Up legs and at 'em now, Rip her out—chorus!"

> *Till awakened*
> *By the clanging*
> *And the banging*
> *And the whanging*
> *From the cupola o'erhanging,*
> *Of that ancient Gym bell!*

Cheered by the new fifth-formers, who came laughing to the windows to hail them, the stage went gloriously around the Circle and came to a stop.

"Here we are back at the same old grind," said Butcher Stevens.

"Frightful, isn't it?" said Stover; and the rest made answer:

THE VARMINT

"Back at the grindstone!"
"Hard luck!"
"We're all slaves!"
"Nothing to eat!"
"Nothing to do!"
"Stuck in a mudhole!"

XI

At the Kennedy steps The Roman was waiting for him. Stover shook hands or, rather, allowed The Roman to pump him, as was the custom.

"Why, dear me—dear me—this is actually Stover!" said The Roman. "Well, well! How you have grown—shouldn't have known you. Had a pleasant vacation? Yes? Glad to have you in the Kennedy. It's a good House—good boys—manly, self-reliant, purposeful. You'll like 'em."

The Roman released Stover's hand, which had grown limp in the process, and said with a twinkle to his quick little eyes:

"Don't put too much ginger into them, Stover."

This remark confirmed Stover's darkest suspicions.

"I'll scatter a little ginger around all right," he said under his breath, as he climbed the stairs to his room. "He thinks he has the laugh on me, does he? Well, we'll see who laughs last!"

On the third floor the Tennessee Shad and Dennis de Brian de Boru Finnegan, from their respective trunks, were volubly debating the

THE VARMINT

merits of Finnegan's victory—the Tennessee Shad claiming that the external application of cream puffs was equivalent to doping and invalidated the result.

"Hello!" said Dink.

"Why, it's my honorable roommate," said the Tennessee Shad, emerging with a load of flannels.

"It's the Dink himself," said Dennis, gamboling up. "Welcome to our city!"

"I hear I'm rooming with you," said Stover, shaking hands with the Shad.

"You certainly are, my bounding boy."

"Where's the room?"

"Straight ahead, turret room, finest on the campus, swept by ocean breezes and all that sort of thing."

"Why, Dink," said Dennis de Brian de Boru in affectionate octaves, "you old, slab-sided, knock-kneed, baby-cheeked, wall-eyed, battling Dink. You've grown ee-normously."

"How's your muscle?" said the Tennessee Shad, with an ulterior motive.

"Feel it," said Stover, who had consecrated the summer to the same.

"Hard as a goat," said Dennis after an admiring whistle. "All nice little cast-iron, jerky bunches, ready and willing. Been in training, Dink?"

"Yes, just so."

"Feels sort of soft to me," said the Tennessee Shad pensively.

"Oh, it does?"

"Question: what can you do with it? Lift a trunk as heavy as this?"

"Huh!" said Stover, bending down. "Where do you want it?"

"Gee! I do believe he can carry it almost to the room," said the Tennessee Shad, whose theory of life was to admire others do his work for him.

Stover bore it proudly on his shoulders and set it down. Dennis, planting himself arms akimbo, surveyed him with melancholy disapproval.

"Too bad, Dink! I had expected better things from you. You're still green, Dink. Been too much with the cows and chickens. Don't do it; don't do it!"

Stover glanced at the Tennessee Shad, who, satisfied, had curled himself up on the bed, to rest himself after the exertion of walking.

"I guess I am still a sucker," he said, scratching his head with a foolish grin, "I'll not be so easy next time."

"Never mind, Dink," said Dennis comfortingly. "Your education's been neglected, but

THE VARMINT

I'm here. Remember that, Dennis is here, ready and willing."

Presently the Gutter Pup and Lovely Mead came tumbling in, and then the lumbering proportions of P. Lentz, King of the Kennedy, crowded through the doorway, and the conversation continued in rapid crossfire.

"Who's seen the Waladoo Bird?"

"Jock Hasbrouck's dropped into the third form."

"What do you think of the electric lights they've given us?"

"They've stuck an arc light in the Circle, too."

"We'll fix that."

"How's the new material, King?"

"Rotten!"

"Think we've a chance for the House championship?"

"A fine chance—to finish last."

"Say, who do you think they've stuck us with?"

"Who?"

"Beekstein."

"Suffering Moses!"

"Never mind. We've got the Dink."

"What's he do?"

"He's the champion truckman—carry your trunk for you anywhere you want."

Dink, thus brought unwillingly into the conversation, blushed a warm red.

THE VARMINT

"Truckman?" said P. Lentz, mystified.

"Champion," said Finnegan. "The mysterious champion truckman of Broad Street Station, Philadelphia. Stand up, Dink, my man, and twitch your muscles."

Stover squirmed uneasily on his chair. There was no malice in the teasing, and yet he was at a loss how to turn it.

The Gutter Pup, as president of the Sporting Club and chief authority on the life and works of the late Marquis of Queensberry, examined the embarrassed Stover, running professional fingers over his legs and arms.

"You're the fellow who tried to fight the whole Green House, aren't you?" he said, immensely interested.

"Why, yes."

"Good nerve," said the Gutter Pup. "You've got something the style of Beans Middleton, who stood up to me for ten rounds in the days of the old Seventy-second Street gang. I'll train you up some time. You'd do well with the crouching style—good reach, quick on the trigger and all that sort of thing. Like fighting?"

"Why, I—I don't know," said Stover helplessly, unable to make out whether the Gutter Pup spoke in jest.

"Modest and brave!" said the irrepressible Finnegan.

The conversation drifted away; Stover, with

a sigh of relief, obliterated himself in a corner, feeling immense distances between himself and the laughing group that continued to exchange rapid banter.

"Dennis, they tell me you're fresher than ever."

"Sir, you compliment me."

"Say, Boru, have they put you on the bottle yet?"

"Not yet, Lovely. Waiting for you to drop it."

It was not particularly brilliant, but it was good-natured, and there was a certain trick to it that he had lost in the long weeks of Coventry.

Presently the group departed to take the keen edge off the approaching luncheon pangs by a trip to the Jigger Shop, the center of social life.

"Coming, Dink?" said the Gutter Pup.

"I—I'll be over a little later," said Stover, who did and did not want to go.

Left alone, half angry at his own enforced aloofness, and yet desiring solitude, Stover stood among the litter of boxes and gaping trunks and surveyed the four bare walls that spelled for him the word home.

"It's a bully room—bully," he said to himself with a tender feeling of possession. "The Shad's a bully fellow—bully! Dennis is a

THE VARMINT

corker! I'm going to make good; see if I don't! But I'm going slow. They've got to come to me. I won't break in until they want me. Gee! What a peach of a room!"

He went to the window and looked out at the whole panorama of the school that ran beneath him, from the long, rakish lines of the Upper, by Memorial Hall, to the chapel and the circle of Houses that ended at the rear with the Dickinson. Below, boys were streaking across the green depths like water-bugs over limpid surfaces, or hallooing joyfully from window to terrace, greeting one another with bearlike hugs, tumbling about in frolicking heaps. He was on the mountain, they on the plain. His was the imaginative perspective and the troubled vision of one who finds a strange city at his feet.

"It's all there," he said lamely, confused by his own impressions. "All of it."

"Homesick?" said a thin voice behind him.

He turned to find Finnegan eyeing him uncertainly.

"Why, you wild Irishman," Dink said, surprised. "Thought you'd gone with the crowd. Hello, what's up now?"

Finnegan, with an air of great mystery, locked the door, extracted the key and, returning, enthroned himself on a chair which he had previously planted defiantly on a trunk.

THE VARMINT

"That's so you can't throw me out."

"Well?"

"I'm going to be fresh as paint."

"You are?" said Stover, mystified and amused.

"Fact," said Finnegan, who, having crossed his legs, plunged his hands into his pockets and cocked one eye, said impressively: "Dink, you're wrong."

"I am—am I?"

"But never mind; I'm here. Dennis de Brian de Boru Finnegan—ready and willing."

"Irishman, I do believe you're embarrassed," said Stover, surprised.

"I'm not," said Finnegan indignantly. "Only —only, I want to be impressive. Dink, you're getting in wrong again."

"What in thunder——"

"You are, Dink, you are. But don't worry; I'm here. In the first place, you can't forget what every one else has forgotten."

"Forget what?"

"The late unpleasantness," said Finnegan, with an expelling wave of his hand. "That's over, spiked, dished, set back, covered up, cobwebbed, no flowers and no tombstone."

"I know."

"No, you don't—that's just it. You've got it on your mind—brooding and all that sort of thing."

THE VARMINT

Stover sat down and stared at the Lilliputian philosopher.

"Well, I like your nerve!"

"Don't—don't start in like that," said Finnegan, rolling up his sleeves over his funny, thin forearms, "cause I shall have to thrash you."

"Well, go on," said Stover suddenly.

"You're not in Coventry—you never have been. You're one of us," said Dennis glibly. "BUT—I repeat BUT—you can't be one of us if you don't believe in your own noddle that you are one of us! Get that? That's deep—no charge, always glad to oblige a customer."

"Keep on," said Stover, leaning back.

"With your kind permission, directly. It's all in this—you haven't got the trick."

"The trick?"

"The trick of conversation. That's not just it. The trick of answering back. Aha, that's better! Scratch out first sentiment. Change signals!"

"There's something in that," said Stover, genuinely amazed.

"You blush."

"What?"

"The word was blush," said Finnegan firmly. "I saw you—Finnegan saw you and grieved. And why? Because you didn't have the trick of answering back."

"Dennis de Brian de Boru Finnegan," said

THE VARMINT

Stover slowly, "I believe you are a wholehearted little cuss. Also, you're not so far off, either. Now, since this is a serious conversation, this is where I stand: I went through Hades last spring—I deserved it and it's done me good. I've come back to make good. Savez? And that's a serious thing, too. Now if you have one particular theory about your art of conversation to elucidate—eluce."

"One theory!" said Finnegan, chirping along as he perceived the danger-point passed. "I'm a theorist, and a real theorist doesn't have one theory; he has dozens. Let me see; let me think, reflect, cogitate, tickle the thinker. Best way is to start at the A, B, C—first principles, all that sort of thing. Supposin', supposin' you come into the room with that hat on—it's a bum hat, by the way—and some one pipes up; 'Get that at the fire sale?' What are you going to answer?"

"Why, I suppose I'd grin," said Stover slowly, "and say: 'How did you guess it?'"

"Wrong," said Finnegan. "You let him take the laugh."

"Well, what?"

"Something in this style: 'Oh, no, I traded it for luck with a squint-eyed, humpbacked biter-off of puppy-dog tails that got it out of Rockefeller's ashcan.' See?"

THE VARMINT

"No, Dennis, no," said Stover, bewildered. "I see, but there are some things beyond me. Every one isn't a young Shakspere."

"I know," said Finnegan, accepting the tribute without hesitation. "But there's the principle. You go him one better. You make him look like a chump. You show him what you could have said in his place. That shuts him up, makes him feel foolish, spikes the gun, corks the bottle."

"By Jove!"

"It's what I call the Superiority of the Superlative over the Comparative."

"It sounds simple," said Stover pensively.

"When you know the trick."

"You know, Dennis," said Stover, smiling reminiscently, "I used to have the gift of gab once, almost up to you."

"Then let's take a few crouching starts," said Dennis, delighted.

"Go ahead."

"Room full of fellows. You enter."

"I enter."

"I speak: 'Dink, I bet Bill here a quarter that you used a toothbrush.'"

"You lose," said Stover; "I use a whiskbroom."

"Good!" said Dennis professionally, "but a little quicker, on the jump, get on the springboard. Try again. 'Why, Dink, how *do* you get such pink cheeks?'"

"That's a hard one," said Dink.

"Peanuts!"

"Let me think."

"Bad, very bad."

"Well, what would you say?"

"Can't help it, Bill; the girls won't let me alone!"

"Try me again," said Stover, laughing.

"Say, Dink, did your mamma kiss you good-by?"

"Sure, Mike," said Stover instantly; "combed my hair, dusted my hands, and told me not to talk to fresh little kids like you."

"Why, Dick, come to my arms," said Dennis, delighted. "A Number 1. Mark 100 for the term. That's the trick."

"Think I'll do?"

"Sure pop. Of course, there are times when the digestion's jumping fences and you get sort of in the thunder glums. Then just answer, 'Is that the best you can do to-day?' or 'Why, you're a real funny man, aren't you?' sarcastic and sassy."

"I see."

"But better be original."

"Of course."

"Oh, it's all a knack."

THE VARMINT

"And to think that's all there is to it!" said Stover, profoundly moved.

"When you know," said Dennis in correction.

"Dennis, I have a thought," said Stover suddenly. "Let's get out and try the system."

"Presto!"

"The Jigger Shop?"

"Why tarry?"

On the way over Dink stopped short with an exclamation.

"What now?" said Finnegan.

"Tough McCarty and a female," said Stover in great indignation.

They stood aside, awkwardly snatching off their caps as McCarty and his companion passed them on the walk. Stover saw a bit of blue felt with the white splash of a wing across, a fluffy shirtwaist, and a skirt that was a skirt, and nothing else. His glance went to McCarty, meeting it with the old, measuring antagonism. They passed.

"Damn him!" said Stover.

"Why, Dink, how shocking!"

"He's grown!"

In the joy of his own increased stature he had never dreamed that like processes of Nature produce like results.

"Ten pounds heavier," said Dennis. "He ought to make a peach of a tackle this year!"

THE VARMINT

"Bringing girls around!" said Stover scornfully, to vent his rage.

"More to be pitied than blamed," sang Dennis on a popular air. "It's his sister. Luscious eyes—quite the figure, too."

"Figure—huh!" said Stover, who hadn't seen.

At the Jigger Shop the Gutter Pup, looking up from a meringue entirely surrounded by peach jiggers, hailed them:

"Hello, Rinky Dink! Changed your mind, eh? Thought you were homesick."

"Sure I was, but Dennis came in with a bucket and caught the tears," said Stover gravely. "I'll call you in next time. Al, how be you? Here's what I owe you. Set 'em up."

"*Très bien!*" said Dennis de Brian de Boru Finnegan.

That night, as they started on the problem of interior decorations, Stover threw himself on the bed, rolling with laughter.

"Well, I'm glad you've decided to be cheerful; but what in blazes are you hee-hawing at?" said the Tennessee Shad, mystified.

"I'm laughing," said Stover, loud enough for Dennis down the hall to hear, "at the Superiority of the Superlative over the Comparative."

XII

"Why, look at the Dink!" said Lovely Mead the next afternoon, as Stover emerged in football togs which he had industriously smeared with mud to conceal their novelty.

"He must be going out for the 'Varsity!" said Fatty Harris sarcastically.

"By request," said the Gutter Pup.

"Why, who told you?" said Stover.

"You trying for the 'Varsity?" said Lovely Mead incredulously. "Why, where did you play football?"

"Dear me, Lovely," said Stover, lacing his jacket, "thought you read the newspapers."

"Huh! What position are you trying for?"

"First substitute scorer," said Stover, according to Finnegan's theory. "Any more questions?"

Lovely Mead, surprised, looked at Stover in perplexity and remained silent.

Dink, laughing to himself at the ease of the trick, started across the Circle for the 'Varsity football field, whither already the candidates were converging to the first call of the season.

He had started joyfully forth from the skeptics on the steps, but once past the chapel and in

THE VARMINT

sight of the field his gait abruptly changed. He went quietly, thoughtfully, a little alarmed at his own daring, glancing at the padded figures that overtopped him.

The veterans with the red L on their black sweaters were apart, tossing the ball back and forth and taking playful tackles at one another. Stover, hiding himself modestly in the common herd, watched with entranced eyes the lithe, sinuous forms of Flash Condit and Charlie DeSoto—greater to him than the faint heroes of mythology—as they tumbled the Waladoo Bird gleefully on the ground. There was Butcher Stevens of the grim eye and the laconic word, a man to follow and emulate; and the broad span of Turkey Reiter's shoulders, a mark to grow to. Meanwhile, Garry Cockrell, the captain, and Mr. Ware, the new coach from the Princeton championship eleven, were drawing nearer on their tour of inspection and classification. Dink knew his captain only from respectful distances—the sandy hair, the gaunt cheek bones and the deliberate eye, whom governors of states alone might approach with equality, and no one else. Under the dual inspection the squad was quickly sorted, some sent back to their House teams till another year brought more weight and experience, and others tentatively retained on the scrubs.

THE VARMINT

"Better make the House team, Jenks," said the low, even voice of the captain. "You want to harden up a bit. Glad you reported, though."

Then Dink stood before his captain, dimly aware of the quick little eyes of Mr. Ware quietly scrutinizing him.

"What form?"

"Third."

The two were silent a moment studying not the slender, wiry figure, but the look in the eyes within.

"What are you out for?"

"End, sir."

"What do you weigh?"

"One hundred and fifty—about," said Dink.

A grim little twinkle appeared in the captain's eyes.

"About one hundred and thirty-five," he said, with a measuring glance.

"But I'm hard, hard as nails, sir," said Stover desperately.

"What football have you played?"

Stover remained silent.

"Well?"

"I—I haven't played," he said unwillingly.

"You seem unusually eager," said Cockrell, amused at this strange exhibition of willingness.

THE VARMINT

"Yes, sir."

"Good spirit; keep it up. Get right out for your House team——"

"I won't!" said Stover, blurting it out in his anger and then flushing: "I mean, give me a chance, won't you, sir?"

Cockrell, who had turned, stopped and came back.

"What makes you think you can play?" he said not unkindly.

"I've got to," said Stover desperately.

"But you don't know the game."

"Please, sir, I'm not out for the 'Varsity," said Stover confusedly. "I mean, I want to be in it, to work for the school, sir."

"You're not a Freshman?" said the captain, and the accents of his voice were friendly.

"No, sir."

"What's your name?" said Cockrell, a little thrilled to feel the genuine veneration that inspired the "sir."

"Stover—Dink Stover."

"You were down at the Green last year, weren't you?"

"Yes, sir," said Stover, looking down with a sinking feeling.

"You're the fellow who tried to fight the whole House?"

"Yes, sir."

THE VARMINT

"Well, Dink, this is a little different—you can't play football on nothing but nerve."

"You can if you've got enough of it," said Stover, all in a breath. "Please, sir, give me a chance. You can fire me if I'm no good. I only want to be useful. You've got to have a lot of fellows to stand the banging and you can bang me around all day. I do know something about it, sir; I've practiced tackling and falling on the ball all summer, and I'm hard as nails. Just give me a chance, will you? Just one chance, sir."

Cockrell looked at Mr. Ware, whose eye showed the battling spark as he nodded.

"Here, Dink," he said gruffly, "I can't be wasting any more time over you. I told you to go back to the House team, didn't I?"

Stover, with a lump in his throat, nodded the answer he could not utter.

"Well, I've changed my mind. Get over there in the squad."

The revulsion of feeling was so sudden that tears came into Stover's eyes.

"You're really going to let me stay?"

"Get over there, you little nuisance!"

Dink went a few steps, and then stopped and tightened his shoelaces a long minute.

"Too bad the little devil is so light," said Cockrell to Mr. Ware.

THE VARMINT

"Best player I ever played against had no right on a football field."

"But one hundred and thirty-five!"

"Yes, that's pretty light."

"What the deuce were you chinning so long about?" said Cheyenne Baxter to Dink, as he came joyfully into the squad.

"Captain wanted just a bit of general expert advice from me," said Dink defiantly. "I've promised to help out."

The squad, dividing, practiced starts. Stover held his own, being naturally quick; and though Flash Condit and Charlie DeSoto distanced him, still he earned a good word for his performances.

Presently Mr. Ware came up with a ball and, with a few words of introduction, started them to falling on it as it bounded grotesquely over the ground, calling them from the ranks by name.

"Hard at it, Stevens."

"Dive at it."

"Don't stop till you get it."

"Oh, squeeze the ball!"

Stover, moving up, caught the eye of Mr. Ware intently on him, and rose on his toes with the muscles in his arms strained and eager.

"Now, Stover, hard!"

The ball with just an extra impetus left the hand of Mr. Ware. Stover went at it like a terrier, dove and came up glorious and muddy with the pigskin hugged in his arms. It was the extent of his football knowledge, but that branch he had mastered on the soft summer turf.

Mr. Ware gave a grunt of approval and sent him plunging after another. This time as he dove the ball took a tricky bounce and slipped through his arms. Quick as a flash Dink, rolling over, recovered himself and flung himself on it.

"That's the way!" said Mr. Ware. "Follow it up. Can't always get it the first time. Come on, Baxter."

The real test came with the tackling. He waited his turn, all eyes, trying to catch the trick, as boy after boy in front of him went cleanly or awkwardly out to down the man who came plunging at him. Some tackled sharply and artistically, their feet leaving the ground and taking the runner off his legs as though a scythe had passed under him; but most of the tackling was crude, and often the runner slipped through the arms and left the tackler prone on the ground to rise amid the jeers of his fellows.

"Your turn, Stover," said the voice of the captain. "Wait a minute." He looked over the squad and selected McCarty, saying: "Here,

THE VARMINT

Tough, come out here. Here's a fellow thinks all you need in this game is nerve. Let's see what he's got."

Dink stood out, neither hearing nor caring for the laugh that went up. He glanced up fifteen yards away where Tough McCarty stood waiting the starting signal. He was not afraid, he was angry clean through, ready to tackle the whole squad, one after another.

"Shall I take it sideways?" said Tough, expecting to be tackled from the side as the others had been.

"No, head on, Tough. Let's see if you can get by him," said Cockrell. "Let her go!"

McCarty, with the memory of past defiances, went toward Stover head down, full tilt. Ordinarily in practice the runner slackens just before the tackle; but McCarty, expecting slight resistance from a novice, arrived at top speed.

Stover, instead of hesitating or waiting the coming, hurled himself recklessly forward. Shoulder met knee with a crash that threw them both. Stunned by the savage impact, Stover, spilled head over heels, dizzy and furious, instinctively flung himself from his knees upon the prostrate body of McCarty, as he had followed the elusive ball a moment before.

"That's instinct, football instinct," said Mr. Ware to Cockrell, as they approached the spot where Dink, still dazed, was clutching Tough McCarty's knees in a convulsive hug.

"Let go! Let go there, you little varmint," said Tough McCarty, considerably shaken. "How long are you going to hold me here?"

Some one touched Dink on the shoulder; he looked up through the blur to see the captain's face.

"All right, Dink, get up."

But Stover released his grip not a whit.

"Here, you young bulldog," said Cockrell with a laugh, "it's all over. Let go. Stand up. Sort of groggy, eh?"

Dink, pulled to his feet, felt the earth slip under him in drunken reelings.

"I missed him," he said brokenly, leaning against Mr. Ware.

"H'm, not so bad," said the coach gruffly.

"How do you feel?" said Garry Cockrell, looking at him with his quiet smile.

Dink saw the smile and misjudged it.

"Give me another chance," he cried furiously. "I'll get him."

"What! Ready for another tackle?" said the captain, looking at him intently.

"Please, sir."

"Well, get your head clear first."

"Let me take it now, sir!"

"All right."

THE VARMINT

"Hit him harder than he hits you, and grip with your hands," said the voice of Mr. Ware in his ear.

Dink stood out again. The earth was gradually returning to a state of equilibrium, but his head was buzzing and his legs were decidedly rebels to his will.

The captain, seeing this, to give him time, spoke to McCarty with just a shade of malice.

"Well, Tough, do you want to take it again?"

"Do I?" said McCarty sarcastically. "Oh, yes, most enjoyable! Don't let me interfere with your pleasure. Why don't you try it yourself?"

"Would you rather watch?"

"Oh, no, of course not. This is a real pleasure, thank you. The little devil would dent a freight train."

"All ready, Stover?" said Cockrell.

The players stood in two lines, four yards apart. No one laughed. They looked at Stover, thrilling a little with his communicated recklessness, grunting forth their approval.

"Good nerve."

"The real stuff."

"Pure grit."

"Little devil."

Stover's face had gone white, the eyes had dwindled and set intensely, the line of the mouth was drawn taut, while on his forehead the wind lifted the matted hair like a banner. In the middle of the lane, crowding forward, his arms out, ready to spring, his glance fixed on Mc-Carty, he waited like a champion guarding the pass.

"All right, Stover?"

Some one near him repeated the question.

"Come on!" he answered.

McCarty's one hundred and seventy pounds came rushing down. But this time the instinct was strong. He slacked a bit at the end as Stover, not waiting his coming, plunged in to meet him. Down they went again, but this time it was the force of Stover's impact that threw them.

When Cockrell came up, Dink, altogether groggy, was entwined around one leg of McCarty with a gaunt grin of possession.

They hauled him up, patted him on the back and walked him up and down in the cool breeze. Suddenly, after several minutes, the mist rose. He saw the fields and heard the sharp cries of the coaches prodding on the players. Then he looked up to find Garry Cockrell's arm about him.

"All right now?" said the captain's voice.

Stover hastily put the arm away from him.

"I'm all right."

"Did I give you a little too much, youngster?"

"I'm ready again," said Stover instantly.

Cockrell laughed a short, contented laugh.

"You've done enough for to-day."

"I'll learn how," said Dink doggedly.

"You know the real things in football now, my boy," said the captain shortly. "We'll teach you the rest."

Dink thought he meant it sarcastically.

"You will give me a chance, won't you?" he said.

"Yes," said the captain, laying his hand on his shoulder with a smile. "You'll get chance enough, my boy. Fact is, I'm going to start you in at end on the scrub. You'll get all the hard knocks you're looking for there. You won't get any credit for what you do—but you boys are what's going to make the team."

"Oh, sir, do you mean it?"

"I'm in the habit of meaning things."

"I'll—I'll——" began Stover, and then stopped before the impossibility of expressing how many times his life should be thrown to the winds.

"I know you will," said the captain, amused. "And now, you young bulldog, back to your room and shake yourself together."

"But I want to go on; I'm feeling fine."

"Off the field," said the captain with terrific sternness.

THE VARMINT

Dink went like a dog ordered home, slowly, unwillingly, turning from time to time in hopes that his captain would relent.

When he had passed the chapel and the strife of the practice had dropped away he felt all at once sharp, busy pains running up his back and over his shoulders. But he minded them not. At that moment with the words of the captain—*his* captain forever now—ringing in his ears, he would have gone forth gratefully to tackle the whole team, one after another, from wiry little Charlie DeSoto to the elephantine P. Lentz.

Suddenly a thought came to him.

"Gee, I bet I shook up Tough McCarty, anyhow," he said grimly. And refreshed by this delightful thought he went briskly across the Circle.

At the steps Finnegan, coming out the door, hailed him excitedly:

"Hi, Dink, we've got a Freshman who's setting up to jiggers and éclairs. Hurry up!"

"No," said Dink.

"What?" said Dennis faintly.

"I can't," said Dink, bristling; "I'm in training."

XIII

The Tennessee Shad, reclining in an armchair softened by sofa cushions, gave critical directions to Dink Stover and Dennis de Brian de Boru Finnegan, to whom, with great unselfishness, he had surrendered all the privileges of the hanging committee.

"Suppose *you* agitate yourself a little," said Dink, descending from a rickety chair which, placed on a table, had allowed him to suspend a sporting print from the dusty moulding.

"The sight of you at hard labor," said Finnegan, from a bureau on the other side of the room, "would fill me with cheer, delectation and comfort."

The Tennessee Shad, by four convulsive processes, reached his feet.

"Oh, very well," he said carelessly. "Thought you preferred to run this show yourselves."

Picking up a poster, he selected with malicious intent the most unsuitable spot in the room and started to climb the bureau, remarking:

"This is about it, I should say."

The artistic souls of Dink and Dennis protested.

"Murder, no!"

"You chump!"

"Too big for it."

"Well, if you know so much," said the Tennessee Shad, halting before the last upward struggle and holding out the poster, "where would you put it?"

Stover and Dennis indignantly bore the poster away and with much effort and straining tacked it in an appropriate place.

"Why, that is better," said the Tennessee Shad admiringly, regaining his chair, not too openly. "Much better. Looks fine! Great! Say, I've got an idea. Stick the ballet girl under it."

"What?"

"You're crazy!"

"Well, where would you put it?"

"Here, you chump.'

"Why, that's not half bad, either," said the Tennessee Shad, once more back among the cushions. "A trifle more to the left, down—now up—good—make fast. First rate; guess you have the best eye. Now where are you going to put this?"

By this process of self-debasement and generous exterior admiration the Tennessee Shad successfully perceived the heavy hanging and arranging brought to a satisfactory conclusion.

THE VARMINT

The vital touches were given, the transom was hung with heavy black canvas; a curtain of the same was so arranged as to permit its being drawn over the telltale cracks of the door. Dennis and Stover, sent to reconnoiter from the hall, waited while the Tennessee Shad passed a lighted candle back and forth over the sealed entrance. One traitor crack was discovered and promptly obliterated.

"Now we're secure," said the Tennessee Shad. "Cave of Silence and all that sort of thing. The Old Roman would have to smell us to get on."

"How about the windows?" said Dink.

"They're a cinch," said the Shad. "When you get the shade down and the shutters closed a blanket will fix them snug as a bug in a rug. Now, at nine o'clock we can go to bed without suffering from drafts. Ha, ha—joke."

"Burn the midnight oil, etceteray—etcetera."

"To-morrow," said the Tennessee Shad, "Volts Mashon is going to install a safety light for us."

"Elucidate," said Dink.

"A safety light is a light that has a connection with the door. Shut door, light; open door, where is Moses? Midnight reading made a pleasure."

"Marvelous!"

THE VARMINT

"Oh, I've heard of that before," said Finnegan.

The Tennessee Shad, meanwhile, had been busy stretching a string from his bed to the hot-air register and from a stick at the foot of his bed to a pulley at the top.

Stover and Finnegan waited respectfully until the Shad, having finished his operations, deigned to give a practical exhibition.

"This thing is simple," said he, stretching out on his bed and pulling a string at one side. "Opens hot-air register. No applause necessary. But this is a little, comforting idea of my own. Protection from sudden change of temperature without bodily exposure." Extending his hand he pulled the other rope, which, running through the pulley over his head, brought the counterpane quickly over him. "How's that? No sitting up, reaching down, fumbling about in zero weather."

"That's good as far as it goes," said Dennis, whose natural state was not one of reverence; "but how about the window? Some one has to get up and shut the window."

"Simple as eggs," said the Shad, yawning disdainfully. "A string and a pulley do the trick, see? Down comes the window. All worked at the same exchange. Well, Dink, you may lead the cheer."

THE VARMINT

Now, Stover suddenly remembered a device he had been told of, and, remembering it, to give it the appearance of improvisation he pretended to deliberate.

"Well," said the Tennessee Shad, surprised, "my humble little inventions don't seem to impress you."

"Naw."

"They don't, eh! Why not?"

"Oh, it's the right principle," said Stover, assuming a deliberate look; "but crude, very crude, backwoods, primitive, and all that sort of thing."

The Tennessee Shad, amazed, looked at Finnegan, who spoke:

"Crude, Dink?"

"Why, yes. All depends on whether the Shad wakes up or not. And then, why hand labor?"

"I suppose you have something more recherché to offer," said the Tennessee Shad cuttingly, having recovered.

"Why, yes, I might," said Stover coolly. "A real inventor would run the whole thing by machinery. Who's got an alarm clock?"

Dennis, mystified, returned running with his.

Stover, securing it with strings, fastened it firmly on the table, which he moved near the scene of operations. He then lowered the upper half of the window, assuring himself that a slight impetus would start it. To the sash he attached a stout string which he ran through a pulley fixed to the top of the window frame; to the string he fastened a weight which he carefully balanced on the edge of a chair; to the weight, thus fastened, he attached another string which he led to the clock and made fast to the stem that wound the alarm. Then he straightened up, cast a glance over the Shad's handiwork and went to the register.

"When the window shuts it should open the register, of course—first principles," he said crushingly. He disconnected the string from the bed and arranged it on the window. Having wound the clock he addressed his audience:

"It's a simple little thing," he said with a wave of his hand. "I happened to remember that the key of an alarm clock turns as the alarm works. That's all there is to it. Set the alarm when you want to wake up—see—like this. Alarm goes off, winds up spring, throws weight off balance, weight falls, shuts the window, opens the register and you stay under the covers. Practical demonstration now proceeding."

The mechanism worked exactly as he had predicted. The Tennessee Shad and the Wild Irishman, transfixed with awe, watched with dropped mouths the operation. Finnegan, the first to recover, salaamed in true Oriental fashion.

"Mr. Edison," he said in a whisper, "don't

take advantage of two innocent babes in the wood. Did you honestly just work this out?"

"Oh, no, of course not," said Dink loftily. "My father told me,—it cost him a fortune; he gave years of his life to perfecting it!"

"And this to me!" said the exponent of the superlative reproachfully.

The Tennessee Shad rose and offered his hand with a gesture worthy of Washington.

"Sir to you. I am your humble servant. Wonderful! Marvelous! Smashing! Terrific! Sublime!"

"Do it again," said Dennis de Brian de Boru.

The alarm being wound and set, the operation was repeated with the same success, while Dennis danced about excitedly and the Tennessee Shad contemplated it with dreamy absorption.

"Jemima!" said Dennis. "And it works for any time?"

"Any time," said Dink, with one hand gracefully resting on his hip.

"Cracky!" exclaimed Dennis, prancing excitedly toward the door. "I'll get the whole House up."

"Dennis!"

Finnegan stopped, surprised at the note of authority in the Tennessee Shad's voice.

"Dennis de Brian de Boru Finnegan; back and sit down."

THE VARMINT

"What's wrong?"

"You would call in the whole House, would you?"

"Why not?" said Dink, thirsting for the applause of the multitude.

"Dink, oh, Dink!" said the Shad, in profound sorrow. "You would throw away a secret worth millions, would you?"

Dink looked at Dennis, who returned the look, and then with a simultaneous motion they sat down.

"This invention has millions in it, millions," said the Tennessee Shad, promoter. "It is simple, but revolutionary. Every room in the school must be equipped with it."

"Then there's all the apartment houses," said Dennis eagerly.

"That will come later," said the Tennessee Shad.

"We'll patent it," said Stover, seeing clouds of gold.

"Certainly," said the promoter. "We will patent the principle."

"Let's form a company."

The three rose and solemnly joined hands.

"What shall we call it?"

"The Third Triumvirate?" said Dennis.

"Good!" said the Tennessee Shad.

"What shall we charge?" said Dink.

THE VARMINT

"We must make a dollar profit on each," said the Tennessee Shad. "That means—four hundred fellows in the school—allowing for roommates; we should clear two hundred and ten dollars at the lowest. That means seventy dollars apiece profit."

"Let's begin," said Dennis.

"I'm unalterably opposed," said Dink, "to allowing Doc Macnooder in the firm."

"Me, too," said Dennis.

"Doc is strong on detail," said the Tennessee Shad doubtfully.

"I'm unalterably opposed," said Dink, "to allowing Doc Macnooder to swallow this firm."

"Me, too," said Dennis.

"Doc has great business experience," said the Tennessee Shad; "wonderful, practical mind."

"I'm unalterably——" said Dink and stopped, as the rest was superfluous.

"Me, too," said Dennis.

"Some one's got to work for us in the other Houses."

"Make him our foreign representative," said Stover.

"And give him a commission?"

"Sure—ten per cent."

"No more," said Dennis. "Even that cuts down our profits."

"All right," said the Tennessee Shad. "As

you say, so be it. But still I think Doc Macnooder's business sagacity——"

At this moment Doc Macnooder walked into the room. The three future millionaires responded to his greeting with dignity, keeping in mind that distance which should separate a board of directors from a mere traveling man.

"Hello," said Macnooder glibly. "All shipshape and ready for action. Tea served here and chafing-dish ready for the midnight rabbit. Ha, ha, Dink, still got the souvenir toilet set, I see."

"Still, but not long," said Dink. "But that story comes later. Sit down, Doc, and pay attention."

"Why so much chestiness?" said Doc, puzzled. "I haven't sold anything to any of you, have I?"

"Doc," said Stover, "we have formed a company and we want to talk business."

"What company?"

"The Third Triumvirate Manufacturing Company," said Dennis.

"What does it manufacture?"

"This," said Stover, indicating the appliance. "A combined window closer and alarm clock that also opens the register."

"Let's see it," said Macnooder, all excitement.

The demonstration took place. Macnooder the

enthusiast was conquered, but Macnooder the financier remained cold and controlled. He sat down, watched by three pairs of eyes, took from his pocket a pair of spectacles, placed them on his nose and said indifferently:

"Well?"

"What do you think of it?"

"It's a beaut!"

"I say, Doc," said Finnegan, "now, won't every fellow in the school be crying for one, won't be happy till he gets it, and all that sort of thing?"

"Every fellow in the school will have one," said Macnooder carefully, making a distinction which was perceived only by the Tennessee Shad.

"Now, Doc," said Dink, still glowing with his triumph over the Tennessee Shad, "let's talk business."

Macnooder took off the glasses and minutely polished them with his handkerchief.

"You've formed a company, eh?"

"The Third Triumvirate—the three of us."

"Well, where do I come in?"

"You're to be our foreign representative."

"Commission ten per cent," added Finnegan carefully.

The Tennessee Shad said nothing, waiting expectantly. Macnooder rose whistling through his teeth and stood gazing down at the alarm clock.

THE VARMINT

"Foreign representative, commission ten per cent," he said softly.

"We thought we'd give you first whack at it," said Stover in a careless, business-like way.

"So. What's your idea of developing it?"

"Why, we thought of installing it for a dollar."

"With the clock?"

"Oh, no! The clock extra."

"Charging a dollar for string and pulley?"

"And the invention."

"Humph!"

"Well, Doc, is it a go?" said Dink, observing him fall into a revery.

"No, I guess I'm not much interested in this," said Macnooder, taking up his hat. "There's no money in it."

"Why, Doc," said Finnegan, aghast, "you said yourself every fellow would have to have it."

"Would have it," said Macnooder in correction. "The invention's all right, but it's not salable."

"Why not?"

"Nothing to sell. First fellow who sees it can do it himself."

Finnegan looked at Stover, who suddenly felt his pockets lighten.

"Doc is very strong on detail," said the Tennessee Shad softly, in a reminiscent way.

"You might sell it to one fellow," said Macnooder, "without telling him. But soon as you set it up every one will copy it."

"Great business head," continued the Tennessee Shad.

"It's a good idea," said Macnooder condescendingly. "You might get a vote of thanks, but that's all you would get. Do you see the rub?"

"I see," said Dink.

"Me, too," said Dennis.

"And a wonderful practical mind," concluded the Tennessee Shad dreamily.

"Well, let's be public benefactors then," said Dennis in a melancholy tone.

"And such a beautiful idea," said Dink mournfully.

"I move the Third Triumvirate disband," said the Tennessee Shad; and there was no objection.

"Now," said Doc Macnooder briskly, sitting down, "I'll put my own proposition to you amateurs. There's only one way to make the thing go, and I've got the way. I take all responsibility and all risks. All I ask is control of the stock—fifty-one per cent."

Ten minutes later the Third Triumvirate Manufacturing Company was reformed on the following basis:

THE VARMINT

President . . . . Doc Macnooder, 51 shares.
Advisory Board . The Third Triumvirate.
Treasurer . . . Doc Macnooder.

Paid-up Capital

Macnooder	$5.10
The Tennessee Shad	1.70
Dink Stover	1.70
Dennis de B. de B. Finnegan	1.50

"Now," said Macnooder, when the articles were safely signed and the capital paid up, "here's the way we work it. We've got to do two things: first, conceal the way it's done until we sell it; and second, keep those who buy from letting on."

"That's hard," said the Tennessee Shad.

"But necessary. I'm thinking out a plan."

"Of course the first part is a cinch," said Dennis. "A few extras, etcetera, etceteray. It's putting the ribbons in the lingerie, that's all."

"Exactly."

"You don't think it's selling goods under false pretenses?"

"Naw," said Macnooder. "Same principle as the patent medicine—the only wheel that goes round there is a nice, fat temperance measure of alcohol, isn't it? We'll have the first public demonstration to-morrow afternoon. I'll distribute a few more pearls to-night. Ta, ta."

The three sat quietly, listening to the fall of his departing steps.

"If we'd asked him in the first place," said the Tennessee Shad, gazing out the window, "we'd only given up twenty-five per cent.—great business head, Doc; great mind for detail."

XIV

Macnooder, that night, formed the Eureka Purchasing Company, incorporated himself, and secured, at jigger rates, every second-hand alarm clock on which he could lay his hands—but more of that hereafter.

At five o'clock the next afternoon the combined Kennedy House packed itself into the Tennessee Shad's room, where Doc Macnooder rose and addressed them:

"Gentlemen of the Kennedy: I will only detain you an hour or so; I have only a few thousand words to offer. We are gathered here on an auspicious occasion, a moment of history—the moment *is* historical. Your esteemed Housemate, Mr. Dink Stover, has completed, after years of endeavor, an invention that is destined to be a household word from the northernmost wilds of the Davis House to the sun-kissed fragrance of the Green, from the Ethiopian banks of the fur-bearing canal to the Western Tins of Hot-dog Land! Gentlemen, I will be frank——"

"Cheese it!" said a voice.

"I will be frank," repeated Macnooder, turning on them a countenance on which candor

THE VARMINT

struggled with innocence. "I did not wish or encourage the present method of procedure. As a member of the Dickinson House I combated the proposition of Mr. Stover and his associates to make this invention a Kennedy House sinecure. I still combat it—but I yield. If they wish to give away their profits they can. Gentlemen, in a few moments I shall have the pleasure of placing before you an opportunity to become shareholders in one of the most epoch-making inventions the world has ever known."

"What's it called?" said a voice.

"It's called," said Macnooder slowly, secure now of the attention of his audience, "it's called The Complete Sleep Prolonger. The title itself is a promise and a hope. I will claim nothing for this wonderful little invention. It not only combats the cold, but it encourages the heat; it prolongs not only the sleep, but the existence; it will increase the stature, make fat men thin, thin men impressive, clear the complexion, lighten the eye and make the hair long and curly."

"Let's have it," cried several voices.

"Gentlemen," said Macnooder, seeing that no further delay was possible, "our first demonstration will be entitled The Old Way."

Dennis de Brian de Boru Finnegan, in pajamas, appeared from a closet, went to the

THE VARMINT

window, opened it, shut the register, yawned, went to his bed and drew the covers over his head. The faint sounds of a mandolin were heard from the expert hands of the Tennessee Shad.

"Scene," said Macnooder, fitting his accents to low music as is the custom of vaudeville—"scene represents the young Lawrenceville boy, exhausted by the preparation of the next day's lessons, seeking to rest his too conscientious brain. The night passes, the wind rises. It grows cold. Hark the rising bell. He hears it not. What now? He rises in his bed, the room is bitter cold. He bounds to the window over the frozen ground. He springs to the register and back to his bed. He looks at his watch. Heavens! Not a moment to lose. The room is bitter cold, but he must up and dress!"

Finnegan, completing the pantomime, returned with thunders of applause.

"Gentlemen," cried Macnooder, "is this picture a true one?"

And the roar came back:

"You bet!"

"Our next instructive little demonstration is entitled The Scientific Way or The Sleep Prolonger Watches Over Him. Observe now the modest movements of the Dink, the Kennedy House Edison."

THE VARMINT

Dink, thus introduced, connected the hot-air register to the window sash, the window sash to the weight—specially covered with tin foil—and brought forth the table on which was the now completed Sleep Prolonger. Only the face of the clock appeared, the rest was buried under an arrangement of cardboard boxes and perfectly useless spools, that turned with the rope that took a thrice devious way to the alarm key. In front, two Kennedy House flags were prominently displayed.

"Is everything ready, Mr. Stover?" said Macnooder, while the crowd craned forth, amazed at the intricacy of the machine.

"Ready, Mr. President."

"Second demonstration," said Macnooder.

Finnegan again entered, fixed the register, lowered the window and, going to the clock, set the alarm.

"He sets the alarm for half-past seven," said Macnooder in cadence. "One half-hour gained. The night passes. The wind rises. It grows cold. Hark the rising bell. He hears it not; he doesn't have to. The Sleep Prolonger is there."

The alarm shot off with a suddenness that brought responsive jumps from the audience, the weight fell, and to the amazement of all, the window closed and the register opened.

THE VARMINT

"Watch him now, watch him," cried Macnooder, hushing the tumult of applause. "Observe the comfort and the satisfaction in his look. He has not stirred, not a limb of his body has been exposed, and yet the room grows warm. His eye is on the clock; he will rise in time, and he will rise in comfort!

"Gentlemen, this great opportunity is now before you. This marvel of human ingenuity, this baffling example of mechanical intricacy is now within your reach. It can do anything. It is yours. It is yours at prices that would make a miner turn from picking up gold nuggets. It is yours for one dollar and twenty-five cents—twenty-five cents is our profit, gentlemen, and you get one profit-sharing bonus. And, furthermore, each of the first fifteen purchasers who will pay the sum of one-fifty will receive not one, but three eight-per-cent., accumulative, preferred bonuses."

"Bonus for what?" said an excited voice.

"Twenty-five per cent. of the net profits," cried Macnooder, thumping the table, "will be set aside for pro-rata distribution. The device itself remains for three days a secret, until the completion of the patents. Orders from the model set up and installed in twenty-four hours now acceptable, cash down. No crowding there, first fifteen get three bonuses—one at a time;

keep back there—no crowding, no pushing—no pushing, boys. Here, stop! Owing to the extraordinary demand, have I the advisory board's consent to give every purchaser present who pays one-fifty three bonuses? I have? Let her go! Mr. Finnegan, take down the names. Cash, right over here!"

"I don't like this idea of bonuses," said Finnegan, when the rooms had returned to their quiet again.

"Twenty-five per cent., Doc!" said the Tennessee Shad reproachfully.

"Why, you chump," said Macnooder proudly, "that's what's called the profit-sharing system. It keeps 'em quiet, and it also keeps 'em from going out and giving the game away. Mark my words."

"But twenty-five per cent.," said the Tennessee Shad, shaking his head.

"Of the profits—net profits," said Macnooder. "There's a way to get around that. I'll show you later."

"We must get to work and round up some alarm clocks," said Stover.

"I've already thought of that," said Doc, as he took his leave. "Don't worry about that. Now I'll canvas the Dickinson."

"A slight feeling of uneasiness," said the Tennessee Shad solemnly, when Macnooder had departed—"a slight feeling of uneasiness is stealing over me, as the poet says."

"Let's have a look at the articles of incorporation," said Stover, who sat down with Dennis to study them.

"We're the advisory board," said Dennis stoutly.

"He's got fifty-one per cent. of the stock, though," said Dink.

"But we've got forty-nine!"

The Tennessee Shad, who had not risen from his chair as it involved extraordinary exertion, was heard repeating in a lonely sort of way to himself:

"A slight feeling of uneasiness."

By the next nightfall every room in the Kennedy was equipped with a Complete Sleep Prolonger. Their reception was exactly as Macnooder had foreseen. At first a roar went up as soon as the simplicity of the device was unearthed, but the thought of the precious bonuses soon quelled the revolt.

Besides, there was no doubt of the great humanizing effects of the invention, and the demand that it would awaken throughout the whole school.

But an obstacle arose to even the deep-laid plans of Macnooder himself. As the Third Triumvirate Manufacturing Company had bought

THE VARMINT

its stock from the Eureka Purchasing Company—which had cornered the alarm-clock market—it followed that the alarm clocks were distinctly second rate.

The consequence was that, though all were set for half-past seven, the first gun went off at about quarter-past two in the morning, bringing Mr. Bundy, the assistant house master, to the middle of the floor in one terrified bound, and starting a giggle that ran the darkened house like an epidemic.

At half-past three another explosion took place, aggravated this time by the fact that, the window pulleys being worn, the sash flew up with enough force to shatter most of the glass.

At four o'clock, when three more went off in friendly conjunction, The Roman met Mr. Bundy in the hall in light marching costume, and made a few very forcible remarks on the duties of subordinates—the same being accentuated by the wailing complaint of the youngest Roman which resounded through the house.

From then on the musketry continued intermittently until half-past seven, when such a salvo went off that the walls of the house seemed jarred apart.

The Third Triumvirate went down to breakfast with small appetite. To add to their apprehension, during the long wakeful reaches of the

THE VARMINT

night there had been borne to their ears faint but unmistakable sounds from the opposite Dickinson and the Woodhull, which had convinced them that there, too, the great invention of the age had been betrayed by defective supplies.

The Roman looked haggard; Mr. Bundy haggard and aggressive.

"Northwester coming," said the Tennessee Shad under his breath. "I know the signs."

"It's all Macnooder," said Stover bitterly.

At first recitation The Roman flunked Stover on the review, on the gerund and gerundive, on the use of hendiadys—a most unfair exhibition of persecution—on several supines, and requested him to remain after class.

"Ahem, John," he said, bringing to bear the batteries of his eyes on the embattled Dink, "you were, I take it, at the bottom, so to speak, of last night's outrage. Yes? Speak up."

"May I ask, sir," said Dink, very much aggrieved—for masters should confine themselves to evidence and not draw deductions—"I should like to know by what right you pick on me?"

The Roman, knowing thoroughly the subject under hand, did not condescend to argue, but smiled a thin, wan smile.

"You were, John, weren't you?"

"I was—that is, I invented it."

"Invented it?" said The Roman, sending one eyebrow toward the ceiling. "Invented what?"

THE VARMINT

"The Sleep Prolonger," said Dink very proudly.

"Prolonger!" said The Roman, with the jarring memories of the night upon him. "Explain, sir!"

Dink went minutely over the detailed construction of the invention of the age. By request, he repeated the same while The Roman followed, tracing a plan upon his pad. At the conclusion Dink waited aggressively, watching The Roman, who continued to stare at his sketch.

"One question, John," he said, without raising his eyes. "Was the Kennedy the only house thus favored?"

"No, sir. Macnooder installed them in the Dickinson and the Woodhull."

"Ah!" As though finding comfort in this last statement, The Roman raised his head and said slowly: "Dear me! I see, I see now. Quite a relief. It is evident from your recital, John, that at least there was no concerted effort to destroy the property of the school. I withdraw the term outrage, in so far as it may suggest outrages of pillage or anarchy. As to the continued usefulness of what you so felicitously term the Sleep Prolonger, that will have to be a subject of consultation with the Doctor, but—but, as your friend, I should advise you, for the present, not to risk any further capital in the venture. Don't do it, John, don't do it."

THE VARMINT

"Tyrant!" said Stover to himself. Aloud he asked: "Is that all, sir?"

"One moment—one moment, John. Are you contemplating any further inventions?"

"Why, no, sir."

"On your honor, John?"

"Why, yes, sir."

"Good—very good. You may go now."

At noon, by virtue of an extraordinary order from headquarters, all alarm clocks were confiscated and ordered to be surrendered.

"It's all the Old Roman," said Stover doggedly. "He knew it was my invention. He's got it in for me, I tell you."

"Anyhow," said Finnegan, "since Doc planted a few Prolongers in the Dickinson and the Woodhull we ought to be able to stack up a few nice, round plunks."

The Tennessee Shad looked very thoughtful.

At this moment the Gutter Pup and P. Lentz, representing the profit-sharing stockholders, called to know when the surplus was to be divided.

"Macnooder is now at work on the books," said Dink. "We expect him over at any time."

But when at eight o'clock that evening no word had been received from the president, the Third Triumvirate held a meeting and sent the Tennessee Shad over to the Dickinson, with orders to return only with the bullion, for which

THE VARMINT

purpose he was equipped with a small, black satchel.

Just before lights the Tennesse Shad's dragging step was heard returning.

"I don't like the sound," said Dink, listening.

"He always shuffles his feet," said Dennis, clinging to hope.

The door opened and the Tennessee Shad, carrying the black satchel, solemnly entered. Dink flung himself on the bag, wrenched it open and let it drop, exclaiming:

"Nothing!"

"Nothing?" said Dennis, rising.

"Nothing," said the Tennessee Shad, sitting down.

"But the profits?"

"The profits," said the Tennessee Shad, pointing sarcastically to the bag, "are in there."

"Do you mean to say——" began Dink and stopped.

"I mean to say that the Third Triumvirate Manufacturing Company is insolvent, bankrupt, busted, up the spout."

"But then, who's got the coin?"

"Doc Macnooder," said the Tennessee Shad, "and it's all legal."

"Legal?"

"All legal. It's this way. Our profits depended upon the price we paid for alarm clocks.

THE VARMINT

See? Well, when Doc Macnooder, as president of the Third Triumvirate Manufacturing Company looked around for clocks, he found that Doc Macnooder, as president of the Eureka Purchasing Company, had cornered the market and could dictate the price."

"So that?" said Stover indignantly.

"So that each clock was charged up to us at a rate ranging from one dollar and forty cents to one dollar and fifty."

"By what right?" said Dennis.

"It's what is called a subsidiary company," said the Tennessee Shad. "It's quite popular nowadays."

"But where's the stock we subscribed?" said Dennis, thinking of his one dollar and fifty cents. "We get that back?"

"No."

"What!" said the two in unison.

"It's this way. Owing to executive interference, the Third Triumvirate Manufacturing Company is liable to the Eureka Purchasing Company for ten alarm clocks, which it has ordered and can't use."

"But then, out of the whole, blooming mess," said Dennis, quite overcome, "where do I stand?"

The Tennessee Shad unfolded a paper and read:

THE VARMINT

"You owe the Eureka, as your share of the assessment, two dollars and forty cents."

"Owe!" said Finnegan with a scream.

"Just let him come," said Dink, doubling up his fists. "Let him come and assess us!"

The three sat in long silence. Finally the Tennessee Shad spoke:

"I am afraid Doc was sore because we tried to freeze him out at first. It was a mistake."

No one noticed this.

"Great Willie Keeler!" said Dennis suddenly. "If this thing had been a success we'd have been ruined!"

"But what right," said Dink, unwilling to give up the fight, "had he to pay the Eureka such prices. Who authorized him?"

"A vote of fifty-one per cent. of the stock," said the Tennessee Shad.

"But he never said anything to us—the forty-nine per cent. Has the minority no rights?"

"The minority," said the Tennessee Shad, speaking beyond his horizon, "the minority has only one inalienable right, the right to indorse."

"I'll get even with him," said Dink, after a blank period.

"I suppose," said Dennis de Brian de Boru Finnegan, "that's what's called Finance."

And the Tennessee Shad nodded assent:

"Higher Finance, Dennis."

XV

During the busy October week Dink found little time to vent the brewing mischief within him. The afternoons were given over to the dogged pursuit of the elusive pigskin. In the evenings he resolutely turned his back on all midnight spreads or expeditions to the protecting shadows of the woods to smoke the abhorrent cigarette, for the joy of the risk run. At nine o'clock promptly each night he dove into bed, wrapped the covers about his head and, leaving the Tennessee Shad deep in the pages of Dumas, went soaring off into lands where goals are kicked from the center of the field, winning touchdowns scored in the last minute of play and bonfires lighted for his special honor. He was only end on the scrub, eagerly learning the game; but with the intensity of his nature that territory, which each afternoon he lined up to defend, was his in sacred trust; and he resolved that the trust of his captain should not be misplaced if it lay in his power to prevent it.

However, the busy mind was not entirely inactive. With the memory of his financial disappointment came the resolve to square himself

THE VARMINT

with The Roman and turn the tables on Doc Macnooder.

The opportunity to do the first came in an unexpected way.

One evening P. Lentz came in upon them in great agitation.

"Why, King," said Dennis, who was lolling around, "you're excited, very, very much excited!"

"Shut up!" said the King of the Kennedy, who was in anything but a good humor. "It's the deuce to pay. I've had a first warning."

At this every one looked grave, and Dink, the loyalist, said:

"Oh, King, how could you!"

For another warning meant banishment from the football team and all the devastation that implied.

"That would just about end us," said Dennis. "Might as well save Andover the traveling expenses."

"I know, I know!" said P. Lentz furiously. "I've had it all said to me. Beautifully expressed, too. Question is, what's to be done? It's all the fault of old Baranson. He's been down on me ever since we licked the Woodhull."

"We must think of something," said the Tennessee Shad.

"How about a doctor's certificate?"

THE VARMINT

"Rats!"

"We might get up a demonstration against Baranson."

"Lot's of good that'll do me!"

Various suggestions were offered and rejected.

"Well, King," said the Tennessee Shad at last, "I don't see there's anything to it but you'll have to buckle down and study."

"Study?" said P. Lentz. "Is that the best you can produce?"

"It seems the simplest."

"I came here for consolation," said P. Lentz, who thereupon departed angrily.

"Still, it'll come to that," said the Tennessee Shad.

"P. Lentz study?" said Finnegan contemptuously. "Can a duck whistle?"

"Then we'll have to tutor him."

"What says Dink?"

"Don't bother me, I'm thinking."

"Gracious, may I watch you?"

"Shad," said Stover, ignoring Dennis, "did it ever occur to you how unscientific this whole game is?"

"What game?"

"This chasing the Latin root, wrestling with the unknown equation, and all that sort of thing."

"Proceed."

THE VARMINT

"Why are we smashed up? Because we are discouraged all fighting alone, unscientifically. Does the light dawn?"

"Very slowly," said the Tennessee Shad. "Keep dawning."

"I am thinking of organizing," said Stover impressively, "The Kennedy Co-operative Educational Institute."

"Aha!" said the Tennessee Shad. "*Video, je vois,* I see. All third-formers in the house meet, divide up the lesson and then fraternize."

"Where do I come in?" said Finnegan, who was two forms below.

"A very excellent idea," said the Tennessee Shad in final approval.

"I've a better one now," said Stover.

"Why, Dink!"

"It begins by chucking the Co-operative idea."

"How so?"

"There's no money in that," said Stover. "We must give the courses ourselves, see?"

"Give?" said the Tennessee Shad. "We two shining marks!"

"No," said Stover contemptuously. "We hire the lecturers and collect from the lectured."

"Why, Shad," said Finnegan, in wide-eyed admiration, "our boy is growing up!"

"He is, he certainly is. I love the idea!"

THE VARMINT

"Why, I think it's pretty good myself," said Dink.

"It has only one error—the lecturers."

"Why, that's the finest of the fine," said Dink indignantly. "You see what I do. Here's Beekstein and Gumbo Binks been laying around as waste material and the whole house kicking because we've been stuck with two midnight-oilers. Now what do I do? I utilize them. I make them a credit to the house, useful citizens."

"True, most true," said the Tennessee Shad. "But why pay? Never pay any one anything."

Stover acknowledged the superior financial mind, while Finnegan remained silent, his greatest tribute.

"I suppose we might lasso them," said Stover, "or bring them up in chains."

"That's only amateurish and besides reprehensible," said the Tennessee Shad. "No, the highest principle in finance, the real cream de la crème, is to make others pay you for what you want them to do."

Stover slowly assimilated this profound truth.

"We'll charge twenty-five cents a week to students and we'll make Beekstein and Gumbo disgorge half a plunk each for letting us listen to them."

"I am ready to be convinced," said Dink, who still doubted.

THE VARMINT

"I'll show you how it's done," said the Tennessee Shad, who, going to the door, called out: "Oh, you Beekstein!"

"Profound, profound mind," said Dennis de Brian de Boru Finnegan. "Doc Macnooder is better on detail, but when it comes to theory the Tennessee Shad is the Willie Keeler boy every time!"

"I've another idea," said Stover, "a way to get even with The Roman, too."

"What's that?"

"To signal the gerund and the gerundive."

"Magnificent and most popular!" said the Tennessee Shad. "We'll put that in as a guaranty. Who'll signal?"

"I'll signal," said Stover, claiming the privilege. "It's my right!"

Beekstein, who might be completely described as a pair of black-rimmed spectacles riding an aquiline nose, now shuffled in with his dictionary under his arm, his fingers between the leaves of a Cicero to which he still clung.

"Mr. Hall," said the Tennessee Shad with a flourish, "take any chair in the room."

Beekstein, alarmed by such generosity, sat down like a ramrod and cast a roving, anxious glance under the beds and behind the screen.

"Beekstein," said the Tennessee Shad, to reassure him, "we have just organized the Kennedy Educational Quick Lunch Institute. The purpose is fraternal, patriotic and convivial. It will be most exclusive and very secret." He explained the working scheme and then added anxiously: "Now, Beekstein, you see the position of First Grand Hot Tamale will be the real thing. He will be, so to speak, Valedictorian of the Kennedy and certainly ought to be elected secretary of the house next year. Now, Beekstein, what we got you here for is this. What do you think of Gumbo for the position? Well, what?"

Beekstein, in his agitation, withdrew his finger from the Orations of Cicero.

"What's the matter with me?" he said directly. "Gumbo is only a second-rater."

"He's very strong in mathematics."

"That's the only thing he beats me on!"

"Yes, but, Beekstein, there is another thing— a delicate subject. I don't know how to approach it. You see, we don't know how you're fixed for the spondulix," said the Tennessee Shad, who knew perfectly well the other's flourishing condition. "You see, this is not only educational, but a very select body, quite a secret society,—with a midnight spread now and then. Of course there are dues, you see. It would cost you a half a week."

"Is that all?" said Beekstein, who had never

belonged to a secret society in his life. "Here's the first month down. Right here."

"I don't know how far we are committed to Gumbo," said the Tennessee Shad, not disdaining to finger the two-dollar bill. "But I'll do everything I can for you."

Gumbo Binks, being consulted as to the qualifications of Beekstein, fell into the same trap. He was a monosyllabic, oldish little fellow, whose cheeks had fallen down and disturbed the balance of his already bald head. He had but one emotion and one enthusiasm, a professional jealousy of Beekstein, who was several points ahead of him in the race for first honors. Under these conditions the Tennessee Shad proceeded victoriously. Having made sure of each, he next informed them that, owing to a wide divergence of opinion, a choice seemed impossible. Each should have two months' opportunity to lecture before the Quick Lunchers before a vote would be taken.

Under these successful auspices the Institute met enthusiastically the following day, both the lecturers and the lectured ignoring the financial status of the others. It was found on careful compilation that, by close and respectful attention to Professors Beekstein and Gumbo, twenty minutes would suffice for the rendering of the Greek and Latin test; while only ten minutes

THE VARMINT

extra were needed to follow the requirements of mathematics.

The clause in the constitution which pledged defiance to The Roman and guaranteed protection on the gerund and gerundive was exceedingly popular. The signals were agreed upon. Absolute rigidity on Stover's part denounced the gerund, while a slight wriggling of his sensitive ears betrayed the approach of the abhorrent gerundive.

In his resolve to destroy forever the peace of mind of The Roman, Dink sat an extra period under Beekstein, stalking and marking down the lair of these enemies of boykind.

On the following morning The Roman lost no time in calling up P. Lentz, who, to his amazement, recited creditably.

"Dear me," said The Roman, quite astonished, "the day of miracles is not over—most astounding! Bring your book to the desk, Lentz—hem! Everything proper! Profuse apologies, Lentz, profuse ones! The suspicion is the compliment. I'm quite upset, quite so. First time such a thing has happened." He hesitated for a moment, debating whether to allow him to retire with the honors, but his curiosity proving strong he said: "And now, Lentz, third line, second word—gerund or gerundive?"

"Gerundive, sir," said P. Lentz promptly, ob-

THE VARMINT

serving Stover's ears in a state of revolution.

"Fortunate youth! Next line, third word, gerund or gerundive?"

"Gerund, sir."

"Still fortunate! Once more, make your bet, Lentz, red or black?" said The Roman, smiling, believing Lentz was risking his fortunes on the alternating system. "Once more. Sixth line, first word, gerund or gerundive?"

"Gerund, sir."

"Is it possible—is it possible?" said The Roman. "Have I lived to see it! Sit down, *Mr.* Lentz, sit down."

He sat silent a moment, his lips twitching, his eyebrows alternately jumping, gazing from the text to P. Lentz and back.

Stover, in the front row, was radiant.

"Gee, that's a stiff one for him to swallow!" he said, chuckling inwardly. "P. Lentz, of all muts!"

As luck would have it the next boy called up, not being from the Kennedy, flunked and somewhat restored The Roman's equanimity.

"Now he feels better," thought Dink. "Wait till the next jolt comes, though!"

"Lazelle," said The Roman.

The Gutter Pup rose, translated fluently and, with his eyes on Dink's admonitory ears, grap-

THE VARMINT

pled with the gerund and threw the gerundive.

"Mead," said The Roman, now thoroughly alert.

Lovely, with a show of insouciance, bagged three gerunds and one gerundive.

The Roman thought a moment and, carefully selecting the experts, sent Beekstein, Gumbo Binks, the Red Dog and Poler Fox to the blackboards. Having thus removed the bird dogs, The Roman called up Fatty Harris.

Stover, struggling to maintain his seriousness, grudgingly admired the professional manner with which The Roman attacked the mystery, the more so as it showed the wisdom of his own planning; for, had the signals been left with either Beekstein or Gumbo, the plot would have been instantly exposed.

As it was, The Roman, to his delighted imagination, at each successful answer seemed to rise under an electric application.

Stover went out radiant, to receive the delighted congratulations of the Institute and the recognition of those who were not in the secret.

"We've got him going," he said, skipping over the campus arm in arm with the Tennessee Shad. "He's nervous as a witch! It's broken him all up. He won't sleep for a week."

"He'll spot it to-morrow," said the Tennessee Shad.

THE VARMINT

"I'll lay a bet on it."

The next day The Roman, at the beginning of the lesson, ordered all the books to the desk and fruitlessly examined them. Macnooder, as spokesman for the justly indignant class, at once expressed the pain felt at this evidence of suspicion and demanded an explanation. This highly strategic manœuver, which would have tripped up a younger master, received nothing but a grim smile from The Roman who waved them to their seats and called up P. Lentz.

"Gerund or gerundive?" he began directly, at the same time rising and scanning the front ranks.

"Why, gerund, sir," said P. Lentz instantly.

"What, again?" said The Roman, who then called upon Stover.

Dink arose, watched with some trepidation by the rest; for being in the front row he could receive no signal.

"First paragraph, third word, gerund or gerundive, Stover?"

Dink took a long time, shifting a little as though trying to glance from side to side, and finally named haltingly:

"Gerund, sir."

"Next line, first word, gerund or gerundive? Look in front of you, Stover. Look at me."

Dink purposely called it wrong, likewise the next; thereby completing the mystification of

THE VARMINT

The Roman, who now concentrated his attention on Macnooder and the Tennessee Shad, as being next in order of suspicion. The day ended victoriously.

"He won't live out the week," announced Dink. "There are circles under his eyes already."

"Better quit for a day or two," said the Tennessee Shad.

"Never!"

Now the advantage of Dink's method of signaling was in its absolute naturalness. For the growing boy wiggles his ears as a pup tries his teeth or a young goat hardens his horns. Moreover, as Dink held to his plan of judicious flunking, The Roman's suspicions were completely diverted. For three days more the lover of the gerund and the gerundive sought to localize and detect the sources of information without avail.

Finally on the sixth day The Roman arrived with a briskness that was at once noted and analyzed. P. Lentz was called and translated.

"We will now take up our daily recreation," said The Roman, in a gentle voice. "It has been a matter of pleasure to me—not unmixed with a little surprise, incredulous surprise—to note the sudden affection of certain members of this class for those elusive forms of Latin grammar known as the gerund and the gerundive. I had despaired, in my unbelief I had despaired, of ever satisfactorily impressing their subtle distinctions on certain, shall we say athletic, imaginations. It seems I was wrong. I had not enough faith. I am sorry. It is evident that these Scylla and Charybdis of prosody have no longer any terrors for you, Lentz. Am I right?"

"Yes, sir," said P. Lentz hesitatingly.

"So—so—no terrors? And now, Lentz, take up your book, take it up. Direct your unfailing glance at the first paragraph, page sixty-two. Is it there?"

"Yes, sir."

"Pick out the first gerund you see."

P. Lentz, beyond the aid of human help, gazed into the jungle and brought forth a supine.

"Is it possible, Lentz?" said The Roman. "Is it possible? Try once more, but don't guess. Don't guess, Lentz; don't do it."

P. Lentz closed the book and sat down.

"What! A sudden indisposition? Too bad, Lentz, too bad. Now we'll try Lazelle. Lazelle won't fail. Lazelle has not failed for a week."

The Gutter Pup rose in a panic, guessed and fell horribly over an ordinary participle.

"Quite mysterious!" said The Roman, himself once more. "Sudden change of weather. Mead, lend us the assistance of your splendid

THE VARMINT

faculties. What? Unable to rise? Too bad. Dear me—dear me—quite the feeling of home again—quite homelike."

The carnage was terrific, the scythe passed over them with the old-time sweep, laying them low. Once maliciously, when Fatty Harris was on his feet, The Roman asked:

"Top of page, fifth word, gerund or gerundive?"

"Gerund," said Harris instantly.

"Ah, pardon——" said The Roman, bringing into play both eyebrows. "My mistake, Harris, entirely my mistake. Go down to the next paragraph and recognize a gerundive. No? Sit down—gently. Too bad—old methods must make way for new ideas. Too bad, then you did have one chance in two and now, where in the whole wide world will you find a friend to help you? Class is dismissed."

"I told you you couldn't beat The Roman," said the Tennessee Shad.

"I made him change his system, though," said Dink gloriously, "and he never caught me."

"Well, if you have, how are you going to spot the gerund and the gerundive?"

"I don't need to; I've learned 'em," said Dink, laughing.

XVI

The Kennedy House Educational Quick Lunch Institute broke up in wrath a week later when an innocent inquiry of Beekstein's for the passwords revealed the direction of the club's finances.

Meanwhile, true to his resolve, Dink, with the assistance of Finnegan and the Tennessee Shad, had started the fad of souvenir toilet sets; which, like all fads, ran its course the faster because of its high qualities of absurdity and uselessness. Dink's intention of recouping himself by selling his own set of seven colors at a big advance was cut short by a spontaneous protest to the Doctor from the house masters, whose artistic souls were stirred to wrath at the hideous invasion. The subject was then so successfully treated from the pulpit, with all the power of sarcasm that it afforded, that the only distinct artistic movement of New Jersey expired in ridicule.

Dink took this check severely to heart and, of course, beheld in this thwarting of his scheme to dispose of the abhorrent set with honor a

THE VARMINT

fresh demonstration of the implacability of The Roman.

He wandered gloomily from Laloo's and Appleby's to the Jigger Shop; where, after pulling his hat over his eyes, folding his arms inconsolably, he confided his desires of revenge on Doc Macnooder to the sympathetic ears of the guardian of the Jigger.

"Why not get up a contest and offer it as a prize?" said Al.

"Have you seen it?" said Dink, who then did the subject full justice.

Al remained very thoughtful for a long while, running back dreamily through the avenues of the past for some stratagem.

"I remember way back in the winter of '88," he said at last, "there was a slick coot by the name of Chops Van Dyne, who got strapped and hit upon a scheme for decoying the shekels."

"What was that?" said Dink hopefully.

"He got up a guessing contest with a blind prize."

"A what?"

"A blind prize all done up in tissue paper and ribbons, and no one was to know what was in it until it was won. It certainly was amazing the number of suckers that paid a quarter to satisfy their curiosity."

"Well, what was inside?" said Dink at once.

THE VARMINT

"There you are!" said Al. "Why, nothing, of course—a lemon, perhaps—but the point is, every one just had to know."

"Not a word!" said Dink, springing up triumphantly.

"Mum as the grave," said Al, accepting his handshake.

Dink went romping back like a young spring goat, his busy mind seizing all the ramifications possible from the central theory. He found the Tennessee Shad and communicated the great idea.

"I don't like the guessing part," said the Tennessee Shad.

"Nor I. We must get up a contest."

"A championship."

"Something devilishly original."

"Exactly."

"Well, what?"

"We must think."

The day was passed in fruitless searching but the next morning brought the answer in the following manner: Dink and the Tennessee Shad—as the majority of trained Laurentians—were accustomed to wallow gloriously in bed until the breakfast gong itself. At the first crash they would spring simultaneously forth and race through their dressing for the winning of the stairs. Now this was an art in itself and many

THE VARMINT

records were claimed and disputed. The Tennessee Shad, like most lazy natures, when aroused was capable of extraordinary bursts of speed and was one of the claimants for the authorized record of twenty-six and a fifth seconds from the bed to the door, established by the famous Hickey Hicks who—as has been related—had departed to organize the industries of his country. Of a consequence Stover was invariably still at his collar button when the thin shadow of the Shad glided out of the door. But on the present morning, the shoe laces of the Tennessee Shad snapping in his hand, Dink reached the exit a bare yard in advance. Suddenly he stopped, clasped the Tennessee Shad by the middle and flung him toward the ceiling.

"I have it," he cried. "We'll organize the dressing championship of the school!"

That very evening a poster was distributed among the houses, thus conceived:

FIRST AMATEUR DRESSING CHAMPIONSHIP OF THE SCHOOL
under the management of that well-known
Sporting Promoter
MR. DINK STOVER
For the Belt of the School
and

THE VARMINT

A Sealed Mysterious Prize
Guaranteed to be Worth Over $3.50
Entrance Fee 25c   Books Close at 6 P. M.
To-morrow
For Conditions and Details Consult
Mr. Dennis de B. de B. Finnegan, Secretary.

While the announcement was running like quicksilver through the school the souvenir toilet set was encased in cotton, packed in the smallest compass, stowed in a wooden box, which was then sewed up in a gunny sacking. This in turn was wrapped in colored paper, tied with bows of pink ribbon and sealed with blue sealing wax stamped with the crest of the school —Virtus Semper Viridis. The whole was placed on a table at the legs of which were grouped stands of flags.

By noon the next day one-half of the school had passed around the table, measuring the mysterious package, touching the seals with itching fingers and wanting to know the reason for such secrecy.

"There are reasons," said Stover, in response to all inquiries. "Unusual, mysterious, excellent reasons. We ask no one to enter. We only guarantee that the prize is worth over three dollars and fifty cents. No one is coaxing you.

THE VARMINT

No one will miss you. The entrance list is already crowded. We are quite willing it should be closed. We urge nobody!"

Macnooder came among the first, scratching his head and walking around the prize as a fox about a tainted trap. Stover, watching from the corner of his eye, studiously appeared to discourage him. Macnooder sniffed the air once or twice in an alarmed sort of way, grunted to himself and went off to try to pump Finnegan.

Finally, just before the closing of the entries, he shambled up with evident dissatisfaction and said:

"Here's my quarter. It's for the championship, though, and not on account of any hocus pocus in the box."

"Do I understand?" said Dink instantly, "that if you win you are willing to let the prize go to the second man?"

"What are you making out of this?" said Doc hungrily, disdaining an answer.

The contest, which began the next afternoon with thirty-one entries, owing to certain features unusual to athletic contests, produced such a furor of interest that the limited admissions to the struggle brought soaring prices.

Everything was conducted on lines of exact formality.

Each contestant was required to don upper

and lower unmentionables, two socks, two shoes, which were to be completely laced and tied, a dickey—formed by a junction of two cuffs, a collar and one button—one necktie, one pair of trousers and one coat. Each contestant was required satisfactorily to wash and dry both hands and put into his hair a recognizable part.

The contestants were allowed to arrange on the chair their wearing apparel according to their own theories, were permitted to fill the wash basin with water, leaving the comb and towel on either side. In order to prevent the formation of two classes, pajamas were suppressed and each contestant, clothed in a nightshirt, was inducted under the covers and his hair carefully disarranged.

Time was taken from the starting gun to the moment of the arrival of the fully clothed, reasonably washed and apparently brushed candidate at the door. Each time was to be noted and the two lowest scores were to compete in the finals. A time limit of forty-five seconds was imposed, after which the contestant was to be ruled out.

The first heat began with the Triumphant Egghead in the bed for the Dickinson, Mr. Dennis de Brian de Boru Finnegan on the stop watch, Mr. Dink Stover as master of ceremonies

THE VARMINT

and Mr. Turkey Reiter, Mr. Cheyenne Baxter and Mr. Charlie DeSoto as jurors.

The entries were admitted by all to be the pick of the school; while the champions most favored, were the Tennessee Shad for the Kennedy, Doc Macnooder for the Dickinson and the White Mountain Canary for the Woodhull.

A certain delay took place on the third heat owing to Susie Satterly, of the Davis House, refusing to compete unless there was less publicity, and being peremptorily ruled out on a demand for a screen.

"The next on the program," said Stover, as master of ceremonies, "is the champion of the Dickinson, the celebrated old-clothes man, Doctor Macnooder."

Macnooder gracefully acknowledged the applause which invariably attended his public performances and asked leave to make a speech, which was unanimously rejected.

"Very well, gentlemen," said Macnooder, taking off his coat and standing forth in a sudden blaze of rainbow underwear. "I will simply draw attention to this neat little bit of color that I have the honor to present to your inspection. It is the latest thing out in dainty fancies and I stand ready to fill all orders. It is rather springy, but why fall when you can spring? Don't applaud—you'll wake the baby.

It is light, it is warm, it gives a sense of exhilaration to the skin. It endears you to your friends, and not even a Lawrenceville suds-lady would bite a hole in it——"

"If you don't get into bed," said Dink, "I'll rule you out."

Macnooder, thus admonished, hastened to his post, merely remarking on the distinction of his garters and impressionistic socks and the fact that he had incurred great expense to afford his schoolmates an equal opportunity.

"Are you ready?" said Turkey Reiter, for the indignant jury.

"One moment."

Macnooder, in bed, glanced carefully at the preparations without, turned on his side and brought his knees up under his chin.

"All ready?"

"Go!"

With a circular kick, something like the flop of a whale's tail, Macnooder drove the covers from him and sprang into the doubled trousers.

A cheer went up from the spectators.

"Gee, what a dive!"

"Faster, Doc!"

"Wash carefully!"

"Behind the ears!"

"Don't forget the buttons!"

"That's the boy!"

THE VARMINT

"Come on, Doc, come on!"

"Oh, you Dickinson!"

"Hurray!"

"Time—twenty-seven seconds flat," said Dennis de Brian de Boru Finnegan. "Best yet. Twenty-seven and four-fifths seconds, next on the list, made by the White Mountain Canary and the Gutter Pup."

"Next contestant," said Dink, in sing-song, "is the champion of the Rouse, Mr. Peanuts Biddle."

But here a difficulty arose.

"Please, sir," said the candidate, who as a freshman was visibly embarrassed at the ordeal before him—"Please, sir, I don't part my hair."

Every eye went to the pompadour, cropped like a scrubbing brush, and recognized the truth of this assertion.

"Please, sir, I don't see why I should have to touch a comb."

A protest broke forth from the other candidates.

"Rats!"

"Penalize him!"

"Why part my hair?"

"I always do that with my fingers when I'm skating down the stairs."

"Why wash till afterward?"

"No favoritism!"

THE VARMINT

The jury retired to deliberate and announced amid cheers that to equalize matters Mr. Peanuts Biddle would be handicapped two-fifths of a second. The candidate took this ruling very much to heart and withdrew.

The Tennessee Shad, closing the list of entries, slouched up to the starting-line amid great excitement to better the record of Doc Macnooder.

He first inspected the washstand, filling the basin higher than customary and exchanging the stiff face towel for a soft bath towel, which would more quickly absorb the moisture.

Doc Macnooder, who followed these preparations with a hostile eye, protested against this last substitution, but was overruled.

The Tennessee Shad then divested himself of his coat and undergarments amid cries of:

"Oh, you ribs!"
"What do they feed you?"
"Oh, you wish-bones!"
"Oh, you shad-bones!"

Macnooder then claimed that the undershirt was manifestly sewed to the coat. The allegation was investigated and disproved, without in the slightest ruffling the composure of the Tennessee Shad, who continued his calculations while making a toothpick dance through his lips. By means of safety pins, he next fastened the

THE VARMINT

back and one wing of his collar to his coat, so that one motion would clothe his upper half.

"I protest," said Doc Macnooder.

"Denied," said Turkey Reiter, as foreman of the jury.

The Tennessee Shad, donning the nightshirt, carefully unloosened the laces of his low shoes, drew them off and arranged the socks inside of them so as to economize the extra movement.

"The socks aren't his!" said Macnooder. "They're big enough for P. Lentz."

"Proceed," said Turkey Reiter.

The Tennessee Shad then unloosened his belt and the trousers slipped down him as a sailor down a greased pole.

Macnooder once more protested and was squelched.

The Tennessee Shad arranged the voluminous trousers, cast a final glance, placed the toothpick on the table and went under the covers.

"All ready?" said Dink.

"Wait!" With the left hand he clutched the covers, with the right his nightshirt, just back of the neck. "Ready now."

"Go!"

With one motion the Tennessee Shad flung the covers from him, tore off his nightshirt and sprang from the bed like Venus from the waves.

The audience burst into cheers:

"Holy Mike."
"Greased lightning!"
"Oh, you Shad!"
"Gee, right through the pants!"
"Suffering Moses!"
"Look at him stab the shoes!"
"Right into the coat!"
"Go it, Shad!"
"Out for the record!"
"Gee, what a wash!"
"Come on, boy, come on!"
"Now for the part!"
"Hurray!"
"Hurrah!"
"Hurroo!"

"Time—twenty-six and one-fifth seconds," cried the shrill voice of Dennis de Brian de Boru. "Equalizing the world's unchallenged professional, amateur and scholastic record made by the late Hickey Hicks! The champion's belt is now the Tennessee Shad's to have and to hold. According to the program the champion and Doc Macnooder, second-best score, will now run another heat for the mysterious sealed prize, guaranteed to be worth over three dollars and fifty cents!"

Macnooder, adopting the Shad's theories of preparation, made an extraordinary effort and brought his record down to twenty-six and four-

THE VARMINT

fifths seconds. The Tennessee Shad then, according to the plan agreed upon with Stover, purposely broke a shoe-lace and lost the match.

Dink, in a speech full of malice, awarded the mysterious sealed prize to Doc Macnooder, with a request to open it at once.

Now, Macnooder, who had been busy thinking the matter over, had sniffed the pollution in the air and, perceiving a wicked twinkle in the eye of Stover, shifted the ground by carrying off the box despite a storm of protests to his room in the Dickinson, where strategically proving his title to Captain of Industry, he charged ten cents admission to all who clamored to see the clearing up of the mystery.

Having thus provided a substantial consolation against discomfiture and joined twenty other curiosity-seekers to his own fortunes, he opened the box and beheld the prodigal souvenir set. At the same moment Dink stepped forward and presented him with his own former bill for three dollars and seventy-five cents.

. . . . .

That night, after Stover had returned much puffed up with the congratulations of his schoolmates on the outwitting of Macnooder, the Tennessee Shad took him to task from a philosophical point of view.

"Baron Munchausen, a word."

"Lay on."

"You must come down to earth."

"Wherefor?"

"You must occasionally, my boy, just as a matter of safeguarding future ventures, start in and scatter a few truths."

"Pooh!" said Stover, with the memory of cheers. "Any fool can tell the truth."

"Yes, but——"

"It's such a lazy way!"

"Still——"

"Enervating!"

"But——"

"Besides, now they expect something more from me."

"True," said the Tennessee Shad, "but don't you see, Dink, if you do tell the truth no one will believe you."

XVII

Oh, we'll push her over
Or rip the cover—
  Too bad for the fellows that fall!
They must take their chances
Of a bruise or two
  Who follow that jolly football.

So sang the group on the Kennedy steps, heralding the twilight; and beyond, past the Dickinson, a chorus from the Woodhull defiantly flung back the challenge. For that week the Woodhull would clash with the Kennedy for the championship of the houses.

The football season was drawing to a close, only the final game with Andover remained, a contest awaited with small hopes of victory. For the season had been disastrous for the 'Varsity; several members of the team had been caught in the toils of the octopus examination and, what was worse among the members, ill-feeling existed due to past feuds.

Stover, in the long grueling days of practice, had won the respect of all. Just how favorable an impression he had made he did not himself suspect. He had instinctive quickness and no

THE VARMINT

sense of fear—that was something that had dropped from him forever. It was not that he had to conquer the impulse to flinch, as most boys do; it simply did not exist with him. The sight of a phalanx of bone and muscle starting for his end to sweep him off his feet roused only a sort of combative rage, the true joy of battle. He loved to go plunging into the unbroken front and feel the shock of bodies as he tried for the elusive legs of Flash Condit or Charley DeSoto.

This utter recklessness was indeed his chief fault; he would rather charge interference than fight it off, waiting for others to break it up for him and so make sure of his man.

Gradually, however, through the strenuous weeks, he learned the deeper lessons of football—how to use his courage and the control of his impulses.

"It's a game of brains, youngster, remember that," Mr. Ware would repeat day after day, hauling him out of desperate plunges. "That did no good; better keep on your feet and follow the ball. Above all, study the game."

His first lesson came when, at last being promoted to end on the scrub, he found himself lined up against Tough McCarty, the opposing tackle. Stover thought he saw the intention at once.

"Put me against Tough McCarty, eh?" he

said, digging his nails into the palms of his hands. "Want to try out my nerve, eh? I'll show 'em!"

Now McCarty did not relish the situation either; foreseeing as he did the long weeks of strenuous contact with the one boy in the school who was vowed to an abiding vengeance. The fact was that Tough McCarty, who was universally liked for his good nature and sociable inclination, had yielded to the irritation Stover's unceasing enmity had aroused and had come gradually into something of the same attitude of hostility. Also, he saw in the captain's assigning Stover to his end a malicious attempt to secure amusement at his expense.

For all which reasons, when the scrub first lined up against the 'Varsity, the alarum of battle that rode on Stover's pugnacious front was equaled by the intensity of his enemy's coldly-calculating glance.

"Here's where I squash that fly," thought McCarty.

"Here's where I fasten to that big stuff," thought Dink, "and sting him until the last day of the season!"

The first direct clash came when the scrubs were given the ball and Dink came in to aid his tackle box McCarty for the run that was signaled around their end.

THE VARMINT

Tough made the mistake of estimating Stover simply by his lack of weight, without taking account of the nervous, dynamic energy which was his strength. Consequently, at the snap of the ball, he was taken by surprise by the wild spring that Stover made directly at his throat and, thrown off his balance momentarily by the frenzy of the impact, tripped and went down under the triumphant Dink, who, unmindful of the fact that the play had gone by, remained proudly fixed on the chest of the prostrate tackle.

"Get off," said the muffled voice.

Stover, whose animal instincts were all those of the bulldog, pressed down more firmly.

"Get off of me, you little blockhead," said McCarty growing furious as he heard the jeers of his teammates at his humiliating reversal.

"Hurry up there, you Stover!" cried the voice of the captain, unheeded, for Dink was too blindly happy with the thrill of perfect supremacy over the hated McCarty to realize the situation.

"Stover! ! !"

At the shouted command Dink looked up and at last perceived the play was over. Reluctantly he started to rise, when a sudden upheaval of the infuriated McCarty caught him unawares

THE VARMINT

and Tough's vigorous arm flung him head over heels.

Down went Dink with a thump and up again with rage in his heart. He rushed up to McCarty as in the mad fight under the willows and struck him a resounding blow.

The next moment not Tough, but Cockrell's own mighty hand caught him by the collar and swung him around.

"Get off the field!"

"What?" said Dink, astounded, for in his ignorance he had expected complimentary pats on his back.

"Off the field!"

Dink, cold in a minute, quailed under the stern eye of the supreme leader.

"I did sling him pretty hard, Garry," said Tough, taking pity at the look that came into Dink's eyes at this rebuke.

"Get off!"

Dink, who had stopped with a sort of despairing hope, went slowly to the side-lines, threw a blanket over his head and shoulders and squatted down in bitter, utter misery. Another was in his place, plunging at the tackle that should have been his, racing down the field under punts that made the blood leap in his exiled body. He did not understand. Why had he been disgraced? He had only shown he wasn't afraid—wasn't that why they had put him opposite Tough McCarty, after all?

The contending lines stopped at last their tangled rushes and straggled, panting, back for a short intermission. Dink, waiting under the blanket, saw the captain bear down upon him and, shivering like a dog watching the approach of his punishment, drew the folds tighter about him.

"Stover," said the dreadful voice, loud enough so that every one could hear, "you seem to have an idea that football is run like a slaughter-house. The quicker you get that out of your head the better. Now, do you know why I fired you? Do you?"

"For slugging," said Dink faintly.

"Not at all. I fired you because you lost your head; because you forgot you were playing football. If you're only going into this to work off your private grudges, then I don't want you around. I'll fire you off and keep you off. You're here to play football, to think of eleven men, not one. You're to use your brains, not your fists. Why, the first game you play in some one will tease you into slugging him and the umpire will fire you. Then where'll the team be? There are eleven men in this game on your side and on the other. No matter what happens don't lose your temper, don't be so stupid, so brainless—do you hear?"

THE VARMINT

"Yes, sir," said Dink, who had gradually retired under his blanket until only the tip of the nose showed and the terror-stricken eyes.

"And don't forget this. You don't count. It isn't the slightest interest to the team whether some one whales you or mauls you! It isn't the slightest interest to you, either. Mind that! Nothing on earth is going to get your mind off following the ball, sizing up the play, working out the weak points—nothing. Brains, brains, brains, Stover! You told me you came out here because we needed some one to be banged around—and I took you on your word, didn't I? Now, if you're going out there as an egotistical, puffed-up, conceited individual who's thinking only of his own skin, who isn't willing to sacrifice his own little, measly feelings for the sake of the school, who won't fight for the team, but himself——"

"I say, Cap, that's enough," said Dink with difficulty; and immediately retired so deep that only the mute, pleading eyes could be discerned.

Cockrell stopped short, bit his lip and said sternly: "Line up now. Get in, Stover, and don't let me ever have to call you down again. Tough, see here." The two elevens ran out. The captain continued: "Tough, every chance you get to-day give that little firebrand a jab, understand? So it can't be seen."

The 'Varsity took the ball and for five minutes

THE VARMINT

Dink felt as though he were in an angry sea, buffeted, flung down and whirled about by massive breakers. Without sufficient experience his weight was powerless to stop the interference that bore him back. He tried to meet it standing up and was rolled head over heels by the brawny shoulders of Cheyenne Baxter and Doc Macnooder. Then, angrily, he tried charging into the offenses and was drawn in and smothered while the back went sweeping around his unprotected end for long gains.

Mr. Ware came up and volunteered suggestions:

"If you're going into it dive through them, push them apart with your hands—so. Keep dodging so that the back won't know whether you're going around or through. Keep him guessing and follow up the play if you miss the first tackle."

Under this coaching Dink, who had begun to be discouraged, improved and when he did get a chance at his man he dropped him with a fierce, clean tackle, for this branch of the game he had mastered with instinctive delight.

"Give the ball to the scrubs," said the captain, who was also coaching.

Stover came in close to his tackle. The third signal was a trial at end. He flung himself at McCarty, checked him and, to his amazement,

THE VARMINT

received a dig in the ribs. His fists clenched, went back and then stopped as remembering, he drew a long breath and walked away, his eyes on the ground; for the lesson was a rude one to learn.

"Stover, what are you doing?" cried the captain, who had seen all.

Dink, who had expected to be praised, was bewildered as well as hurt.

"What are you stopping for? You're thinking of McCarty again, aren't you? Do you know where your place was? Back of your own half. Follow up the play. If you'd been there to push there'd been an extra yard. Think quicker, Stover."

"Yes, sir," said Stover, suddenly perceiving the truth. "You're right, I wasn't thinking."

"Look here, boy," said the captain, laying his hand on his shoulders. "I have just one principle in a game and I want you to tuck it away and never forget it."

"Yes, sir," said Dink reverently.

"When you get in a game get fighting mad, but get cold mad—play like a fiend—but keep cold. Know just what you're doing and know it all the time."

"Thank you, sir," said Dink, who never forgot the theory, which had a wider application than Garry Cockrell perhaps suspected.

THE VARMINT

"You laid it on pretty strong," said Mr. Ware to Cockrell, as they walked back after practice.

"I did it for several reasons," said Garry; "first, because I believe the boy has the makings of a great player in him; and second, I was using him to talk to the team. They're not together and it's going to be hard to get them together."

"Bad feeling?"

"Yes, several old grudges."

"What a pity, Garry," said Mr. Ware. "What a pity it is you can't only have second and third formers under you!"

"Why so?"

"Because they'd follow you like mad Dervishes," said Mr. Ware, thinking of Dink.

Stover, having once perceived that the game was an intellectual one, learned by bounds. McCarty, under instructions, tried his best to provoke him, but met with the completest indifference. Dink found a new delight in the exercise of his wits, once the truth was borne in on him that there are more ways of passing beyond a windmill than riding it down. Owing to his natural speed he was the fastest end on the field to cover a punt, and once within diving distance of his man he almost never missed. He learned, too, that the scientific application of his one hundred and thirty-eight pounds,

THE VARMINT

well timed, was sufficient to counterbalance the disadvantage in weight. He never loafed, he never let a play go by without being in it, and at retrieving fumbles he was quick as a cat.

Meanwhile the house championships had gone on until the Woodhull and the Kennedy emerged for the final conflict. The experience gained in these contests, for on such occasions Stover played with his House team, had sharpened his powers of analysis and given him a needed acquaintance with the sudden, shifting crises of actual play.

Now, the one darling desire of Stover, next to winning the fair opinion of his captain, was the rout of the Woodhull, of which Tough McCarty was the captain and his old acquaintances of the miserable days at the Green were members—Cheyenne Baxter, the Coffee-colored Angel and Butsey White. This aggregation, counting as it did two members of the 'Varsity, was strong, but the Kennedy, with P. Lentz and the Waladoo Bird and Pebble Stone, the Gutter Pup, Lovely Mead and Stover, all of the scrub, had a slight advantage.

Dink used to dream of mornings, in the lagging hours of recitation, of the contest and the sweet humiliation of his ancient foes. He would play like a demon, he would show them, Tough McCarty and the rest, what it was to be up against the despised Dink— and dreaming thus he used to say to himself, with suddenly tense arms:

"Gee, I only wish McCarty would play back of the line so I could get a chance at him!"

But on Tuesday, during the 'Varsity practice, suddenly as a scrimmage ended and sifted open a cry went up. Ned Banks, left end on the 'Varsity, was seen lying on the ground after an attempt to rise. They gathered about him with grave faces, while Mr. Ware bent over him in anxious examination.

"What is it?" said the captain, with serious face.

"Something wrong with his ankle; can't tell yet just what."

"I'll play Saturday, Garry," said Banks, gritting his teeth. "I'll be ready by then. It's nothing much."

The subs carried him off the field with darkened faces—the last hopes of victory seemed to vanish. The gloom spread thickly through the school, even Dink, for a time, forgot the approaching hour of his revenge in the great catastrophe. The next morning a little comfort was given them in the report of Doctor Charlie that there was no sprain but only a slight wrenching, which, if all went well, would allow him to start the game. But the consolation was scant.

THE VARMINT

What chance had Banks in an Andover game? There would have to be a shift; but what?

"Turkey Reiter will have to go from tackle to end," said Dink, that afternoon, as in football togs they gathered on the steps before the game, "and put a sub in Turkey's place."

"Who?"

"I don't know."

"I guess you don't."

"Might bring Butcher Stevens back from center."

"Who'd go in at center?"

"Fatty Harris, perhaps."

"Hello—here's Garry Cockrell now," said P. Lentz. "He don't look particular cheerful, does he?"

The captain, looking indeed very serious, arrived, surveyed the group and called Stover out. Dink, surprised, jumped up, saying:

"You want me, sir?"

"Yes."

Cockrell put his arm under his and drew him away.

"Stover," he said, "I've got bad news for you."

"For me?"

"Yes. I'm not going to let you go in the Woodhull game this afternoon."

Stover received the news as though it had been the death of his entire family, immediate and distant. His throat choked, he tried to say something and did not dare trust himself.

"I'm sorry, my boy—but we're up against it, and I can't take any risks now of your getting hurt."

"It means the game," said Dink at last.

"I'm afraid so."

"We've no one to put in my place—no one but Beekstein Hall," said Stover desperately. "Oh, please, sir, let me play; I'll be awfully careful. It's only a House game."

"Humph—yes, I know these House games. I'm sorry, but there's no help for it."

"But I'm only a scrub, sir," said Stover, pleading hard.

"We're going to play you at end," said Cockrell suddenly, seeing he did not understand, "just as soon as we have to take Banks out; and Heaven only knows when that'll be."

Dink was aghast.

"You're not going—you're not going——" he tried to speak, and stopped.

"Yes, we've talked it over and that seems best."

"But—Turkey Reiter—I—I thought you'd move him out."

"No, we don't dare weaken the middle; it's bad enough now."

"Oh, but I'm so light."

THE VARMINT

The captain watched the terror-stricken look in his face and was puzzled.

"What's the matter? You're not getting shaky?"

"Oh, no, sir," said Dink, "it's not that. It—it seems so awful that you've got to put me in."

"You're better, my boy, than you think," said Cockrell, smiling a little, "and you're going to be better than you know how. Now you understand why you've got to keep on the side-lines this afternoon. You're too fragile to take risks on."

"Yes, I understand."

"It comes hard, doesn't it?"

"Yes, sir, it does; very hard."

When the Kennedy and the Woodhull lined up for play an hour later little Pebble Stone was at end in place of Stover, who watched from his post as linesman the contest that was to have been his opportunity. He heard nothing of the buzzing comments behind, of the cheers or the shouted entreaties. Gaze fixed and heart in throat, he followed the swaying tide of battle, imprisoned, powerless to rush in and stem the disheartening advance.

The teams, now more evenly matched, both showed the traces of tense nerves in the frequent fumbling that kept the ball changing sides and prevented a score during the first half.

THE VARMINT

In the opening of the second half, by a lucky recovery of a blocked kick, the Kennedy scored a touchdown, but failed to kick the goal, making the score four to nothing. The Woodhull then began a determined assault upon the Kennedy's weak end. Stover, powerless, beheld little Pebble Stone, fighting like grim death, carried back and back five, ten yards at a time as the Woodhull swept up the field.

"It's the only place they can gain," he cried in his soul in bitter iteration.

He looked around and caught the eye of Captain Cockrell and sent him a mute, agonizing, fruitless appeal.

"Kennedy's ball," came the sharp cry of Slugger Jones, the umpire.

Dink looked up and felt the blood come back to his body again—on the twenty-five yard line there had been a fumble and the advance was checked. Twice again the battered end of the Kennedy was forced back for what seemed certain touchdowns, only to be saved by loose work on the Woodhull's part. It was getting dark and the half was ebbing fast—three minutes more to play. A fourth time the Woodhull furiously attacked the breach, gaining at every rush over the light opposition, past the forty-yard line, past the twenty-yard mark and triumphantly, in the last minute of play, over the goal

THE VARMINT

for a touchdown. The ball had been downed well to the right of the goal posts and the trial for goal was an unusually difficult one. The score was a tie, everything depended on the goal that, through the dusk, Tough McCarty was carefully sighting. Dink, heartbroken, despairing, leaning on his linesman's staff, directly behind the ball, waited for the long, endless moments to be over. Then there was a sudden movement of McCarty's body, a wild rush from the Kennedy and the ball shot high in the air and, to Stover's horror, passed barely inside the farther goalpost.

"No goal," said Slugger Jones. "Time up."

Dink raised his head in surprise, scarcely crediting what he had heard. The Woodhull team were furiously disputing the decision, encouraged by audible comments from the spectators. Slugger Jones, surrounded by a contesting, vociferous mass, suddenly swept them aside and began to take the vote of the officials.

"Kiefer, what do you say?"

Cap Kiefer, referee, shook his head.

"I'm sorry, Slugger, it was close, very close, but it did seem a goal to me."

"Tug, what do you say?"

"Goal, sure," said Tug Wilson, linesman for the Woodhull. At this, jeers and hoots broke out from the Kennedy.

"Of course he'll say that!"

"He's from the Woodhull."

"What do you think?"

"Justice!"

"Hold up, hold up, now," said Slugger Jones, more excited than any one. "Don't get excited; it's up to your own man. Dink, was it a goal or no goal?"

Stover suddenly found himself in a whirling, angry mass—the decision of the game in his own hands. He saw the faces of Tough McCarty and the Coffee-colored Angel in the blank crowd about him and he saw the sneer on their faces as they waited for his answer. Then he saw the faces of his own teammates and knew what they, in their frenzy, expected from him.

He hesitated.

"Goal or no goal?" cried the umpire, for the second time.

Then suddenly, face to face with the hostile mass, the fighting blood came to Dink. Something cold went up his back. He looked once more above the riot, to the shadowy posts, trying to forget Tough McCarty, and then, with a snap to his jaws, he answered:

"Goal."

XVIII

Dink returned to his room in a rage against everything and every one, at Slugger Jones for having submitted the question, at Tough McCarty for having looked as though he expected a lie, and at himself for ever having acted as linesman.

If it had not been the last days before the Andover match he would have found some consolation in rushing over to the Woodhull and provoking McCarty to the long-deferred fight.

"He thought I'd lie out of it," he said furiously. "He did; I saw it. I'll settle that with him, too. Now I suppose every one in this house'll be down on me; but they'd better be mighty careful how they express it."

For as he had left the field he had heard only too clearly how the Kennedy eleven, in the unreasoning passion of conflict, had expressed itself. At present, through the open window, the sounds of violent words were borne up to him from below. He approached and looked down upon the furious assembly.

"Damn me up and down, damn me all you want," he said, doubling up his fists. "Keep it up, but don't come up to me with it."

THE VARMINT

Suddenly, back of him, the door opened and shut and Dennis de Brian de Boru Finnegan stood in the room.

"I say, Dink——"

"Get out," said Stover furiously, seizing a pillow.

Finnegan precipitately retired and, placing the door between him and the danger, opened it slightly and inserted his freckled little nose.

"I say, Dink——"

"Get out, I told you!" The pillow struck the door with a bang. "I won't have any one snooping around here!"

The next instant Dennis, resolved on martyrdom, stepped inside, saying:

"I say, old man, if it'll do you any good, take it out on me."

Stover, thus defied, stopped and said:

"Dennis, I don't want to talk about it."

"All right," said Dennis, sitting down.

"And I want to be alone."

"Correct," said Dennis, who didn't budge.

They sat in moody silence, without lighting the lamp.

"Pretty tough," said Dennis at last.

Stover's answer was a grunt.

"You couldn't see it the way the umpire did, could you?"

"No, I couldn't."

THE VARMINT

"Pretty tough!"

"I suppose," said Dink finally, "the fellows are wild."

"A little—a little excited," said Dennis carefully. "It was tough—pretty tough!"

"You don't suppose I wanted that gang of muckers to win, do you?" said Stover.

"I know," said Dennis sympathetically.

The Tennessee Shad now returned from the wars, covered with mud and the more visible marks of the combat.

"Hello," he said gruffly.

"Hello," said Stover.

The Tennessee Shad went wearily to his corner and stripped for the bath.

"Well, say it," said Stover, who, in his agitation, had actually picked up a textbook and started to study. "Jump on me, why don't you?"

"I'm not going to jump on you," said the Tennessee Shad, who weakly pulled off the heavy shoes. "Only—well, you couldn't see it as the umpire did, could you?"

"No!"

"What a day—what an awful day!"

Dennis de Brian de Boru Finnegan, with great tact, rose and hesitated:

"I'm going—I—I've got to get ready for supper," he said desperately. Then he went lamely over to Stover and held out his hand: "I know how you feel old man, but—but—I'm glad you did it!"

Whereupon he disappeared in blushing precipitation.

Stover breathed hard and tried to bring his mind to the printed lesson. The Tennessee Shad, sighing audibly, continued his ablutions, dressed and sat down.

"Dink."

"What?"

"Why did you do it?"

Then Stover, flinging down his book with an access of rage, cried out:

"Why? Because you all, every damn one of you, expected me to *lie!*"

. . . . .

The next day Stover, who had firmly made up his mind to a sort of modified ostracism, was amazed to find that over night he had become a hero. By the next morning the passion and the bitterness of the struggle having died away, the house looked at the matter in a calmer mood and one by one came to him and gripped his hand with halting, blurted words of apology or explanation.

Utterly unprepared for this development, Stover all at once realized that he had won what neither courage nor wit had been able to bring him, the something he had always longed for

THE VARMINT

without being quite able to name it—the respect of his fellows. He felt it in the looks that followed him as he went over to chapel, in the nodded recognition of Fifth Formers, who had never before noticed him, in The Roman himself, who flunked him without satire or aggravation. And not yet knowing himself, his impulses or the strange things that lay dormant beneath the surface of his everyday life, Stover was a little ashamed, as though he did not deserve it all.

That afternoon as Dink was donning his football togs, preparing for practice, a knock came at the door which opened on a very much embarrassed delegation from the Woodhull—the Coffee-colored Angel, Cheyenne Baxter and Tough McCarty.

"I say, is that you, Dink?" said the Coffee-colored Angel.

"It is," said Stover, with as much dignity as the state of his wardrobe would permit.

"I say, we've come over from the Woodhull, you know," continued the Coffee-colored Angel, who stopped after this bit of illuminating news.

"Well, what do you want?"

"I say, that's not just it; we're sent by the Woodhull I meant to say, and we want to say, we want you to know—how white we think it was of you!"

"Old man," said Cheyenne Baxter, "we want

to thank you. What we want to tell you is how white we think it was of you."

"You needn't thank me," said Stover gruffly, pulling his leg through the football trousers. "I didn't want to do it."

The delegation stood confused, wondering how to end the painful scene.

"It was awful white!" said the Coffee-colored Angel, tying knots in his sweater.

"It certainly was," said Cheyenne.

As this brought them no further along the Coffee-colored Angel exclaimed in alarm:

"I say, Dink, will you shake hands?"

Stover gravely extended his right.

Cheyenne next clung to it, blurting out:

"Say, Dink, I wish I could make you understand—just—just how white we think it was!"

The two rushed away leaving Tough McCarty to have his say. Both stood awkwardly, frightened before the possibility of a display of sentiment.

"Look here," said Tough firmly, and then stopped, drew a long breath and continued: "Say, you and I have sort of formed up a sort of vendetta and all that sort of thing, haven't we?"

"We have."

"Now, I'm not going to call that off. I don't suppose you'd want it, either."

THE VARMINT

"No, I wouldn't!"

"We've got to have a good, old, slam-bang fight sooner or later and then, perhaps, it'll be different. I'm not coming around asking you to be friends, or anything like that sort of rot, you know, but what I want you to know is this—is this—what I want you to understand is just how darned *white* that was of you!"

"All right," said Stover frigidly, because he was tremendously moved and in terror of showing it.

"That's not what I wanted to say," said Tough, frowning terrifically and kicking the floor. "I mean—I say, you know what I mean, don't you?"

"All right," said Stover gruffly.

"And I say," said Tough, remembering only one line of all he had come prepared to say, "if you'll let me, Stover, I should consider it an honor to shake your hand."

Dink gave his hand, trembling a little.

"Of course you understand," said Tough who thought he comprehended Stover's silence, "of course we fight it out some day."

"All right," said Stover gruffly.

Tough McCarty went away. Dink, left alone, clad in his voluminous football trousers, sat staring at the door, clasping his hands tensely between his knees, and something inside of him

THE VARMINT

welled up, dangerously threatening his eyes—something feminine, to be choked instantly down.

He rose angrily, flung back his hair and filled his lungs. Then he stopped.

"What the deuce are they all making such a fuss for?" he said. "I only told the truth."

He struggled into his jersey, still trying to answer the problem. In his abstraction he drew a neat part in his hair before perceiving the *faux pas*, he hurriedly obliterated the effete mark.

"I guess," he said, standing at the window still pondering over the new attitude toward himself— "I guess, after all, I don't know it all. Tough McCarty—well, I'll be damned!"

Saturday came all too soon and with it the arrival of the stocky Andover eleven. Dink dressed and went slowly across the campus— every step seemed an effort. Everywhere was an air of seriousness and apprehension, strangely contrasted to the gay ferment that usually announced a big game. He felt a hundred eyes on him as he went and knew what was in every one's mind. What would happen when Ned Banks would have to retire and he, little Dink Stover, weighing one hundred and thirty-eight, would have to go forth to stand at the end of the line. And because Stover had learned the

THE VARMINT

lesson of football, the sacrifice for an idea, he too felt not fear but a sort of despair that the hopes of the great school would have to rest upon him, little Dink Stover, who weighed only one hundred and thirty-eight pounds.

He went quietly to the Upper, his eyes on the ground like a guilty man, picking his way through the crowds of Fifth Formers, who watched him pass with critical looks, and up the heavy stairs to Garry Cockrell's room, where the team sat quietly listening to the final instructions. He took his seat silently in an obscure corner, studying the stern faces about him, hearing nothing of Mr. Ware's staccato periods, his eyes irresistibly drawn to his captain, wondering how suddenly older he looked and grave.

By his side Ned Banks was listening stolidly and Charlie DeSoto, twisting a paper-weight in his nervous fingers, fidgeting on his chair with the longing for the fray.

"That's all," said the low voice of Garry Cockrell. "You know what you have to do. Go down to Charlie's room; I want a few words with Stover."

They went sternly and quickly, Mr. Ware with them. Dink was alone, standing stiff and straight, his heart thumping violently, waiting for his captain to speak.

"How do you feel?"

THE VARMINT

"I'm ready, sir."

"I don't know when you'll get in the game—probably before the first half is over," said Cockrell slowly. "We're going to put up to you a pretty hard proposition, youngster." He came nearer, laying his hand on Stover's shoulder. "I'm not going to talk nerve to you, young bulldog, I don't need to. I've watched you and I know the stuff that's in you."

"Thank you, sir."

"Not but what you'll need it—more than you've ever needed it before. You've no right in this game."

"I know it, sir."

"Tough McCarty won't be able to help you out much. He's got the toughest man in the line. Everything's coming at you, my boy, and you've got to stand it off, somehow. Now, listen once more. It's a game for the long head, for the cool head. You've got to think quicker, you've got to out-think every man on the field and you can do it. And remember this: No matter what happens never let up—get your man back of the line if you can, get him twenty-five yards beyond you, get him on the one-yard line,—but get him!"

"Yes, sir."

"And now one thing more. There's all sorts of ways you can play the game. You can charge

THE VARMINT

in like a bull and kill yourself off in ten minutes, but that won't do. You can go in and make grandstand plays and get carried off the field, but that won't do. My boy, you've got to last out the game."

"I see, sir."

"Remember there's a bigger thing than yourself you're fighting for, Stover—it's the school, the old school. Now, when you're on the sidelines don't lose any time; watch your men, find out their tricks, see if they look up or change their footing when they start for an end run. Everything is going to count. Now, come on."

They joined the eleven below and presently, in a compact body, went out and through Memorial and the chapel, where suddenly the field appeared and a great roar went up from the school.

"All ready," said the captain.

They broke into a trot and swept up to the cheering mass. Dink remembered seeing the Tennessee Shad, in his shirt sleeves, frantically leading the school and thinking how funny he looked. Then some one pulled a blanket over him and he was camped among the substitutes, peering out at the gridiron where already the two elevens were sweeping back and forth in vigorous signal drill.

He looked eagerly at the Andover eleven.

THE VARMINT

They were big, rangy fellows and their team worked with a precision and machine-like rush that the red and black team did not have.

"Trouble with us is," said the voice of Fatty Harris, at his elbow, "our team's never gotten together. The fellows would rather slug each other than the enemy."

"Gee, that fellow at tackle is a monster," said Dink, picking out McCarty's opponent.

"Look at Turkey Reiter and the Waladoo Bird," continued Fatty Harris. "Bad blood! And there's Tough McCarty and King Lentz. We're not together, I tell you! We're hanging apart!"

"Lord, will they ever begin!" said Dink, blowing on his hands that had suddenly gone limp and clammy.

"We've won the toss," said another voice. "There's a big wind, we'll take sides."

"Andover's kick-off," said Fatty Harris.

Stover sunk his head in his blanket, waiting for the awful moment to end. Then a whistle piped and he raised his head again. The ball had landed short, into the arms of Butcher Stevens, who plunged ahead for a slight gain and went down under a shock of blue jerseys.

Stover felt the warm blood return, the sinking feeling in the pit of his stomach left him,

THE VARMINT

he felt, amazed, a great calm settling over him, as though he had jumped from out his own body.

"If Flash Condit can once get loose," he said quietly, "he'll score. They ought to try a dash through tackle before the others warm up. Good!"

As if in obedience to his thought Flash Condit came rushing through the line, between end and tackle, but the Andover left halfback, who was alert, caught him and brought him to the ground after a gain of ten yards.

"Pretty fast, that chap," thought Dink. "Too bad, Flash was almost clear."

"Who tackled him?" asked Fatty Harris.

"Goodhue," came the answer from somewhere. "They say he runs the hundred in ten and a fifth."

The next try was not so fortunate, the blue line charged quicker and stopped Cheyenne Baxter without a gain. Charlie DeSoto tried a quarter-back run and some one broke through between the Waladoo Bird and Turkey Reiter.

"Not together—not together," said the dismal voice of Fatty Harris.

The signal was given for a punt and the ball lifted in the air went soaring down the field on the force of the wind. It was too long a punt for the ends to cover, and the Andover back with a good start came twisting through the

THE VARMINT

territory of Ned Banks who had been blocked off by his opponent.

"Watch that Andover end, Stover," said Mr. Ware. "Study out his methods."

"All right, sir," said Dink, who had watched no one else.

He waited breathless for the first shock of the Andover attack. It came with a rush, compact and solid, and swept back the Lawrenceville left side for a good eight yards.

"Good-by!" said Harris in a whisper.

Dink began to whistle, moving down the field, watching the backs. Another machine-like advance and another big gain succeeded.

"They'll wake up," said Dink solemnly to himself. "They'll stop 'em in a minute."

But they did not stop. Rush by rush, irresistibly the blue left their own territory and passed the forty-five yard line of Lawrenceville. Then a fumble occurred and the ball went again with the gale far out of danger, over the heads of the Andover backs who had misjudged its treacherous course.

"Lucky we've got the wind," said Dink, calm amid the roaring cheers about him. "Gee, that Andover attack's going to be hard to stop. Banks is beginning to limp."

The blue, after a few quick advances, formed and swept out toward Garry Cockrell's end.

THE VARMINT

"Three yards lost," said Dink grimly. "They won't try him often. Funny they're not onto Banks. Lord, how they can gain through the center of the line. First down again." Substitute and coach, the frantic school, alumni over from Princeton, kept up a constant storm of shouts and entreaties:

"Oh, get together!"
"Throw 'em back!"
"Hold 'em!"
"First down again!"
"Hold 'em, Lawrenceville!"
"Don't let them carry it seventy yards!"
"Get the jump!"
"There they go again!"
"Ten yards around Banks!"

Stover alone, squatting opposite the line of play, moving as it moved, coldly critical, studied each individuality.

"Funny nervous little tricks that Goodhue's got—blows on his hands—does that mean he takes the ball? No, all a bluff. What's he do when he does take it? Quiet and looks at the ground. When he doesn't take it he tries to pretend he does. I'll tuck that away. He's my man. Seems to switch in just as the interference strikes the end about ten feet beyond tackle, running low—Banks is playing too high; better, perhaps, to run in on 'em now and then before

THE VARMINT

they get started. There's going to be trouble there in a minute. The fellows aren't up on their toes yet—what is the matter, anyhow? Tough's getting boxed right along, he ought to play out further, I should think. Hello, some one fumbled again. Who's got it? Looks like Garry. No, they recovered it themselves—no, they didn't. Lord, what a butter-fingered lot—why doesn't he get it? He has—Charlie De-Soto—clear field—can he make it?—he ought to—where's that Goodhue?—looks like a safe lead; he'll make the twenty-yard line at least—yes, fully that, if he doesn't stumble—there's that Goodhue now—some one ought to block him off, good work—that's it—that makes the touchdown—lucky—very lucky!"

Some one hit him a terrific clap on the shoulder. He looked up in surprise to behold Fatty Harris dancing about like a crazed man. The air seemed all arms, hats were rising like startled coveys of birds. Some one flung his arms around him and hugged him. He flung him off almost indignantly. What were they thinking of—that was only one touchdown—four points—what was that against that blue team and the wind at their backs, too. One touchdown wasn't going to win the game.

"Why do they get so excited?" said Dink Stover to John Stover, watching deliberately

THE VARMINT

the ball soaring between the goalposts; "6 to 0—they think it's all over. Now's the rub."

Mr. Ware passed near him. He was quiet, too, seeing far ahead.

"Better keep warmed up, Stover," he said.

"Biting his nails, that's a funny trick for a master," thought Dink. "He oughtn't to be nervous. That doesn't do any good."

The shouts of exultation were soon hushed; with the advantage of the wind the game quickly assumed a different complexion. Andover had found the weak end and sent play after play at Banks, driving him back for long advances.

"Take off your sweater," said Mr. Ware.

Dink flung it off, running up and down the side-lines, springing from his toes.

"Why don't they take him out?" he thought angrily, with almost a hatred of the fellow who was fighting it out in vain. "Can't they see it? Ten yards more, oh, Lord! This ends it."

With a final rush the Andover interference swung at Banks, brushed him aside and swept over the remaining fifteen yards for the touchdown. A minute later the goal was kicked and the elevens again changed sides. The suddenness with which the score had been tied impressed every one—the school team seemed to have no defense against the well-massed attacks of the opponents.

THE VARMINT

"Holes as big as a house," said Fatty Harris. "Asleep! They're all asleep!"

Dink, pacing up and down, waited the word from Mr. Ware, rebelling because it did not come.

Again the scrimmage began, a short advance from the loosely-knit school eleven, a long punt with the wind and then a quick, business-like line-up of the blue team and another rush at the vulnerable end.

"Ten yards more; oh, it's giving it away!" said Fatty Harris.

Stover knelt and tried his shoelaces and rising, tightened his belt.

"I'll be out there in a moment," he said to himself.

Another gain at Banks' end and suddenly from the elevens across the field the figure of the captain rose and waved a signal.

"Go in, Stover," said Mr. Ware.

He ran out across the long stretch to where the players were moving restlessly, their clothes flinging out clouds of steam. Back of him something was roaring, cheering for him, perhaps, hoping against hope.

Then he was in the midst of the contestants, Garry Cockrell's arm about his shoulders, whispering something in his ear about keeping cool, breaking up the interference if he couldn't get

THE VARMINT

his man, following up the play. He went to his position, noticing the sullen expressions of his teammates, angry with the consciousness that they were not doing their best. Then taking his stand beyond Tough McCarty, he saw the Andover quarter and the backs turn and study him curiously. He noticed the half-back nearest him, a stocky, close-cropped, red-haired fellow, with brawny arms under his rolled-up jersey, whose duty it would be to send him rolling on the first rush.

"All ready?" cried the voice of the umpire. "First down."

The whistle blew, the two lines strained opposite each other. Stover knew what the play would be—there was no question of that. Fortunately the last two rushes had carried the play well over to his side—the boundary was only fifteen yards away. Dink had thought out quickly what he would do. He crept in closer than an end usually plays and at the snap of the ball rushed straight into the starting interference before it could gather dangerous momentum. The back, seeing him thus drawn in, instinctively swerved wide around his interference, forced slightly back. Before he could turn forward his own speed and the necessity of distancing Stover and Condit drove him out of bounds for a four-yard loss.

THE VARMINT

"Second down, nine yards to go!" came the verdict.

"Rather risky going in like that," said Flash Condit, who backed up his side.

"Wanted to force him out of bounds," said Stover.

"Oh—look out for something between tackle and guard now."

"No—they'll try the other side now to get a clean sweep at me," said Stover.

The red-haired halfback disappeared in the opposite side and, well protected, kept his feet for five yards.

"Third down, four to gain."

"Now for a kick," said Stover, as the Andover end came out opposite him. "What the deuce am I going to do to this coot to mix him up. He looks more as though he'd like to tackle me than to get past." He looked over and caught a glance from the Andover quarter. "I wonder. Why not a fake kick? They've sized me up for green. I'll play it carefully."

At the play, instead of blocking, he jumped back and to one side, escaping the end who dove at his knees. Then, rushing ahead, he stalled off the half and caught the fullback with a tackle that brought him to his feet, rubbing his side.

"Lawrenceville's ball. Time up for first half."

THE VARMINT

Dink had not thought of the time. Amazed, he scrambled to his feet, half angry at the interruption, and following the team went over to the room to be talked to by the captain and the coach.

It was a hang-dog crowd that gathered there, quailing under the scornful lashing of Garry Cockrell. He spared no one, he omitted no names. Dink, listening, lowered his eyes, ashamed to look upon the face of the team. One or two cried out:

"Oh, I say, Garry!"

"That's too much!"

"Too much, too much, is it?" cried their captain, walking up and down, striking the flat of his hand with the clenched fist. "By heavens, it's nothing to what they're saying of us out there. They're ashamed of us, one and all! Listen to the cheering if you don't believe it! They'll cheer a losing team, a team that is being driven back foot by foot. There's something glorious in that, but a team that stands up to be pushed over, a team that lies down and quits, a team that hasn't one bit of red fighting blood in it, they won't cheer; they're ashamed of you! Now, I'll tell you what's going to happen to you. You're going to be run down the field for just about four touchdowns. Here's Lentz being tossed around by a fellow that weighs forty pounds less. Why, he's the joke of the game.

THE VARMINT

McCarty hasn't stopped a play, not one! Waladoo's so easy that they rest up walking through him. But that's not the worst, you're playing wide apart as though there wasn't a man within ten miles of you; not one of you is helping out the other. The only time you've taken the ball from them is when a little shaver comes in and uses his head. Now, you're not going to win this game, but by the Almighty you're going out there and going to hold that Andover team! You've got the wind against you; you've got everything against you; you've got to fight on your own goal line, not once, but twenty times. But you've got to hold 'em; you're going to make good; you're going to wipe out that disgraceful, cowardly first half! You're going out there to stand those fellows off! You're going to make the school cheer for you again as though they believed in you, as though they were proud of you! You're going to do a bigger thing than beat a weaker team! You're going to fight off defeat and show that, if you can't win, you can't be beaten!"

Mr. Ware, in a professional way, passed from one to another with a word of advice: "Play lower, get the jump—don't be drawn in by a fake plunge—watch Goodhue."

But Dink heard nothing; he sat in his corner, clasping and unclasping his hands, suffering

THE VARMINT

with the moments that separated him from the fray. Then all at once he was back on the field, catching the force of the wind that blew the hair about his temples, hearing the half-hearted welcome that went up from the school.

"Hear that cheer!" said Garry Cockrell bitterly.

From Butcher Stevens' boot the ball went twisting and veering down the field. Stover went down, dodging instinctively, hardly knowing what he did. Then as he started to spring at the runner an interferer from behind flung himself on him and sent him sprawling, but not until one arm had caught and checked his man.

McCarty had stopped the runner, when Dink sprang to his feet, wild with the rage of having missed his tackle.

"Steady!" cried the voice of his captain.

He lined up hurriedly, seeing red. The interference started for him, he flung himself at it blindly and was buried under the body of the red-haired half. Powerless to move, humiliatingly held under the sturdy body, the passion of fighting rose in him again. He tried to throw him off, doubling up his fist, waiting until his arm was free.

"Why, you're easy, kid," said a mocking voice. "We'll come again."

THE VARMINT

The taunt suddenly chilled him. Without knowing how it happened, he laughed.

"That's the last time you get me, old rooster," he said, in a voice that did not belong to him.

He glanced back. Andover had gained fifteen yards.

"That comes from losing my head," he said quietly. "That's over."

It had come, the cold consciousness of which Cockrell had spoken, strange as the second wind that surprises the distressed runner.

"I've got to teach that red-haired coot a lesson," he said. "He's a little too confident. I'll shake him up a bit."

The opportunity came on the third play, with another attack on his end. He ran forward a few steps and stood still, leaning a little forward, waiting for the red-haired back who came plunging at him. Suddenly Dink dropped to his knees, the interferer went violently over his back, something struck Stover in the shoulder and his arms closed with the fierce thrill of holding his man.

"Second down, seven yards to gain," came the welcome sound.

Time was taken out for the red-haired halfback, who had had the wind knocked out of him.

"Now he'll be more respectful," said Dink, and as soon as he caught his eye he grinned. "Red hair—I'll see if I can't get his temper."

THE VARMINT

Thus checked and to use the advantage of the wind Andover elected to kick. The ball went twisting, and, changing its course in the strengthening wind, escaped the clutches of Macnooder and went bounding toward the goal where Charlie DeSoto saved it on the twenty-five-yard line. In an instant the overwhelming disparity of the sides was apparent.

A return kick at best could gain but twenty-five or thirty yards. From now on they would be on the defensive.

Dink came in to support his traditional enemy, Tough McCarty. The quick, nervous voice of Charlie DeSoto rose in a shriek: "Now, Lawrenceville, get into this, 7—52—3."

Dink swept around for a smash on the opposite tackle, head down, eyes fastened on the back before him, feeling the shock of resistance and the yielding response as he thrust forward, pushing, heaving on, until everything piled up before him. Four yards gained.

A second time they repeated the play, making the first down.

"Time to spring a quick one through us," he thought.

But again DeSoto elected the same play.

"What's he trying to do?" said Dink. "Why don't he vary it?"

Some one hauled him out of the tangled pile. It was Tough McCarty.

THE VARMINT

"Say, our tackle's a stiff one," he said, with his mouth to Stover's ear. "You take his knees; I'll take him above this time."

Their signal came at last. Dink dove, trying to meet the shifting knees and throw him off his balance. The next moment a powerful arm caught him as he left the ground and swept him aside.

"Any gain?" he asked anxiously as he came up.

"Only a yard," said McCarty. "He got through and smeared the play."

"I know how to get him next time," said Dink.

The play was repeated. This time Stover made a feint and then dove successfully after the big arm had swept fruitlessly past. Flash Condit, darting through the line, was tackled by Goodhue and fell forward for a gain.

"How much?" said Stover, rising joyfully.

"They're measuring."

The distance was tried and found to be two feet short of the necessary five yards. The risk was too great, a kick was signaled and the ball was Andover's, just inside the center of the field.

"Now, Lawrenceville," cried the captain, "show what you're made of."

The test came quickly, a plunge between Mc·

THE VARMINT

Carty and Lentz yielded three yards, a second four. The Andover attack, with the same precision as before, struck anywhere between the tackles and found holes. Dink, at the bottom of almost every pile, raged at Tough McCarty.

"He's doing nothing, he isn't fighting," he said angrily. "He does't know what it is to fight. Why doesn't he break up that interference for me?"

When the attack struck his end now it turned in, slicing off tackle, the runner well screened by close interference that held him up when Stover tackled, dragging him on for the precious yards. Three and four yards at a time, the blue advance rolled its way irresistibly toward the red and black goal. They were inside the twenty-yard line now.

Cockrell was pleading with them. Little Charlie DeSoto was running along the line, slapping their backs, calling frantically on them to throw the blue back.

And gradually the line did stiffen, slowly but perceptibly the advance was cut down. Enmities were forgotten with the shadow of the goal-posts looming at their backs. Waladoo and Turkey Reiter were fighting side by side, calling to each other. Tough McCarty was hauling Stover out of desperate scrimmages, patting him on the back and calling him "good old Dink." The fighting blood that Garry Cockrell had called upon was at last there—the line had closed and fought together.

And yet they were borne back to their fifteen-yard line, two yards at a time, just losing the fourth down.

Stover at end was trembling like a blooded terrier, on edge for each play, shrieking:

"Oh, Tough, get through—you must get through!"

He was playing by intuition now, no time to plan. He knew just who had the ball and where it was going. Out or in, the attack was concentrating on his end—only McCarty and he could stop it. He was getting his man, but they were dragging him on, fighting now for inches.

"Third down, one yard to gain!"

"Watch my end," he shouted to Flash Condit, and hurling himself forward at the starting backs dove under the knees, and grabbing the legs about him went down buried under the mass he had upset.

It seemed hours before the crushing bodies were pulled off and some one's arm brought him to his feet and some one hugged him, shouting in his ear:

"You saved it, Dink, you saved it!"

Some one rushed up with a sponge and began dabbing his face.

THE VARMINT

"What the deuce are they doing that for?" he said angrily.

Then he noticed that an arm was under his and he turned curiously to the face near him. It was Tough McCarty's.

"Whose ball is it?" he said.

"Ours."

He looked to the other side. Garry Cockrell was supporting him.

"What's the matter?" he said, trying to draw his head away from the sponge that was dripping water down his throat.

"Just a little wind knocked out, youngster—coming to?"

"I'm all right."

He walked a few steps alone and then took his place. Things were in a daze on the horizon, but not there in the field. Everything else was shut out except his duty there.

Charlie DeSoto's voice rose shrill:

"Now, Lawrenceville, up the field with it. This team's just begun to play. We've got together, boys. Let her rip!"

No longer scattered, but a unit, all differences forgot, fighting for the same idea, the team rose up and crashed through the Andover line, every man in the play, ten—fifteen yards ahead.

"Again!" came the strident cry.

Without a pause the line sprang into place,

THE VARMINT

formed and swept forward. It was a privilege to be in such a game, to feel the common frenzy, the awakened glance of battle that showed down the line. Dink, side by side with Tough McCarty, thrilled with the same thrill, plunging ahead with the same motion, fighting the same fight; no longer alone and desperate, but nerved with the consciousness of a partner whose gameness matched his own.

For thirty yards they carried the ball down the field, before the stronger Andover team, thrown off its feet by the unexpected frenzy, could rally and stand them off. Then an exchange of punts once more drove them back to their twenty-five-yard line.

A second time the Andover advance set out from the fifty-yard line and slowly fought its way to surrender the ball in the shadow of the goalposts.

Stover played on in a daze, remembering nothing of the confused shock of bodies that had gone before, wondering how much longer he could hold out—to last out the game as the captain had told him. He was groggy, from time to time he felt the sponge's cold touch on his face or heard the voice of Tough McCarty in his ear.

"Good old Dink, die game!"

How he loved McCarty fighting there by his side, whispering to him:

THE VARMINT

"You and I, Dink! What if he is an old elephant, we'll put him out the play."

Still, flesh and blood could not last forever. The half must be nearly up.

"Two minutes more time."

"What was that?" he said groggily to Flash Condit.

"Two minutes more. Hold 'em now!"

It was Andover's ball. He glanced around. They were down near the twenty-five-yard line somewhere. He looked at McCarty, whose frantic head showed against the sky.

"Break it up, Tough," he said, and struggled toward him.

A cry went up, the play was halted.

"He's groggy," he heard voices say, and then came the welcome splash of the sponge.

Slowly his vision cleared to the anxious faces around him.

"Can you last?" said the captain.

"I'm all right," he said gruffly.

"Things cleared up now?"

"Fine!"

McCarty put his arm about him and walked with him.

"Oh, Dink, you will last, won't you?"

"You bet I will, Tough!"

"It's the last stand, old boy!"

"The last."

THE VARMINT

"Only two minutes more we've got to hold 'em! The last ditch, Dink."

"I'll last."

He looked up and saw the school crouching along the line—tense drawn faces. For the first time he realized they were there, calling on him to stand steadfast.

He went back, meeting the rush that came his way, half-knocked aside, half-getting his man, dragged again until assistance came. DeSoto's stinging hand slapped his back and the sting was good, clearing his brain.

Things came into clear outline once more. He saw down the line and to the end where Garry Cockrell stood.

"Good old captain," he said. "They'll not get by me, not now."

He was in every play it seemed to him, wondering why Andover was always keeping the ball, always coming at his end. Suddenly he had a shock. Over his shoulder were the goalposts, the line he stood on was the line of his own goal.

He gave a hoarse cry and went forward like a madman, parting the interference. Some one else was through; Tough was through; the whole line was through flinging back the runner. He went down clinging to Goodhue, buried under

THE VARMINT

a mass of his own tacklers. Then, through the frenzy, he heard the shrill call of time.

He struggled to his feet. The ball lay scarcely four yards away from the glorious goalposts. Then, before the school could sweep them up; panting, exhausted, they gathered in a circle with incredulous, delirious faces, and leaning heavily, wearily on one another gave the cheer for Andover. And the touch of Stover's arm on McCarty's shoulder was like an embrace.

XIX

At nine o'clock that night Stover eluded Dennis de Brian de Boru Finnegan and the Tennessee Shad and went across the dusky campus, faintly lit by the low-hanging moon. Past him hundreds of gnomelike figures were scurrying, carrying shadowy planks and barrels, while gleeful voices crossed and recrossed.

"There's a whole pile back of Appleby's."

"We've got an oil barrel."

"Burn every fence in the county!"

"Who cares!"

"Where did you get that plank?"

"Up by the Rouse."

"Gee, we'll have a bonfire bigger'n the chapel!"

"More wood, Freshmen!"

"Rotten lot, those Freshmen!"

"Hold up your end, Skinny. Do you think I'm a pack mule?"

Dink pulled the brim of his hat over his eyes and slunk away, not to be recognized. He went in a roundabout way past the chapel. He had just one desire, to stand under the goalposts they had defended and to feel again the thrill.

THE VARMINT

"Who's that?" The voice was Tough McCarty's.

"It's me. It's Dink," said Stover.

"I came down here," said McCarty, appearing from under the goal-posts and hesitating a little, "well, just to feel how it felt again."

"So did I."

Dink stood by the posts, taking one affectionately in his hand, and said curiously: "They tell me, Tough, we held 'em four times inside the ten-yard line."

"Four times, old boy."

"Funny I don't remember but two. Guess I was groggy."

"You didn't show it."

"It was you pulled me through, Tough."

"Rats!"

"It was. There at the last, I remember when you gripped me." As this was perilously near sentiment he stopped. "I say, how many of us tackled that fellow the last time?"

"The whole bunch. I say, Dink."

"Yes?"

"Stand out here—that's it, knee to knee. Can't you just feel it behind you?"

"Yes," said Dink, surprised that in the big body there was an imagination akin to his own. Then he said abruptly:

"Tough, I guess there won't be any fight."

"No—not after this."

"What the deuce did we get a grudge for, anyway?"

"I always liked you, Dink, but you wouldn't have it."

"I was a mean little varmint!"

"Rats! I say, Dink, we've got two years more on the old team. There's nothing going to get around our end, is there, old boy?"

"You bet there isn't!"

All at once a flame ran up the towering bonfire and belched toward the sky.

"Are you going to let them get you?" said McCarty.

"Me? Oh, Lord, no—I can't make a speech!"

"Neither can I!" said Tough mendaciously. "I wouldn't go back there for the world!"

The thin posts stood out against the sheet of flame, gaunt, rigid, imbued with a certain grandeur.

"I say, Dink," said McCarty.

"Yes?"

"I say, we're going to have some great old fights together. But, do you know, I sort of feel after all, this will be the best."

Then a chorus of thin shrieks rose about them. They started half-heartedly to run, pretending fury. A swarm of determined boyhood rushed

THE VARMINT

over them and flung them kicking, struggling into the air.

"Tough McCarty and Dink Stover!"

"We've got 'em!"

"On to the bonfire!"

"They're ours!"

"Hurray!"

"Help!"

"Help! We've got McCarty and Stover!"

Boys by the score came tearing out. The little knot under Dink became a thick, black shadow, rushing forward with hilarious, triumphant shouts. Then all at once he landed all-fours on a cart before the flaming stack, greeted by fishhorns and rattles, his name shrieked out in a wild acclaim.

"Three cheers for good old Dink!"

"Three cheers for honest John Stover!"

"Three cheers for the little cuss!"

He drew himself up, fumbling at his cap, terrified at the multiplied faces that danced before his eyes.

"I say, fellows——"

"Hurray!"

"Good boy!"

"Orator!"

"I say, fellows, I don't see why you've got me up here."

"You don't!"

THE VARMINT

"We'll show you!"

"Dink, you're the finest ever!"

"You're the stuff!"

"Three cheers for good old Rinky Dink!"

"Fellows, I'm no silver-tongued orator——"

"Don't believe it!"

"You are!"

"Fellows, I haven't got anything to say——"

"That's the stuff!"

"Hurray!"

"Keep it up!"

"Oh, you bulldog!"

"Fellows, they were good——"

A derisive shout went up.

"Fellows, they were very good——"

"Yes, they were!"

"Fellows, they were re-markably good—but *they didn't beat the old school team!* That's all."

He dove headlong into the crowd, unaware that he had repeated for the sixth time the stock oration of the evening.

"Good old Dink! Good old Rinky Dink!"

The cry stuck in his memory all through the jubilant night and long after, when in his delicious bed he tossed and worried over the tackles he had missed.

"It's a bully nickname—bully!" he repeated drowsily, again and again. "It sounds as

THE VARMINT

though they liked you! And Tough McCarty, what a bully chap—bully! We're going to be friends—pals—what a bully fellow! Everything is bully—everything!"

. . . . .

With the close of the football season and the advent of December, with its scurries of snow and sleet, what might be termed the open season for masters began.

A school of four hundred fellows is a good deal like a shaky monarchy: the football and baseball seasons akin to foreign wars; so long as they last the tranquillity of the state is secure, but with the return of peace a state of fermentation and unrest is due.

The three weeks that lead to the Christmas vacation are too filled with anticipation to be dangerous. It is the long reaches after January fifth, the period of arctic night that settles down until the passing of the muddy month of March, that tries the souls of the keepers of these caged menageries.

Since those days a humane direction has built a gymnasium to lighten the condition of servitude, preserve the health and prolong the lives of the Faculty. But at this time, with the shutting of the door on the treadmills of exercise, the young assistant master arranged his warm wrapper and slippers at the side of his bed and went to sleep with one ear raised.

Dink Stover entered this season of mischief with all the ardor and intensity of his nature, the more so because, owing to his weeks of strict training and his virtual isolation of the year before, it was all strange to him. And at that period what is forbidden, dangerous and, above all, untried, must be attempted at least once.

Now, owing to the foresight of a wise father, Dink had never been forbidden to smoke. Of a consequence when, at an early age, he practiced upon an old corncob pipe and found it violently disagreed with him, the desire abruptly ceased and, as the athletic ardor came, he consecrated his years to the duty of growing, with not the slightest regret.

But between smoking under permission and squeezing close to a cold-air ventilator, stealthily, in the pin-drop silences of the night, with frightful risks of detection, was all the difference in the world. One was a disagreeable, thoroughly unsympathetic exercise; the other was a romantic, mediæval adventure.

So when Slops Barnett, who roomed below and was the proprietor of a model air flue with direct, perpendicular draught, said to him with an air of mannish *insouciance:*

"I say, old man, I've got a fat box of 'Gyptians. Glad to have you drop in to-night if you like the weed."

Dink answered with blasé familiarity:

"Why, thankee, I've been aching for just a good old coffin-nail."

He slipped down the creaking, nervous stairs, and found Slops luxuriously reclining before the ventilator, on a mattress re-enforced by yellow and green sofa pillows, that gave the whole somewhat of the devilishly dissipated effect of the scenes from Oriental lands that fascinated him on the covers of cigarette boxes.

Slops made him a sign in the deaf-and-dumb language to extinguish the light and creep to his side.

"Comfy?" said Slops, whispering from the darkness.

"Out of sight!"

"Here's the filthy weed."

"Thanks."

"Always keep the cig in front of the ventilator," said Slops, applying his lips to Dink's ear. "Get a light from mine. Talk in whispers."

Stover filled his cheeks cautiously and blew out after a sufficient period.

"You inhale?"

"Sure."

"Inhale a cigar?"

"Always."

THE VARMINT

"It's awful the way I inhale," said Slops with a melancholy sigh. "I'm undermining my constitution. Ever see my hand? Shakes worse'n jelly. Can't help it, though; can't live without the weed. I'm a regular cig fiend!"

Stover, holding his cigarette gingerly, keeping the sickly smoke at the end of his tongue, looked over at Slops' stupid little face, flashing out of the darkness at each puff. He was no longer the useless Slops Barnett, good only to fetch and carry the sweaters of the team, but Barnett, man of the world, versed in deadly practices.

"I say, Slops——"

"Hist—lower."

"I say, Slops, what would they do if they caught us?"

"Bounce us."

"For good?"

"Sure! P. D. Q."

The cigarette suddenly had a new delight to Dink. He was even tempted to inhale a small, very small puff, but immediately conquered this enthusiastic impulse.

"Isn't this the gay life, though?" said Slops carelessly.

"You bet," said Dink.

From down the flue came three distinct taps.

"That's the Gutter Pup signaling," said Slops,

putting his finger over Dink's mouth. "**Bundy** is snooping around. Mum's the word."

Presently, as Dink sat there in the darkness, trying desperately to breathe noiselessly, the sound of slipping footsteps was heard in the hall. Slops' hand closed over his. The steps stopped directly outside their door, waited a long moment and went on.

"Bundy?" said Dink in a whisper.

"Yes."

"Why did he stop?"

"He's got me spotted. He's seen the nicotine on my finger," said Slops, showing a finger under a sudden glow of his cigarette.

A half-hour later when Dink crept up the stairs, homeward bound, he swelled with a new sensation. Yesterday was months away; then he was a boy, now that he had smoked up a cold-air ventilator, with Bundy outwitted by the door, he had aged with a jump—he must be at last a man.

The next week he added to his stature by going to P. Lentz's room for a midnight session of the national game, where, after a titanic struggle of three hours, he won the colossal sum of forty-eight cents.

Having sunk to these depths he began to listen to the Sunday sermons with a thrill of personal delight—there being not the slightest

THE VARMINT

doubt that they were directly launched at him. Sometimes he wondered how the Doctor and The Roman could remain ignorant of the extent of his debauches, his transgressions were so daring and so complete. He stood shivering up the Trenton road, under the shadow of an icy trunk, of Sunday mornings, and met Blinky, the one-eyed purveyor of illicit cigarettes and the forbidden Sunday newspapers, which had to be wrapped around his body and smuggled under a sweater.

Secretly he rubbed iodine on his fingers to simulate the vicious stain of nicotine that was such a precious ornament to Slops' squat fingers. Only one thing distressed him, and that was his invincible dislike for the cigarette itself.

Being now a celebrity, many doors were thrown invitingly open to him, invitations that flattered him, without his making a distinction. He went over to the Upper at times and into rooms where he had no business, immensely proud that he was called in to share the delights and liberties of the lords of the school.

At the Kennedy he was in constant rebellion against established precedent, constantly called below to be lectured by The Roman. In revenge for which at night he made the life of Mr. Bundy one of constant insomnia, and, by soaping the stairs or strewing tacks in the hall, seriously in-

THE VARMINT

terfered with that inexperienced young gentleman's nightly exercises.

The deeper he went the deeper he was determined to go; doggedly imagining that the whole Faculty, led by The Roman, were bending every effort to bring him down and convict him.

The Tennessee Shad had no inclinations toward sporting life—greatly to Stover's surprise. When Dink urged him to join the clandestine parties he only yawned in a bored way.

"Come on now, Shad, be a sport," said Dink, repeating the stock phrase.

"You're not sports," said the Tennessee Shad in languid derision, "you're bluffs. Besides, I've been all through it, two years ago. Hurry up with your dead-game sporting phase, if you've got to, but get through it; 'cause now you're nothing but a nuisance."

Dink felt considerably grieved at his roommate's flippant attitude toward his career of vice. Secretly, he felt that a word of kindly remonstrance, some friendly effort to pull him back from the frightful abyss into which he was sinking, would have been more like a friend and a roommate.

This same callous indifference to the fate of his roommate's soul so incensed Stover that, to bring before the Shad's eyes the really desperate state of his morals, he appointed a Welsh-rabbit party in their room for the following night.

"Don't mind, do you?" he said carelessly.

"Not if I don't have to eat it!"

"It's going to be a real one," said Stover, making a distinction."

"Come off!"

"Fact. It is not going to be flavored with rootbeer, toothwash, condensed milk or russet polish; it is going to be the genuine, satisfaction guaranteed, or you get your money back."

"With beer?"

"Exactly."

"Yes, it is!"

"It is."

"Where'll you get it?"

"I have ways."

"Oh," said the Tennessee Shad sarcastically, "this is one of your real, sporting-life parties, is it?"

Stover disdained to answer.

"Is that bunch of slums going to be here?"

"Are you referring to my friends?" said Stover.

"I am," said the Tennessee Shad, "and all I ask while this feast of bacchanalian orgies is going on, is that *I* be allowed to sleep."

At eleven o'clock Stover, holding his shoes in his hand, went down the stairs to meet Slops in

Fatty Harris' room and thence into the outlawed night. They stole over the crinkling snow, burying their noses in their sweaters, until, having climbed several fences, they arrived behind a shed of particularly cavernous appearance.

"Make the signal," said Slops, sheltering himself behind Stover.

Blinky appeared like a monster of the night.

"Hist, Blinky, O. K.?" said Slops, who, having his shoulder to Dink's recovered his sporting manner. "Got the booze?"

"I got it," said Blinky in husky accents, with his hand behind his back. "What's youse got?"

"The cash is here all right. How many bots did you bring?"

Blinky slowly brought forward one bottle.

"What, only one?" said Slops the bacchanalian, in dismay.

"All's left," said Blinky, with a double meaning.

"How much?"

"One dollar."

"What! You robber!"

"Take it or leave it—don't care," said Blinky, who sat down and hugged the bottle to him like a baby.

They paid the extortion and slunk back.

"We'll have to cook up a story," said Dink.

"Sure!"

"Still, it's beer."

"It certainly is!"

"It's expulsion if we're caught."

"And a penal offense, don't forget that!"

Somewhat consoled by this delightful thought they cautiously tapped on Fatty Harris' window and, removing their boots, tiptoed upstairs like anarchists with a price on their heads.

In Stover's room three more desperate characters were waiting about the chafing dish, Fatty Harris, Slush Randolph and Pee-wee Norris, all determined on a life of crime—but all slightly nervous.

The Tennessee Shad, rolled into a ball on his bed, was venting his scorn with an occasional snore.

Stover held up the lonely bottle.

"Is that all?" exclaimed the three in indignant whispers.

"All, and mighty lucky to get that," said Dink valiantly. "We were chased by the constable, terrific time, pounced on us, desperate struggle, just got away with our skins."

At this a distinct snort was heard from the direction of the Tennessee Shad's bed.

"I say, isn't it rather—rather dangerous?" said Pee-wee Norris, with his ears horribly strained.

"What of it?"

THE VARMINT

"Suppose he goes to the Doctor?"

"We'll have to take the risk."

"I say, though, let's be quick about it."

An uncongenial chill began to pervade the room. Fatty Harris, as master cook, visibly hastened the operations.

The Tennessee Shad was now heard to say in a mumbled jumble:

"Hurrah for crime! Never say die, boys— dead game sports—give us a drink, bartender!"

The revelers stood at the bed looking wrathfully down at the cynic, who snored heavily and said drowsily:

"Talks in his sleep, he talks in his sleep, poor old Pol!"

"Don't pay any attention to him," said Stover angrily. "He's a cheap wit. What are you doing at the door, Pee-wee?"

"I'm listening," said Norris, turning guiltily.

"You're afraid!"

"I'm not; only let's hurry it up."

Fatty Harris, watching the swirling yellow depths of the rabbit with evident anxiety, emptied a third of the beer into it and held out the bottle, saying:

"Here, sports, fill up the glasses with the good old liquor."

When the three glasses and two toothmugs had received their exact portion of the bitter

THE VARMINT

stuff, which had been allowed to foam copiously in order to eke out, the five desperadoes solemnly touched glasses and Slops Barnett, who had visited in Princeton, led them in that whispered toast that is the acme of devilment:

> *" Then stand by your glasses steady,*
> *This world is a world full of lies.*
> *Then here's to the dead already dead,*
> *And here's to the next man who dies!"*

It was terrific. Stover, quite moved, looked about the circle, thought that Pee-wee looked the nearest to the earthworm and repeated solemnly:
"To the next man who dies."
At this moment the Tennessee Shad was heard derisively intoning:

> *" Ring around a rosie,*
> *Pocket full of posie.*
> *Oats, peas, beans and barley grows.*
> *Open the ring and take her in*
> *'And kiss her when you get her in!"*

They paid no heed. They felt too acutely the solemnity of life and the fleeting hour of pleasure to be deterred by even the lathery aspect of their own faces, which emerged from the suds of the beer ready for the barber.

THE VARMINT

"Dish out the bunny," said Slops, putting down his mug with a reckless look.

Suddenly there came an impressive knock and the voice of Mr. Bundy saying:

"Open the door, Stover!"

In a thrice the revelry broke up, the telltale bottle and glasses were stowed under the window-seat, the visiting sporting gentlemen precipitately groveled to places of concealment, while Stover extinguished the lights and softly stole into bed.

"Open the door at once!"

"Who's there?" said Dink with a start.

"Open the door!"

All sleepy innocence Dink opened the door, rubbing his eyes at the sudden glow.

"Up after lights?" said Mr. Bundy, marching in.

"I, sir?" said Dink, astounded.

All at once Mr. Bundy perceived the chafing-dish and descended upon it. Stover's heart sank—if he tasted it they were lost; no power could save them. Mr. Bundy turned and surveyed the room; one by one the terrified roués were dragged forth and recognized, while the Tennessee Shad sat on the edge of his bed, reflectively sharpening his fingers on the pointed knee-caps.

Then, to the horror of all, Mr. Bundy, sniffing

THE VARMINT

the chafing-dish, inserted a spoon and tasted it. Immediately he set the spoon down with a crash, gave a furious glance at Stover and departed, after ordering them to their rooms.

The dead game sports, white and shaky, went without stopping.

"They're a fine sample of vicious bounders, they are!" said the Tennessee Shad. "Bet that Slops Barnett is weeping to his pillow now!"

"I'm sorry I got you into this," said Stover gloomily.

"You've brought my gray hairs in sorrow to the grave!" said the Tennessee Shad solemnly.

"Don't jest," said Dink in a still voice. "It's all up with me, but I'll square you."

"Don't worry," said the Tennessee Shad, smiling. "I may not be a tin sport, but I keep my thinker going all the time."

"Why, what do you mean?"

"I mean you'll get twigged for a midnight spread, that's all."

"But the beer. Bundy tasted the beer."

"Taste it yourself," said the Tennessee Shad, with a wave of his hand.

Stover hurriedly dipped in a spoon, tasted it and uttered an execration.

"Murder, what did you put in it?"

"About half a bottle of horse liniment," said the Tennessee Shad, crawling back into bed.

THE VARMINT

"Only, don't tell the others if you want to see how much dead game sportiness there is in them by to-morrow morning."

The affair made a great noise and, as Stover suppressed the transformation worked by the Tennessee Shad, Slops Barnett and his companions did not exactly show those qualities of Stoic resignation which might be expected from brazen characters with their view of life.

Meanwhile, the skies cleared and the earth hardened, and the air resounded with the cries of baseball candidates.

Much to his surprise, Dink found at the end of the strenuous day no impelling desire to plunge into fast life. Still the conviction remained for a long time that his soul had been surrendered, that not only was he destined for the gallows in this world, but that only the prayers of his mother might save him from being irrevocably damned in the next. It was a terrific thought, and yet it brought a certain pleasure. He was different from the rest. He was a man of the world. He had known—LIFE!

The episode ended as episodes in the young days end—in a laugh.

"I say, Dink," said the Tennessee Shad one afternoon in April, as, gloriously reveling on the warm turf, they watched the 'Varsity nine.

"Say it."

THE VARMINT

"In your dead-game sporting days did you ever, by chance, paint your nicotine fingers with iodine?"

"How in blazes did you know?"

"Used to do it myself," said the Shad reminiscently. Then he added: "Thought yourself a lost soul?"

Stover began to laugh.

"All alone in a cold, cold world—wicked, very wicked?"

"Perhaps."

"And it was rather a nice feeling, too, wasn't it?"

"I didn't know you——" said Dink, blushing to find himself back in the common herd.

"Me, too," said the Tennessee Shad, sucking a straw. "Good old sporting days!" Presently he began mischievously:

"*Then stand by your glasses steady,*
 This world is a——"

But here Dink, rising up, tumbled him over.

XX

With the complete arrival of the spring came also a lessening of Dink's requested appearances at Faculty meetings, his little evening chats in The Roman's study on matters of disciplinary interpretation and the occasional summons through the gates of Avernus to quail before the all-seeing eye.

It was not that the spirit of Spartacus was faint, or that his enmity had weakened toward The Roman—who, of course, without the slightest doubt, was always the persecutor responsible for his summons before the courts of injustice. The truth was, Stover had suddenly begun to age and to desire to put from himself youthful things. This extraordinary phenonenon that somehow does happen was in some measure a reflex action.

Ever since the stormy afternoon on which he had decided against his own eleven, he had slowly come to realize that he had won a peculiar place in the estimation of the school—somewhat of the dignity of the incorruptible judges that existed in former days. He became in a small way a sort of court of arbitration before which questions of more or less gravity were submitted. This deference at first embarrassed, then amused, then finally pleased him with an acute, mannish pleasure.

The consequence was that Stover, who until this time had only looked forward and up at the majestic shadows of the fourth and fifth formers, now looked backward and down, and became pleasurably aware that leagues below him was the large body of the first and second forms. Having perceived this new adjustment he woke with a start and, rubbing his eyes, took stock of his amazing knowledge of life and again said to himself that now, finally, he certainly must have arrived at man's estate.

On top of which, having been asked to referee several disputes in his character of Honest John Stover, Dink, while holding himself in reserve to direct operations on a dignified and colossal scale against the Natural Enemy, decided that it was unbecoming of a man of his position, age and reputation, who had the entrée of the Upper House, to go skipping about the midnight ways, in undignified costume, with such rank shavers as Pebble Stone and Dennis de B. de B. Finnegan.

So when Dennis arrived after lights, like a will-o'-the-wisp, with a whispered:

"I say, Dink, all ready."

THE VARMINT

Stover replied:

"All ready in bed."

"What," said Dennis aghast, "you're not with us?"

"No."

"Aren't you feeling well?"

"First rate."

"But I say, Dink, there's half a dozen of us. We've got all the laundry bags in the house heaped up just outside of Beekstein's door and, I say, we're going to pile 'em all up on top of him and then jump on and pie him, and scoot for our rooms before old Bundy can jump the stairs and nab us. It'll be regular touch and go—a regular lark! Come on!"

A snore answered him.

"You won't come?"

"No."

"Are you mad at me?"

"No, I'm sleepy!"

"Sleepy!" said Dennis in such amazement that he no longer had any strength to argue, and left the room convinced that Stover was heroically concealing an agony of pain.

Stover immediately settled his tired body, sunk his nose to the level of the covers and floated blissfully off into the land of dreams. The next night and the next it was the same. For a whole month Dink slept, wasting not a one of the pre-

THE VARMINT

cious moments of the night, sleeping through th‚ slow-moving recitations, sleeping on the green turf of afternoons, pillowed on Tough McCarty or the Tennessee Shad, and watching others scampering around the diamond in incomprehensible activity; but the month was the month of April and his years sixteen. In the first week of May Stover awakened, the drowsiness dropped from him and the spirit of perpetual motion again returned. Still, the distance between himself and his past remained. He had changed, become graver, more laconic, moving with sedateness, like Garry Cockrell, whose tricks of speech and gestures he imitated, holding himself rather aloof from the populace, curiously conscious that the change had come, and sometimes looking back with profound melancholy on the youth that had now passed irrevocably away.

During this period of somewhat fragile self-importance, the acquaintance with Tough McCarty had strengthened into an eternal friendship in a manner that had a certain touch of humor.

McCarty, after the close of the football season, had repeatedly sought out his late antagonist, but, though Dink at the bottom of his soul was thrilled with the thought that here at last was the friend of friends, the Damon to his Pythias, the chum who was to stand shoulder to his shoulder, and so on, still there was too much self-conscious pride in him to yield immediately to this feeling.

McCarty perceived the reserve without quite analyzing it, and was puzzled at the barriers that still intervened.

During the winter, when Dink was resolutely set in the pursuit of that beau-ideal, which had a marked resemblance with a certain creation of Bret Harte's, Mr. Jack Hamlin, "gentleman sport," as Dennis would have called him, McCarty found little opportunity for friendly intercourse. He disapproved of many of Dink's friendships, not so much from a moralistic point of view as from Stover's not exercising the principle of selection. As this phase was intensified and Stover became the object of criticism of his classmates for hanging at the heels of fifth-formers and neglecting his own territory, McCarty resolved that the plain duty of a friend required him to administer a moral lecture.

This heroic resolve threw him into confusion for a week, for, in the first place, he had been accustomed to receive rather than to give words of warning and, in the second place, he was fully aware of the difficulties of opening up the subject at all.

After much anxious and gloomy cogitation he

THE VARMINT

hit upon a novel plan and, approaching Stover at the end of the last recitation, gave him a mysterious wink.

"What's up?" said Dink instantly.

McCarty pulled him aside:

"I've got a couple of A. No. 1 millionaire cigars," he said in a whisper. "If you've got nothing better, why, come along."

"I'm yours on the jump," said Dink, trying to give to his words a joy which he was far from feeling in his stomach.

"You smoke cigars?"

"Do I!"

"Come on, then!"

It was the last day of March, which had gone out like a lamb, leaving the ground still chill and moist with the memory of departed snows. They went down by the pond in the shelter of the grove and McCarty proudly produced two cigars coated with gilt foil.

"They look the real thing to me," said Dink, eying the long projectiles with a rakish, professional look.

Now, Dink had never smoked a cigar in his life and was alarmed at the thought of the task before him; but he was resolved to die a lingering death rather than allow that humiliating secret to be discovered.

"You bet they're the real thing," said Tough

THE VARMINT

McCarty, slipping off the foil. "Real, black beauties! Get the flavor?"

Dink approached the ominous black cigar to his nose, sniffed it rapturously and cocked a knowing eye.

"Aha!"

"Real Havanas!"

"They certainly smell good!"

"Swiped 'em off my brother-in-law, forty-five centers."

"I believe it. Say, what do you call 'em?"

"Invincibles."

The name threw a momentary chill over Stover, but he instantly recovered.

"I say, we ought to have a couple of hatpins," he said, turning the cigar in his fingers.

"What for?"

"Smoke 'em to the last puff!"

"We'll use our penknives."

"All right—after you."

Stover cautiously drew in his first puff. To his surprise nothing immediate happened.

"How is it?" said McCarty.

"Terrific!"

"Do you inhale?"

"Sometimes," said Stover, with an inconsequential wave of his hand.

This gave McCarty his opening; besides, he was deceived by Stover's complete manner.

THE VARMINT

"Dink, I'm afraid you're smoking too much," he said earnestly, puffing on his cigar.

"Oh, no," said Dink, immensely flattered by this undeserved accusation from McCarty, who smoked forty-five-cent cigars.

"Yes, you are. I know it. Trouble with you is, old boy, you never do anything by halves. I know you."

"Oh, well," said Stover loftily.

"You're smoking too much, and that's not all, Dink. I—I've wanted to have a chance at you for a long while, and now I'm going for you."

"Hello——"

"Now, look here, boy," said Tough McCarty, filling the air with the blue smoke, "I'm not a mammy boy nor a goody-goody, and I don't like preaching; but you've got too much ahead of you, old rooster, to go and throw it away."

"What do you mean?" said Dink, champing furiously on his cigar, as he had seen several stage villains do.

"I mean, old socks," said Tough, frowning with his effort—"I mean there are some fellows here who are worth while and some who are not, who won't do you any good, who don't amount to a row of pins, and aren't up to you in any way you look at it."

"Are you criticising my friends?" said Stover,

THE VARMINT

who had just passed an even more unflattering judgment, due to the Welsh-rabbit episode.

"I am," said McCarty, passing his hand over his forehead with difficulty.

Stover was just about to make an angry reply when he looked at McCarty, who suddenly leaned back against the tree. At the same moment a feeling of insecurity overtook him. He started again to make an angry answer and then all pugnacious thoughts left him. He sat down suddenly, his head swam on his shoulders and about him the woods danced in drunken reelings, sweeping grotesque boughs over him. Only the earth felt good, the damp, muddy earth, which he all at once convulsively embraced.

"Dink!"

The sound was far off, weak and fraught with mortal distress.

"Has it hit you, too?"

Dink's answer was a groan. He opened one eye; McCarty, prone at his side, lay on his stomach, burying his head in his arms.

At this moment a light patter sounded about them.

"It's beginning to rain."

"I don't care!"

"Neither do I."

Stover lay clutching the earth, that somehow

THE VARMINT

wouldn't kept still, that moved under him, that swayed and rose and fell. Then things began to rush through his brain: armies of football-clad warriors, The Roman whirling by on one leg of his chair, Dennis de Brian de Boru Finnegan prancing impishly, sticking out his tongue at him, whole flocks of Sunday preachers gesticulating in his direction, crowds of faces, legs, arms, an old, yellow dog with a sausage in his mouth——

Suddenly near him McCarty began to move.

"Where are you going?" he managed to say. "For Heaven's sake, don't leave me."

"To the pond—drink."

McCarty, on his hands and knees, began to crawl. Stover raised himself up and staggered after. The rain came down unheeded—nothing could add to his misery. They reached the pond and drank long copious drinks, plunging their dripping heads in the water.

Gradually the vertigo passed. Faint and weak they sat propped up opposite each other, solemnly, sadly, glance to glance, while unnoticed the rain spouted from the ends of their noses.

"Oh, Dink!" said Tough at last.

"Don't!"

"I thought I was going to die."

"I'm not sure of it yet."

"I had a lot I wanted to say to you," said

THE VARMINT

Tough painfully, feeling the opportunity was slipping away.

"You said I was smoking too much," said Dink maliciously.

"Ugh! Don't—no, that wasn't it."

"Shut up, old cockalorum," said Dink pleasantly. "I know all you want to say—found it out myself—it's all in one word—swelled head!"

"Oh!" said Tough deprecatingly, now that Dink had turned accuser.

"I've been a little, fluffy ass!" said Dink, marvelously stimulated to repentance by the episode which had gone before. "But that's over. My head's subsiding."

"What?"

The two burst into sympathetic laughter.

"You—you didn't mind my sailing into you, old horse?" said Tough.

"Not now."

McCarty looked mystified.

"Tough," said Dink with a queer look, "if you had smoked that black devil and I hadn't—all would have been over between us. As it is——"

"Well?" said Tough.

"As it is—Tough, here's my hand—let's swear an eternal friendship!"

"Put it there!"

"I say, Tough——"

THE VARMINT

"What?"

"Now, on your honor—did you ever smoke a cigar before?"

"Never," said McCarty. "And I'll never smoke another. So help me."

"Nor I. I say, what was that name?"

"Invincibles."

"That's where we should have stopped!"

"Dink, I begin to feel a little chilly."

"Tough, that's a good sign; let's up."

Arm in arm, laughing uproariously, they went, still a little shaky, back toward the school.

"I say, Tough," said Dink, throwing his arm affectionately about the other's shoulders. "I've been pretty much of a jackass, haven't I?"

"Oh, come, now!"

"I'm afraid I'm not built for a sport," said Dink, with a lingering regret. "But I say, Tough——"

"What?"

"I may be the prodigal son, but you're the devil of a moral lecturer, you are!"

XXI

One Wednesday afternoon, as Dink was lolling gorgeously on his window-seat, sniffing the alert air and waiting for the moment to go skipping over to the 'Varsity field for the game with a visiting school, a voice from below hailed him:

"Oh, you, Rinky Dink!"

Stover languidly extended his head and beheld Tough McCarty.

"Hello there, Dink."

"Hello yourself."

"Come over to the Woodhull and meet my family."

"What!" said Dink in consternation.

"They're over for the game. Hurry up now and help me out!"

Dink tried frantically to call him back, but Tough, as though to shut off a refusal, disappeared around the house. Dink returned to the room in a rage.

"What's the matter?" said the Tennessee Shad.

"I've got to go over and meet a lot of women," said Dink in disgust. "Confound Tough McCarty! That's a rotten trick to play on me. I'll wring his neck!"

THE VARMINT

"Go on now, make yourself beautiful!" said the Tennessee Shad, delighted. "Remember the whole school will be watching you."

"Shut up!" said Dink savagely, making the grand toilet, which consisted in putting on a high collar, exchanging his belt for a pair of suspenders and donning a pair of patent-leathers. "The place for women is at home! It's an outrage!"

He tied his necktie with a vicious lunge, ran the comb once through the tangled hair, glanced at his hands, decided that they would pass muster, slapped on his hat and went out, kicking the door open.

At the Woodhull, Tough hailed him from his window. Dink went up, bored and rebellious. The door opened, he found himself in Tough McCarty's room in the vortex of a crowd of fellow-sufferers. Over by the window-seat two fluffy figures, with skirts and hats on, were seated. He shook hands with both; one was Mrs. McCarty, the other was the daughter, he wasn't quite sure which. He said something about the delight which the meeting afforded him, and, gravitating into a corner, fell upon Butsey White, with whom he gravely shook hands.

"Isn't this awful?" said Butsey in a confidential whisper.

THE VARMINT

"Frightful!"

"What the deuce's got into Tough?"

"It's a rotten trick!"

"Let's hook it."

"All right. Slide toward the door."

But at this moment, when deliverance seemed near, Tough bore down and, taking Stover by the arm, drew him aside.

"I say, stick by me on this, old man," he said desperately. "Take 'em to the game with me, will you?"

"To the game!" cried Dink in horror. "Oh, Tough, come now, I say, I'm no fusser. I'm tongue-tied and pigeon-toed. Oh, I say, old man, do get some one else!"

But as Tough McCarty kept a firm grip on the lapel of his coat Dink suddenly found himself, with the departure of the other guests, a helpless captive. The first painful scraps of conversation passed in a blur. Before he knew it he was crossing the campus, actually walking, in full view of the school, at the side of Miss McCarty.

Her unconsciousness was paralyzing, perfectly paralyzing! Dink, struggling for a word in the vast desert of his brain, was overwhelmed with the ease with which his companion ran on. He stole a glance under the floating azure veil and decided, from the way the brilliant blue parasol swung from her hand, that she must be a woman of the world—thirty, at least.

He extracted his hands precipitately from the trousers pockets in which they had been plunged and buttoned the last button of his coat. Somehow, his hands seemed to wander all over his anatomy, like jibs that had broken loose. He tried to clasp them behind his back, like the Doctor, or to insert one between the first and second button of his coat, the characteristic pose of the great Corsican, according to his history. For a moment he found relief by slipping them, English fashion, into his coat pockets; but at the thought of being detected thus by the Tennessee Shad he withdrew them as though he had struck a hornet's nest.

The school, meanwhile, had gamboled past, all snickering, of course, at his predicament. In this state of utter misery he arrived at last at the field, where, to his amazement, quite a group of Fifth-Formers came up and surrounded Miss McCarty, chattering in the most bewildering manner. Dink seized the opportunity to drop back, draw a long sigh, reach madly behind for his necktie, which had climbed perilously near the edge of his collar, and shoot back his cuffs. He saw the Tennessee Shad and Dennis de Boru grinning at him from the crowd, and showed them his fist with a threatening gesture.

THE VARMINT

Then the game began and he was seated by Miss McCarty, unutterably relieved that the tension of the contest had diverted the entire attention of the school from his particular sufferings.

The excitement of the play for the first time gave him an opportunity to study his companion. His first estimate was undoubtedly correct; she was plainly a woman of the world. No one else could sit at such perfect ease, the cynosure of so many eyes. Her dress was some wonderful creation, from Paris, no doubt, that rustled with an alluring sound and gave forth a pleasant perfume.

The more he looked the more his eye approved. She was quite unusual—quite. She had style— a very impressive style. He had never before remembered any one who held herself quite so well, or whose head carried itself so regally. There was something Spanish, too, about her black hair and eyes and the flush of red in her cheeks.

Having perceived all this Dink began to recover from his panic and, with a desire to wipe out his past awkwardness, began busily to search for some subject with which gracefully to open up the conversation.

At that moment his eye fell upon his boot carelessly displayed and, to his horror, beheld there a gaping crack. This discovery drove all desire for conversation at once out of his head. By a covert movement he drew the offending shoe up under the shadow of the other.

"You hate this, don't you?" said a laughing voice.

He turned, blushing, to find Miss McCarty's dark eyes alive with amusement.

"Oh, now, I say, really——" he began.

"Of course, you loathe being dragged out this way," she said, cutting in. "Confess!"

Dink began to laugh guiltily.

"That's better," said Miss McCarty approvingly. "Now we shall get on better."

"How did you know?" said Dink, immensely mystified.

Miss McCarty wisely withheld this information, and before he knew it Dink was in the midst of a conversation, all his embarrassment forgot. The game ended—it had never been really important—and Dink found himself, actually to his regret, moving toward the Lodge.

There, as he was saying good-by with a Chesterfieldian air, Tough plucked him by the sleeve.

"I say, Dink, old man," he said doubtfully, "I'd like you to come over and grub with us. But I don't want to haul you over, you know——"

THE VARMINT

"My dear boy, I should love to!" said Dink, squeezing his arm eagerly.

"Honest?"

"Straight goods!"

"Bully for you!"

He had three-quarters of an hour to dress before dinner. He went to his room at a gallop, upsetting Beekstein and Gumbo on his volcanic way upward. Then for half an hour the Kennedy was thrown into a turmoil as the half-clothed figure of Dink Stover flitted from room to room, burrowed into closets, ransacked bureaus and departed, bearing off the choicest articles of wearing apparel. Meanwhile, the corridors resounded with such unintelligible cries as these:

"Who's got a collar, fourteen and a half?"

"Darn you, Dink, bring back my pants!"

"Who swiped my blue coat?"

"Who's been pulling my things to pieces?"

"Hi there, bring back my shoes!"

"Dinged if he hasn't gone off with my cuff buttons, too!"

"Oh you robber!"

"Body snatcher!"

"Dink, the fusser!"

"Who'd have believed it!"

Meanwhile, Dink, returning to his room laden with the spoils of the house, proceeded to adorn

THE VARMINT

himself on the principle of selection, discarding the Gutter Pup's trousers for the gala breeches of the Tennesse Shad, donning the braided cutaway of Lovely Mead's in preference to an affair of Slush Randolph's which was too tight in the chest.

The Tennessee Shad, the Gutter Pup and Dennis de Brian de Boru watched the proceedings, brownie fashion, across the transom, volunteering advice.

"Why, look at Dink wash!"

"It's a regular annual, isn't it?"

"Look out for my pants!"

"I say, Dink, your theory's wrong. You want to begin by parting your hair—soak it into place, you know."

Stover, struck by this expert advice, approached the mirror and seized his comb and brush with determination. But the liberties of a rebellious people, unmolested for sixteen years, were not to be suddenly abolished. The more he brushed the more the indignant locks rose up in revolt. He broke the comb and threw it down angrily.

"Wet your hair," said the Tennessee Shad.

"Soak it in water," said the Gutter Pup.

"Soak it in witch-hazel," said Dennis. "It will make it more fragrant.

Dink hesitated:

THE VARMINT

"Won't it smell too much?"

"Naw. It evaporates."

Stover seized the bottle and inundated his head, made an exact part in the middle and drew the sides back in the fashion of pigeon wings.

"Now clap on a dicer," said the Gutter Pup approvingly, "and she'll come up and feed from your hand."

"Are you really in love?" said Dennis softly.

Stover, ignoring all comments, tied a white satin four-in-hand with forget-me-not embossings, which had struck his fancy in Fatty Harris' room, and inserted a stick-pin of Finnegan's.

"You ought to have a colored handkerchief to stick in your breast pocket," said the Gutter Pup, who began to yield to the excitement.

"Up his sleeve is more English, don't you know," said Dennis.

Stover stood brazenly before the mirror, looking himself over. The scrubbing he had inflicted on his face had left red, shining spots in prominent places, while his hair, slicked back and plastered down, gave him somewhat the look of an Italian barber on a Sunday off. He felt the general glistening effect without, in his innocence, knowing the remedy.

"Dink, you are bee-oo-tiful!" said Dennis.

THE VARMINT

"Be careful how you sit down," said the Tennessee Shad, thinking of the trousers.

"How are the shoes?" asked the Gutter Pup solicitously.

"Tight as mischief," said Dink, with a wry face.

"Walk on your heels."

Stover, with a last deprecating glance, opened the door and departed, amid cheers from the contributing committee.

When he arrived at the Lodge the dusky waitress who opened the door started back, as he dropped his hat, and sniffed the air. He went into the parlor, spoiling his carefully-planned entrance by tripping over the rug.

"Heavens!" said Tough, "what a smell of witch-hazel. Why, it's Dink. What have you been doing?"

Stover felt the temperature rise to boiling.

"We had a bit of a shindy," he said desperately, trying to give it a tragic accent, "and I bumped my head."

"Well, you look like a skinned rat," said Tough to put him thoroughly at his ease.

The angel, however, came to his rescue with solicitous inquiries and with such a heavenly look that Stover only regretted that he could not appear completely done up in bandages.

They went in to dinner, where Dink was so

overwhelmed by the vision of Miss McCarty in all her transcendent charms that the effort of swallowing became a painful physical operation.

Afterward, Tough and his mother went over to Foundation House for a visit with the Doctor, and Dink found himself actually alone, escorting Miss McCarty about the grounds in the favoring dusk of the fast-closing twilight.

"Let's go toward the Green House," she said. "Will you take my cloak?"

The cloak settled the perplexing question of the hands. He wondered uneasily why she chose that particular direction.

"Are you sure you want to go there?" he said.

"Quite," she said. "I want to see the exact spot where the historic fight took place."

Stover moved uneasily.

"Dear me, what's the matter?"

"I never go there. I hate the place."

"Why?"

"I was miserable there," said Dink abruptly. "Hasn't Tough told you about it?"

"Tell me yourself," said the angelic voice.

Stover felt on the instant the most overpowering desire to confide his whole life's history, and being under the influence of a genuine emotion as well as aided by the obliterating hour, he began straight forward to relate the story of his

THE VARMINT

months of Coventry in tense, direct sentences, without pausing to calculate either their vividness or their effect. Once started, he withheld nothing, neither the agony of his pride nor the utter hopelessness of that isolation. Once or twice he hesitated, blurting out:

"I say, does this bore you?"

And each time she answered quickly:

"No, no—go on."

They went back in the fallen night to the campus, and there he pointed out the spot where he had stood and listened to the singing on the Esplanade and made up his mind to return. All at once, his story ended and he perceived, to his utter confusion, that he had been pouring out his heart to some one whose face he couldn't see, some one who was probably smiling at his impetuous confidence, some one whom he had met only a few hours before.

"Oh, I say," he said in horror, "you must think me an awful fool to go on like this."

"No."

"You made me tell you, you know," he said miserably, wondering what she could think of him. "I never talked like this before—to any one. I don't know what made me confide in you."

This was untrue, for he knew perfectly well what had led him to speak. So did she and,

[326]

THE VARMINT

knowing full well what was working in the tense, awkward boy beside her, she had no feeling of offense, being at an age when such tributes, when genuine, are valued, not scorned.

"I can just feel how you felt—poor boy," she said, perhaps not entirely innocent of the effect of her words. "But then, you have won out, haven't you?"

"I suppose I have," said Stover, almost suffocated by the gentleness of her voice.

"Charlie's told me all about the rest," she said. "Every one looks up to you now—it's quite a romance, isn't it?"

He was delighted that she saw it thus, secretly wondering if she really knew every point that could be urged in his favor.

"I suppose I'll kick myself all over the lot to-morrow," he said, choosing to be lugubrious.

"Why?" she said, stopping in surprise.

"For talking as I've done."

"You don't regret it?" she said softly, laying her hand on his arm.

Stover drew a long breath—a difficult one.

"No, you bet I don't," he said abruptly. "I'd tell you anything!"

"Come," she said, smiling to herself, "we must go back—but it's so fascinating here, isn't it?"

He thought he had offended her and was in a panic.

"I say, you did not understand what I meant."

"Oh, yes, I did."

"You're not offended?"

"Not at all."

This answer left Stover in such a state of bewilderment that all speech expired. What did she mean by that? Did she really understand or not?

They walked a little way in silence, watching the lights that fell in long lines across the campus, hearing through the soft night the tinkling of mandolins and the thrumming of guitars, a vibrant, feverish life that suddenly seemed unreal to him. They were fast approaching the Lodge. A sudden fear came to him that she would go without understanding what the one, the only night had been in his life.

"I say, Miss McCarty," he began desperately.

"Yes."

"I wish I could tell you——"

"What?"

"I wish I could tell you just what a privilege it's been to meet you."

"Oh, that's very nice."

THE VARMINT

He felt he had failed. He had not expressed himself well. She did not understand.

"I shall never forget it," he said, plunging ahead.

She stopped a little guiltily and looked at him.

"You queer boy," she said, too pleasantly moved to be severe. "You queer, romantic boy! Why, of course you're going to visit us this summer, and we're going to be good chums, aren't we?"

He did not answer.

"Aren't we?" she repeated, amused at a situation that was not entirely strange.

"No!" he said abruptly, amazed at his own audacity; and with an impulse that he had not suspected he closed the conversation and led the way to the Lodge.

When at last he and Tough were homeward bound he felt he should die if he did not then and there learn certain things. So he began with Machiavellian adroitness:

"I say, Tough, what a splendid mother you've got. I didn't get half a chance to talk to her. I say, how long will she be here?"

"They're going over to Princeton first thing in the morning," said Tough, who was secretly relieved.

THE VARMINT

A button on the borrowed vest popped with Stover's emotion.

"How did you get on with Sis?"

"First rate. She's—she's awful sensible," said Dink.

"Oh, yes, I suppose so."

"I say," said Dink, seeing that he made no progress, "she's been all around—had lots of experience, hasn't she?"

"Oh, she's bounded about a bit."

"Still, she doesn't seem much older than you," said Dink craftily.

"Sis—oh, she's a bit older."

"About twenty-two, I should say," said Dink hopefully.

"Twenty-four, my boy," said Tough unfeelingly. "But I say, don't give it away; she'd bite and scratch me all over the map for telling."

Stover left him without daring to ask any more questions—he knew what he wanted to know. He could not go to his room, he could not face the Tennessee Shad, possessor of the trousers. He wanted to be alone—to wander over the unseen earth, to gulp in the gentle air in long, feverish breaths, to think over what she had said, to grow hot and cold at the thought of his daring, to reconstruct the world of yesterday and organize the new.

He went to the back of chapel and sat down

on the cool steps, under the impenetrable clouds of the night.

"She's twenty-four, only twenty-four," he said to himself. "I'm sixteen, almost seventeen—that's only seven years' difference."

XXII

When Stover awoke the next morning it was to the light of the blushing day. He thought of the events of the night before and sprang up in horror. What had he been thinking of? He had made an ass of himself, a complete, egregious ass. What had possessed him? He looked at himself in the glass and his heart sunk at the thought of what she must be thinking. He was glad she was going. He did not want to see her again. He would never visit Tough McCarty. Thank Heaven it was daylight again and he had recovered his senses.

Indignant at every one, himself most of all, he went to chapel and to recitations, profoundly thankful that he would not have to face her in the mocking light of the day. That he never could have done, never, never!

As he left second recitation Tough McCarty joined him.

"I say, Dink, they both wanted to be remembered to you, and here's a note from Sis."

"A note?"

"Here it is."

Stover stood staring at a violet envelope, inscribed in large, flowing letters: "Mr. John H. Stover."

Then he put it in his pocket hastily and went to his room. Luckily the Tennessee Shad was poaching in the village. He locked the door, secured the transom and drew out the note. It was sealed with a crest and perfumed with a heavenly scent. He held it in his hand a long while, convulsively, and then broke the seal with an awkward finger and read:

Dear Mr. Stover: Just a word to thank you for being my faithful cavalier. Don't forget that you are to pay us a good, long visit this summer, and that we are to become the best of chums.

Your very good *friend*,
JOSEPHINE MCCARTY.

P. S. Don't dare to "kick yourself about the place," whatever that may mean.

When Dink had read this through once he immediately began it again. The second reading left him more bewildered than ever. It was the first time he had come in contact with a manifestation of the workings of the feminine mind. What did she intend him to understand?

"I'll read it again," he said, perching on the back of a chair. "Dear Mr. Stover!" He stopped and considered. " My dear Mr. Stover—Dear Mr. Stover—well, that's all right. But what the deuce does she mean by 'faithful cavalier'—I wonder now, I wonder. She wants me to visit her—she can't be offended then. 'Your very good friend,' underlined twice, that sounds as though she wanted to warn me. Undoubtedly I made a fool of myself and this is her angelic way of letting me down. 'Friend'—underlined twice—of course that's it. What a blooming, sentimental, moon-struck jay I was. Gee, I could kick myself to Jericho and back!" But here his eye fell on the postscript and his jaw dropped. " Now how did she guess that? That sounds different from the rest, as though—as though she understood."

He went to the window frowning, and then to the mirror, with a new interest in this new Mr. John H. Stover who received perplexing notes on scented paper.

"I must get some decent collars," he said pensively. " How the deuce does Lovely Mead keep his tie tight—mine's always slipping down, showing the stud." He changed his collar, having detected a smirch, and tried the effect of parting his hair on the side, like Garry Cockrell.

"She's a wonderful woman—wonderful," he said softly, taking up the letter again. "What eyes! Reminds me of Lorna Doone. Josephine

THE VARMINT

—so that's her name, Josephine—it's a beautiful name. I wish the deuce I knew just what she did mean by this!"

By nightfall he had written a dozen answers which had been torn up in a panic as soon as written. Finally, he determined that the craftiest way would be to send her his remembrances by Tough—that would express everything as well as show her that he could be both discreet and dignified.

In the afternoon he added a dozen extra high collars to his wardrobe and examined hesitatingly the counter of Gent's Bon-Ton socks, spring styles, displayed at Bill Appleby's.

The collars, the latest cut, he tried on surreptitiously. They were uncomfortable and projected into his chin, but there was no question of the superior effect. Suddenly a new element in the school came to his notice—fellows like Lovely Mead, Jock Hasbrouk and Dudy Rankin, who wore tailor-made clothes, rainbow cravats, who always looked immaculate and whose trousers never bagged at the knees.

No sooner was this borne in upon him than he was appalled at the state of his wardrobe. He had outgrown everything. Everything he had bagged at the elbows as well as the knees. His neckties were frazzeled and his socks were all earthy-browns and oat-meal grays.

THE VARMINT

His first step was to buy a blacking brush and his next to press his trousers under his mattress, with the result that, being detected and diverted by Dennis, they appeared next morning with a cross-gartered effect.

At nights, especially moonlight nights, under pretense of insomnia, he drew his bed to the open window and gazed sentimentally into the suddenly discovered starry system.

"What the deuce are you mooning about?" said the Tennessee Shad on the first occasion.

"I'm studying astronomy," said Dink with dignity.

The Tennessee Shad gave a snort and soon went loudly off to sleep.

Dink, unmolested, soared away into his own domain. It is true that, having read Peter Ibbetson, he tried for a week to emulate that favored dreamer, throwing his arms up, clasping his hands behind his head and being most particular in the crossing of the feet. He dreamed, but only discouraging, tantalizing dreams, and the figure his magic summoned up was not the angelic one, but invariably the elfish eyes and star-pointing nose of Dennis de Brian de Boru Finnegan.

But the dreams that lay like shadows between the faltering eyelids and the shut were real and magic. Then all the difficulties were swept

THE VARMINT

away, no cold chill ran up his back to stay the words that rushed to his lips. Conversations to defy the novelist were spun out and, having periodically saved her from a hundred malignant deaths, he continued each night anew the heroic work of rescue with unsatiated delight. At times, in the throbs of the sacred passion, he thought with a start of his blackened past and the tendencies to crime within him.

"Lord!" he said with a gasp, thinking of the orgy in beer, "what would have become of me—it's like an act of Providence. I wish I could let her know what a—what a good influence she's been. I don't know what I'd 'a' done—if I hadn't met her! I was in a dreadful way!"

By this time, having had the advantage of countless midnight walks, not to mention the familiarizing effect of several scores of desperate adventures, the character of Miss Lorna Doone McCarty had been completely unfolded to the reverential Dink. He saw her, he conversed with her, he knew her. She was a sort of heavenly being, misunderstood by her family—especially her brother, who had not the slightest comprehension. She was like Dante's Beatrice, as the pictures, not the dreadful text, represent that lady—and only seven years older than Mr. John H. Stover. There was Napoleon, who had married a woman older than he was—Napoleon and hosts of others.

With the sudden fear of being dropped a year he began to study with such assiduity that, as is the way with newly-sprouted virtue in a cynical world, his motives were suspected by the masters, who, of course, could know nothing of the divine transformation, and by his classmates, who secretly credited him with some new method of cribbing.

Meanwhile, as the year neared its close, the inventive minds of Dennis de Brian de Boru Finnegan and the Tennessee Shad conceived the idea of a monster mass meeting and illustrative parade, which should down the hereditary foe—the steam laundry.

Up to this time the columns of *The Lawrence* had been flooded with communications couched in the style of the oration against Catiline, demanding to know how long the supine Lawrenceville boy would bear in silence the return of his shirt with added entrances and exits, and collars that enclosed the neck with a cheval-de-frise.

This verbal, annual outbreak was succeeded, as usual, by House to House mutinies on the occasion of the arrival of the weekly boxes, without the protest taking further head or front. But at the opening of the last week of the school year, whether a machine had suddenly jumped

THE VARMINT

its fences or whether the ladies of the washtubs desired to open the way for the new summer styles; however it may have been, the laundry returned like the battle flags of the republic to the outraged school. Windows were flung open and indignant boys appeared, with white shreds in hand, and vociferously appealed to the heavens above and the green lands below for justice and indemnification.

A meeting of determined spirits was speedily held under the leadership of the Tennessee Shad and Doc Macnooder, and it was decided that a demonstration should take place instanter, the Houses to form and march with complete exhibits to the Upper House, where the fifth-formers should likewise display their grievances and join them in a mammoth protest.

Dink, at the first sounds of martial organization, pricked up his ears and summoned the Tennessee Shad and Dennis de Brian de Boru Finnegan to explain why he had been left out of such an important enterprise.

"Why have we left you out?" said the Tennessee Shad indignantly. "What's happened to you these last three weeks? You've had a fighting grouch—no one dared to speak to you for fear of being bitten!"

"In fact," said Dennis, with his sharp, little glance, "you are under the gravest suspicion."

THE VARMINT

Seeing his secret in peril, Stover assumed a melancholy, injured air.

"You don't know what I've had to worry me," he said, looking out the window, "family matters—financial reverses."

"Oh, I say, Dink, old boy," said the Tennessee Shad, in instant contrition.

"You don't mean it's anything that might keep you from coming back next year?" said Dennis, aghast. "Oh, Dink!"

"I had rather not talk about it," said Stover solemnly.

Dennis and the Shad were overwhelmed with remorse—they offered him at once the Grand Marshalship, which he refused with still offended dignity, but promised his fertile brain to the common cause.

Now Dink's sentimental education, which had progressed with a rush, had just begun to languish on insufficiency of food and a little feeling of staleness on having exhausted the one thousand and one possible methods of saving a heroine's life and wringing the consent of her parents.

He felt a species of guilt in the accusation of his roommate and a sudden longing to be back among mannish pursuits. In an hour, with delighted energy, he had organized the banner and effigy committees of the demonstration and had

THE VARMINT

helped concoct the fiery speech of protest that Doc Macnooder, as spokesman, was solemnly pledged to deliver for the embattled school.

Four hours later the Kennedy House, led by Toots Cortell and his famous Confederate bugle, defiled and formed the head of the procession. Each member carried a pole attached to which was some article that had been wholly or partly shot to pieces. The Dickinson contingent, led by Doc Macnooder, marched in a square, supporting four posts around which ran a clothesline decked out with the dreadful débris of the house laundry.

The Woodhull proudly bore as its battle flag a few strings of linen floating from a rake, with this inscription underneath:

THE GRAND OLD SHIRT OF THE WOODHULL! WASHED 16 TIMES AND STILL IN THE GAME!

Several poles, adorned with single hosing in the fashion of liberty caps, were labeled:

WHERE IS MY WANDERING SOCK TO-NIGHT?

The Davis House was headed by Moses Moseby in a tattered nightshirt, backed up by an irreverent placard:

HOLY MOSES!

THE VARMINT

But the premier exhibit of the parade was admitted by all to be the Kennedy float, conceived and executed by the Honorable Dink Stover.

On a platform carried by eight hilarious members, was displayed Dennis de Brian de Boru Finnegan, clothed in a suit of dark gymnasium tights, over which were superimposed a mangled set of upper and lower unmentionables, whose rents and cavities stood admirably out against the dark background, while the Irishman sat on a chair and alternately stuck a white foot through the bottomless socks that were fed him.

Above the platform was the flaring ensign:

RATHER FRANK NUDITY THAN THIS!

Now it happened that at the auspicious moment when Dink Stover led the apparently scantily-clothed Finnegan and the procession of immodest banners around to the Esplanade of the Upper, the Doctor suddenly appeared through the shrubbery that screens Foundation House from the rest of the campus, with a party of ladies, relatives, as it unfortunately happened, of one of the trustees of the school.

One glance of horror and indignation was sufficient for him to wave back the more modest

THE VARMINT

sex and to advance on the astounding procession with fury and determination.

Before Jove's awful look the spirit of '76 vanished. There was a cry of warning and the hosts hesitated, shivered and scampered for shelter.

Now, at any other time the Doctor—who suffered, too, from the common blight—would have secretly if not openly enjoyed the joke; but at that moment the circumstances were admittedly trying. Besides, there was the delicate explanation to be offered to the ladies, who were relatives of one of the influential members of the board of trustees of the Lawrenceville School, John C. Green Foundation. As a consequence, in a towering rage, he summoned the ringleaders, chief among whom he had recognized Dink Stover and, corraling them in his study that night, exposed to them the enormity of their offense against the sex of their mothers and sisters, common decency, morals and morality, the ideals of the school, and the hope that the Nation had a right to place in a body of young men nurtured in such homes and educated at such an institution.

The ringleaders, being veterans, viewed the speech from the point of view of artists, and were unanimous in their appreciation. The episode had for Stover, however, unfortunate com-

THE VARMINT

plications. With the closing of the scholastic season came the elections in the Houses. The Kennedy House, unanimously and with much enthusiasm, chose the Honorable Honest John Stover to succeed the Honorable King Lentz as administrator and benevolent despot for the ensuing year.

This election, coming as it did as a complete surprise to Stover, was naturally a source of deep gratification. His enjoyment, however, was rudely shocked when, the next morning after chapel, the Doctor stopped him and said:

"Stover, I am considerably surprised at the choice of the Kennedy House and I am not at all sure that I shall ratify it. Nothing in your career has indicated to me your fitness for such a place of responsibility. I shall have a further talk with Mr. Hopkins and let him know my decision."

The Roman! Of course it was The Roman! Of course he had been raging at the thought of his elevation to the presidency! Dink, forgetting the hundred and one times he had met the Faculty in the Monday afternoon deliberations, rushed out to spread the news of The Roman's vindictive persecution. Every one was indignant, outraged at this crowning insult to a free electorate. The whole House would protest *en masse* if the despot's veto was exercised.

"NOTHING IN YOUR CAREER HAS INDICATED TO ME
YOUR FITNESS FOR SUCH A PLACE
OF RESPONSIBILITY"

THE VARMINT

At the hour of these angry threats The Roman, persecutor of Dink, was actually saying to the tyrant:

"Doctor, I think it would be the best thing—the very best. It will bring out the manliness, the serious earnestness that is in the boy."

"What, you say that!" said the Doctor, a little impatiently, for it was only the morrow of the parade. "I should think your patience would be exhausted. The scamp has been in more mischief than any other boy in the school. He's incorrigibly wild!"

"No—no. I shouldn't say that. Very high spirited—excess of energy—too much imagination—that's all. There's nothing vicious about the boy."

"But as president, Hopkins, not as president!"

"No one better," said The Roman firmly. "The boy is bound to lead. I know what's in him—he will rise to his responsibility. Doctor, you will see. I have never lost confidence in him."

The Doctor, unconvinced, debated at length before acceding. When he finally gave his ratification he added with a smile:

"Well, Hopkins, I do this on your judgment. You may be right, we shall see. By the way,

THE VARMINT

Stover must have led you quite a dance over in the Kennedy. What is it you like in him?"

The Roman reflected and then, his eye twitching reminiscently:

"Fearlessness," he said, "and—and a diabolical imagination."

When The Roman returned to the Kennedy he summoned Stover to his study. He knew that Dink misunderstood his attitude and he would have liked to enlighten him. Unfortunately, complete confidence in such cases is sometimes as embarrassing as the relations between father and son. The Roman, pondering, twisted a paper-cutter and frowned in front of him.

"Stover," he said at last. "I have talked with the Doctor. He has seen best to approve of your election."

Dink, of course, perceiving the hesitation, went out gleefully, persuaded that the decision was gall and wormwood to his inveterate foe.

The last day of school ended. He drove to Trenton in a buggy with Tough McCarty as befitted his new dignity. He passed the Green House with a strange thrill. The humiliation of a year before had well been atoned, and yet the associations somehow still had power to rise up and wound him.

"Lord, you've changed!" said Tough, following his thoughts.

THE VARMINT

"Improved!" said Dink grimly.

"I was an infernal nuisance myself when I landed," said Tough, President of the Woodhull, evasively. "I say, Dink, next year we'll be licking the cubs into shape ourselves."

"That's so," said Stover. "Well, by this time next year I probably won't be so popular."

"Why not?"

"I'm going to put an end to a lot of nonsense," said Dink solemnly. "I'm going to see that my kids walk a chalk-line."

"So am I," said McCarty, with equal paternity. "What a shame we can't room together, old boy!"

"That'll come in the Upper, and afterward!"

They drove sedately, amid the whirling masses of the school that went hilariously past them. They were no longer of the irresponsible; the cares of the state were descending on their shoulders and a certain respect was necessary.

"Good-by, old Sockbuts," said Tough, departing toward New York. "Good-by, old geezer!"

"Au revoir."

"Mind now—fifteenth of July and you come for one month."

"You bet I will!"

"Take care of yourself!"

"I say, Tough," said Dink, with his heart in

his mouth. McCarty, laden with valises, stopped:

"What is it?"

"Remember me to your mother, will you?"

"Oh, sure."

"And—and to all the rest of the family!" said Dink, who thereupon bolted, panic-stricken.

XXIII

When John Stover, President of the Kennedy House, arrived at the opening of the new scholastic year, he arrived magnificently in a special buggy, his changed personal appearance spreading wonder and incredulity before him. He was stylishly encased in a suit of tan whipcord, with creases down his trousers front that cut the air like the prow of a ship. On his head, rakishly set, was a Panama hat, over his arm was a natty raincoat and he wore gloves.

"Who is it?" said the Tennessee Shad faintly.

"It's the gas inspector," said Dennis de Brian de Boru, who, though now long of trousers, continued short of respect.

"Goodness gracious," said the Tennessee Shad, "can it be the little Dink who came to us from the Green House?"

Stover approached serenely and shook hands.

"Heavens, Dink," said the Gutter Pup, "what has happened? Have you gone into the clothing business?"

"Like my jibs?" said Stover, throwing back his coat. "Catch this!"

The front rank went over like so many nine pins. Stover, pleased with the effect, waved his

THE VARMINT

hand and disappeared to pay his militant respects to The Roman who led him to the light and looked him over with unconcealed amazement.

When Dink had gone to his old room the Tennessee Shad, the Gutter Pup and Dennis de Brian de Boru Finnegan were already awaiting him, with heads critically slanted.

"Tell us the worst," said the Gutter Pup.

"Are you married?" said the Tennessee Shad.

"Let's see her photograph," said Dennis de Brian de Boru Finnegan.

Now, Stover had foreseen the greeting and the question and had come prepared. He opened his valise and, taking out a case, arranged a dozen photographs on his bureau, artfully concealing the one and only in a temporarily subordinate position.

The three village loungers arose and stationed themselves in front of the portrait gallery.

"Why, he must be perfectly irresistible!" said the Gutter Pup.

"Dink," said Dennis, "do all these girls love you?"

Stover, disdaining a reply, selected another case.

"Razors!" said the Tennessee Shad.

"What for?" said Dennis.

"Oh, I shave, too," said the Gutter Pup, in

THE VARMINT

whom the spirit of envy was beginning to work.

"And now, boys," said Stover briskly, taking off his coat, folding it carefully over a chair and beginning to unpack, "sit down. Don't act like a lot of hayseeds on a rail, but tell me what the Freshmen are like."

The manner was complete—convincing, without a trace of embarrassment. The three wits exchanged foolish glances and sat down.

"What do you weigh?" said the Gutter Pup faintly.

"One hundred and fifty-five, and I've grown an inch," said Stover, ranging on a ring a score of flashy neckties.

"I wish Lovely Mead could see those," said the Gutter Pup with a last appearance of levity.

"Call him up. Look at them yourself," said Stover, tendering the neckwear. "I think they're rather tasty myself."

Before such absolute serenity frivolity died of starvation. They made no further attempt at sarcasm, but sat awed until Stover had departed to carry the glad news of his increased weight to Captain Flash Condit.

"Why he's older than The Roman," said the Tennessee Shad, the first to recover.

"He's in love," said Dennis, who had intuitions.

THE VARMINT

"No, be-loved," said the Gutter Pup with a sigh, who was suffering from the first case, but not from the second.

The amazement of rolling, old Sir John Falstaff at the transformation of Prince Hal was nothing to the consternation of the Kennedy House at the sudden conversion of Dink Stover, the fount of mischief, into a complete disciplinarian.

Now the cardinal principle of House government is the division of the flock by the establishing of an age line. The control of the youngsters is almost always vigorously enforced, and though the logical principles involved are sometimes rather dubious they are adequate from the fact that they are never open to argument. Occasionally, however, under the leadership of some president either too indolent or incapable of leadership, this strict surveillance over the habits and conduct of youth is relaxed, with disastrous results to the orderly reputation of the House.

Stover, having been the arch rebel and fomenter of mischief, had the most determined ideas as to the discipline he intended to enforce and the respect he should exact.

The first clash came with the initial House Meeting, over which he presided. Now in the past these occasions had offered Dennis de Brian de Boru Finnegan and his attendant imps unlimited amusement, as King Lentz had been almost totally ignorant of the laws of parliamentary procedure.

Of a consequence, no sooner was a meeting fairly under way, than some young scamp would rise and solemnly move the previous question, which never failed to bring down a storm of hoots at the complete mystification of the perplexed chairman, who never to his last day was able to solve this knotty point of procedure.

Now, Dennis, while he had been impressed by Stover's new majesty, retained still a feeling of resistance. So the moment the gavel declared the meeting open he bobbed up with a wicked gleam and shrilly announced:

"Mr. Chairman, I move the previous question."

"Mr. Finnegan will come to order," said Stover quietly.

"Oh, I say, Dink!"

"Are you addressing the chair?" said Stover sternly.

"Oh, no," said Finnegan, according to his usual manner, "I was just whistling through my teeth, gargling my larynx, trilling——"

Crash came the gavel and the law spoke forth:

"Mr. Finnegan will come to order?"

"I won't!"

"Mr. Finnegan either apologizes to the chair,

THE VARMINT

or the chair will see that Mr. Finnegan returns to short trousers and stays there. Mr. Finnegan has exactly one minute to make up his mind."

Dennis, crimson and gasping, stood more thoroughly amazed and nonplussed than he had ever been in his active existence. He opened his mouth as though to reply, and beheld Stover calmly draw forth his watch. Had it been any one else, Dennis would have hesitated; but he knew Stover of old and what the chilly, metallic note was in his voice. He chose the lesser of two evils and gave the apology.

"The chair will now state," said Stover, replacing his watch, "for the benefit of any other young, transcendent jokers that may care to display their side-splitting wit, that the chair is quite capable of handling the previous question, or any other question, and that these meetings are going to be orderly proceedings and not one-ring circuses for the benefit of the Kennedy Association of Clowns. The question before the House is the protest against compulsory bath. The chair recognizes Mr. Lazelle to make a motion."

The cup of Finnegan's bitterness was not yet filled. Stover's first act of administration was to forbid the privileges of the cold-air flues and the demon cigarette to all members of the House

THE VARMINT

who had not attained, according to his judgment, either a proper age or a sufficient display of bodily stature. Among the proscribed was Dennis de Brian de Boru Finnegan, whose legs, clothed in new dignity, fairly quivered under the affront, as he tearfully protested:

"I say, Dink, it's an outrage!"

"Can't help it. It's for your own good."

"But I'm fifteen."

"Now, see here, Dennis," said Stover firmly, "your business is to grow and to be of some use. No one's going to know about it unless you yell it out, but I'm going to see that you turn out a decent, manly chap and not another Slops Barnett."

"But you went with Slops yourself."

"I did—but you're not going to be such a fool."

"Why, you're a regular tyrant!"

"All right, call it that."

"And I elected you," said Dennis, the aggrieved and astounded modern politician. "This is Goo-gooism!"

"No, it isn't," said Stover indignantly. "I'm not interfering with any fellow who's sixteen—they can do what they darn please. But I'm not going to have a lot of kids in this House starting sporting life until they've grown up to it, savez? They're going to be worth living with

THE VARMINT

and having around, and not abominations in the sight of gods and men. Pass the word along."

The revolt, for a short while, was furiously indignant, but the prestige of Stover's reputation forestalled all thought of disobedience. In such cases absolute power is in the hands of him who can wield it, and Stover could command.

In short order he had reduced the youngsters to respect and usefulness, with the following imperial decrees:

1. All squabs are to maintain in public a deferential and modest attitude.

2. No squab shall talk to excess in the presence of his elders.

3. No squab shall habitually use bad language, under penalty of an application of soap and water.

4. No squab shall use tobacco in any form.

5. No squab shall leave the House after lights without express permission.

These regulations were not simply an excercise of arbitrary authority, for in the House itself were certain elements which Dink perfectly understood, and whose spheres of influence he was resolved to confine to their own limits.

"How're you going to enforce, Sire, these imperial decrees?" asked the Tennessee Shad, who, however, thoroughly approved.

THE VARMINT

"I have a method," said Stover, with an interior smile. "It's what I call a Rogues' Gallery."

"I don't see," said the Tennessee Shad, puzzled.

"You will."

The first rebel was a Freshman, Bellefont, known as the Millionaire Baby, who, due to a previous luxurious existence, had acquired manly practices at an early age. Bellefont was detected with the odor of tobacco.

"Young squab, have you been smoking?" said Stover.

"Well, what are you going to do about it?" said the youngster defiantly.

"Gutter Pup, get your camera," said Stover.

The Gutter Pup, mystified, returned. The autocrat seized the young rebel, slung him paternally across his knee and with raised hand spoke:

"Gutter Pup, snap a couple of good ones. We'll make this Exhibit A in our Rogues' Gallery."

Bellefont, at the thought of this public perpetuation, set up a howl and kicked as though mortally stung. Stover held firm. The snapshots were taken, developed and duly posted.

From that moment, in public at least, Stover's slightest gesture was obeyed as promptly as the lifting of an English policeman's finger.

THE VARMINT

The yoke once accepted became popular alike with the older members, who ceased to be annoyed, and with the squabs themselves, who, finding they were protected from bullying or unfair exactions, soon adopted toward Stover an attitude of reverent idolatry that was not without its embarrassments. He was called upon at all hours to render decisions on matters political and philosophical, with the knowledge that his opinion would instantly be adopted as religion. Before him were brought all family quarrels, some serious, some grotesque; but each class demanding a settlement in equity.

One afternoon Dennis maliciously piloted to his presence Pee-wee Norris and his new roommate, a youngster named Berbacker, called Cyclops from the fact that one eye was glass, a gift that brought him a peculiar admiration and envy.

Stover, observing the cunning expression on Finnegan's face, scented a trap. The matter was, indeed, very grave.

"See here, Dink," said Pee-wee indignantly; "I leave it to you. How would you like to stumble upon a loose eye all over the room?"

"A what?"

"A loose eye. This fellow Cyclops is all the time leaving his glass eye around in my diggin's and I don't like it. It's the deuce of a thing to find it winking up at you from the table or the window-seat. It gives me the creeps."

"What have you got to say, Cyclops?" said Stover, assuming a judicial air.

"Well, I've always been used to takin' the eye out," said Cyclops, with an injured look. "Most fellows are glad to see it. But, I say, I'm the fellow who has the kick. The whole thing started by Norris hiding it on me."

"Did you swipe his eye?" said Stover severely.

"Well, yes, I did. What right's he got to let it out loose?"

"I want him to leave my eye alone," said Cyclops.

"I want him to keep his old eye in his old socket," said Pee-wee.

"Oh, Solomon, what is thy judgment?" said Dennis, who had engineered it all.

"I'll give my judgment and it'll settle it," said Dink firmly. "But I'll think it over first."

True to his word, he deliberated long and actively and, as the judgment had to be given, he called the complaining parties before him and said:

"Now, look here, Pee-wee and Cyclops; you fellows are rooming together and you've got to get on. If you fight, keep it to yourselves; don't shout it around. But get together—

agree. You've got to go on, and the more you agree—ahem—the less you'll disagree, see? It's just like marriage. Now you go back and live like a respectable married couple, and if I hear any more about this glass eye I'll spank you both and have you photographed for the Rogues' Gallery."

Among the members of the Kennedy House there were two who defied his authority and gave him cause for dissatisfaction—the Millionaire Baby, who was a nuisance because he had been pampered and impressed with his own divine right, and a fellow named Horses Griffin, who was unbearable because, owing to his size and strength, he had never had the blessing of a good thrashing.

Now when Stover promulgated his laws for the protection of Squabs he had served notice on the sporting centers that he expected their adherence. Fellows like Slops Barnett and Fatty Harris, who, to do them justice, approved of segregation, made no defiance. Griffin, though, who was a hulking, rather surly, self-conscious fellow, secretly rebelled at this act of authority, and gave asylum to Bellefont, from whom he was glad to accept the good things that regularly arrived in boxes from a solicitous mother.

Stover had seen from the first how the issue

THE VARMINT

would have to be met, and met it at the first opportunity. Griffin having defied his authority by openly inviting the Millionaire Baby up for the nefarious practice of matching pennies, Dink marched up the stairs and entered the enemy's room.

A moment later the group expectantly gathered in the hall heard something within that resembled an itinerant cyclone, then the door blew open and Griffin shot out and raced for the stairs, while behind him—like an angry tom-cat —came Stover, in time to give to the panicky champion just that extra impetus that allowed him, as Dennis expressed it, to establish a new record—flying start—for the twenty-six steps. After this little explanation Griffin showed a marked disinclination for the company of Bellefont, and became, indeed, quite a useful member of the community, though he always retained such acute memories that an angry tone from Stover would cause him to fidget and calculate the distance to the door.

Griffin subdued, the Millionaire Baby still remained. The problem was a knotty one, for as Bellefont was still of sub-stature the means of correction were limited.

"What worries your Majesty?" said Dennis de Brian de Boru, perceiving Stover in stern meditation. "Is it that beautiful specimen of flunky-raised squab entitled the Millionaire Baby?"

"It is," said Dink. Between him and Dennis peace had long since been concluded.

"He is a very precious hothouse flower," said Dennis sarcastically.

"He is the most useless, pestiferous, conceited little squirt I ever saw," said Dink.

"I love him not."

"But I'll get that flunky smell out of him yet!"

"The pity is he has such fat, juicy boxes from home."

"He has—how often?"

"Every two weeks."

"It oughtn't to be allowed."

"What are you going to do? You can't take 'em by force."

"No—that wouldn't do."

"Still," said Dennis regretfully, "he's so young it is just ruining his little digestion."

They sat a moment deliberating. Finally Dink spoke rapturously:

"I have it. We'll organize the Kennedy Customs House."

"Aha!"

"Everything imported must pass the Customs House."

"Pass?"

THE VARMINT

"Certainly; everything must be legal."

"What am I to be?"

"Appraiser."

"I'd rather be first taster."

"Same thing."

"You said pass," said Dennis obstinately. "I don't like that word."

"Purely technical sense."

"But there will be duties imposed?"

"Certainly."

"Aha!" said Dennis brightening. "Very high duties?"

"The maximum duty on luxuries," said Dink. "We're all good Republicans, aren't we?"

"I am, if I can write the tariff schedule," said Dennis, who, as may be seen, was orthodox.

When, on the following week, young Bellefont received his regular installment of high-priced indigestibles he was amazed to see the Gutter Pup and Lovely Mead appear with solemn demeanor.

"Hello," said the Millionaire Baby, placing himself in front of the half-open box.

"See these badges," said Lovely Mead, pointing to their caps, around which were displayed white bandages inscribed "inspector."

"Sure."

"We're in the Customs House."

"Well, what?"

THE VARMINT

"And we have received information that you are systematically smuggling goods into this territory."

The Millionaire Baby looked as though a ghost had arisen.

"Aha!" said the Gutter Pup, perceiving the box. "Here's the evidence now. Officer, seize the goods and the prisoner."

"What are you going to do to me?" said the culprit in great alarm.

"Take you before the Customs Court."

The Customs Court was sitting, without absentees, in Stover's room—appraisers, weighers, adjusters and consulting experts, all legally ticketed and very solemn. The prisoner was stood in a corner and the contents of the box spread on the floor.

"First exhibit—one plum cake," announced Beekstein, who was in a menial position.

"Duty sixty-five per cent," said Dennis de Brian de Boru Finnegan, consulting a book. "Raisins and spices."

"Two bottles of anchovy olives."

"Duty fifty per cent, imported fruits."

"Only fifty per cent?" said Stover, who had a preference for the same.

"That's all."

"What's it on?"

"Imported fruits."

THE VARMINT

"How about spiced fish?" said the Tennessee Shad, coming to the rescue, "and, likewise, Italian glass?"

The Millionaire Baby gave a groan.

"Imported fish, forty per cent," said Dennis, "glass—Venetian glass—thirty-five per cent. He owes us thirty per cent on this."

"Continue," said Stover, casting a grateful glance at the Tennessee Shad.

"Two boxes of candied prunes, that's vegetables, twenty-five per cent."

"They're preserved in sugar, aren't they?"

"Sure."

"There's a duty of fifty per cent on sugar."

"Long live the Sugar Trust."

"Doggone robbers!" said the Millionaire Baby tearfully.

"Three boxes salted almonds, one large box of chocolate bonbons, one angel cake and six tins of candied ginger."

The judges, deliberating, assessed each article. Stover rose to announce the decree.

"The clerk of the court will return to the importer thirty-five per cent of the plum cake, twenty-five per cent of the candied prunes, one box of salted almonds and two tins of ginger."

The Millionaire Baby breathlessly contained his wrath.

THE VARMINT

Dennis de Brian de Boru Finnegan addressed the court:

"Your Honor."

"Mr. Finnegan."

"I beg to call to your Honor's attention that these goods have been seized and are subject to a fine."

"True," said Stover, glancing sternly at the frothing Bellefont. "I would be inclined to be lenient, but I am informed that this is not the defendant's first offense. The clerk of the court will, therefore, confiscate the whole."

The Millionaire Baby, with a howl, began to express himself in the language of the stables.

"Gag him," said Stover, "and let him be informed that the duties will be lightened if in the future he declares his imports."

The government then applied the revenues to the needs of the department of the interior.

"The duty on anchovy olives is too high," said Finnegan, looking fondly down a bottle.

"How so?"

"It will stop the imports."

"True—we might reduce it."

"We must encourage imports," said the Gutter Pup firmly.

And the chorus came full mouthed:

"Sure!"

The Millionaire Baby received three more

boxes—that is, he received the limited portion that a paternal government allowed him. Then, being chastened, he took a despicable revenge—he stopped the supply.

"Well, it was sweet while it lasted," said Dennis regretfully.

"We've stopped toadyism in the House," said Stover virtuously. "We have eliminated the influence of money."

"That is praiseworthy, but it doesn't fill me with enthusiasm."

"Dink," said the Tennessee Shad, "I must say I consider this one of your few failures. You're a great administrator, but you don't understand the theory of taxation."

"I don't, eh? Well, what is the theory?"

"The theory of taxation," said the Tennessee Shad, "is to soak the taxed all they'll stand for, but to leave them just enough, so they'll come again."

XXIV

No sooner had Mr. John H. Stover returned from the serious developments of the summer, arranged his new possessions and brought forward the photograph of Miss McCarty to a position on the edge of his bureau, where he could turn to it the last thing at night and again behold it with his waking glance, than a horrible coincidence appeared.

Among the festive decorations that made the corporate home of Dink and the Tennessee Shad a place to visit and admire was, as has been related, a smashing poster of a ballet dancer in the costume of an amazon parader. Up to now Dink had shared the just pride of the Tennessee Shad in this rakish exhibit that somehow gave the possessor the reputation of having an acquaintance with stage entrances. But on the second morning when his faithful glance turned to the protecting presence of Miss McCarty resting among the brushes, it paused a moment on the representative of the American dramatic profession, who was coquettishly trying to conceal one foot behind her ear.

Then he sat bolt upright with a start. By

THE VARMINT

some strange perversion of the fate that delights in torturing lovers, the features of the immodestly clothed amazon bore the most startling resemblance to that paragon of celestial purity, Miss Josephine McCarty.

The more he gazed the more astounding was the impression. He gazed and then he did not gaze at all—it seemed like a profanation. The resemblance, once perceived, positively haunted him; stand where he might his eyes could see nothing but the seraphic head of Miss McCarty upon the unspeakable body of the amazon—and then those legs!

For days this centaurian combination tortured him without his being able to evolve a satisfactory method of removing the blasphemous poster. A direct attack was quite out of the question, for manifestly the Tennessee Shad would demand an adequate explanation for the destruction of his treasured possession. There could be no explanation except the true one, and such a confession was unthinkable, even to a roommate under oath.

For two solid weeks Stover, brooding desperately, sought to avert his glance from the profane spectacle before chance came to his rescue. One Saturday night, after a strenuous game with the Princeton Freshmen, Dink, afraid of going stale, decided to quicken his jaded appetite by an application of sardines, deviled ham and rootbeer.

The feasting-table happened to be directly beneath the abhorrent poster, so that Stover, as he lifted the bottle to open it, beheld with fury the offending tights. He gave the bottle instinctively a shake and with that disturbing motion suddenly came his plan.

"This rootbeer has been flat as the deuce lately," he said.

"They're selling us poor stuff," said the Tennessee Shad, with the tail of a sardine disappearing within.

"I wonder if I could put life in the blame thing if I shook it up a bit," said Stover, suiting the action to the word.

Now, the Tennessee Shad knew from experience what that result would be, but as Stover was holding the bottle he dissembled his knowledge.

"Give it a shake," he said.

Stover complied.

"Shake her again."

"How's that?"

"Once more. It'll be just like champagne."

Stover gave it a final vigorous shake, pointed the nozzle toward the poster and cut the cork. There was an explosion and then the contents rose like a geyser and spread over the ceiling

THE VARMINT

and the luckless ballet dancer who dared to resemble Miss McCarty.

By the next morning the poster was unrecognizable under a coating of dried reddish spots and was ignominiously removed, to the delight of Stover, whose illusions were thus preserved, as well as his secret.

Now, the month spent at the McCartys' had strengthened his honorable intentions and given them that definite purpose that is sometimes vulgarly ticketed—object matrimony.

It is not that Dink could return over the romantic days of his visit and lay his finger on any particular scene or any definite word that could be construed as binding Miss McCarty. But, on the other hand, his own actions and expressions, he thought, must have been so capable of but one interpretation that, as a man of honor, he held himself morally as well as willingly bound. Of course, she had understood his attitude; she must have understood. And, likewise, there were events that made him believe that she, in her discreet way, had let him see by her actions what she could not convey by her words. For, of course, in his present position of dependence on his father, nothing could be said. He understood that. He would not have changed it. Still, there were unmistakable memories of the preference he had enjoyed. There had been, in particular, an ill-favored dude, called Ver Plank, who had always been hanging around with his tandem and his millions, who had been sacrificed a dozen times by the unmercenary angel to his, John H. Stover's, profit. That was clear enough, and there had been many such incidents.

The only thing that disappointed Dink was the polite correctness of her letters. But then something, he said to himself, must be allowed for maiden modesty. His own letters were the product of afternoons and evenings. The herculean difficulty that he experienced in covering four sheets of paper—even when writing a flowing hand and allowing half a page for the signature—secretly worried him. It seemed as though something was lacking in his character or in the strength of his devotion.

On the day after the final disappearance of the brazen amazon Dink pounced upon a violet envelope in the well-known handwriting and bore it to a place of secrecy. It was in answer to four of his own painful compositions.

He gave three glances before reading, three glances that estimate all such longed-for epistles. There were five pages, which brought him a thrill; it was signed "as ever, Josephine," which brought him a doubt; and it began "Dear Jack," which brought him nothing at all.

THE VARMINT

Having thus passed from hot to cold, and back to a fluctuating temperature, he began the letter—first, to read what was written, and second, to read what might be concealed between the lines:

DEAR JACK: Since your last letter I've been in a perfect whirl of gayety—dances, coaching parties and what-not. Really, you would say that I was nothing but a frivolous butterfly of fashion. Next week I am going to the Ver Planks' with quite a party and we are to coach through the Berkshires. The Judsons are to be along and that pretty Miss Dow, of whom I was so jealous when you were here, do you remember? I met a Mr. Cockrell, who, it seems, was at Lawrenceville. He told me you were going to be a phenomenal football player, captain of the team next year, and all sorts of wonderful things. He *admires* you *tremendously*. I was so pleased! Don't forget to write soon.

As ever,
JOSEPHINE.

This letter, as indeed all her letters did, left Dink trapezing, so to speak, from one emotion to another. He had not acquired that knowledge, which indeed is never acquired, of valuing to a nicety the intents, insinuations and complexities of the feminine school of literature.

THE VARMINT

There were things that sent him soaring like a Japanese kite and there were things, notably the reference to Ver Plank, that tumbled him as awkwardly down.

He immediately seized upon pen and paper. It had, perhaps, been his fault. He would conduct the correspondence on a more serious tone. He would be a little—daring.

At the start he fell into the usual inky deliberation. "Dear Josephine" was so inadequate. "My dear Josephine" had—or did it not have —just an extra little touch of tenderness, a peculiar claim to possession. But if so, would it be too bold or too sentimental? He wrote boldly:

"My dear Josephine:"

Then he considered. Unfortunately, at that time the late lamented Pete Daly, in the halls of the likewise lamented Weber and Fields, was singing dusky love songs to a lady likewise entitled "My Josephine." The connection was unthinkable. Dink tore the page into minute bits and, selecting another, sighed and returned to the old formula.

Here another long pause succeeded while he searched for a sentiment or a resolve that would raise him in her estimation. It is a mood in which the direction of a lifetime is sometimes bartered for a phrase. So it happened with

THE VARMINT

Dink. Suddenly his face lit up and he started to write:

DEAR JOSEPHINE: Your letter came to me just as I was writing you of a plan I have been thinking of for weeks. I have decided not to go to college. Of course, it would be a great pleasure and, perhaps, I look upon life too seriously, as you often tell me; but I want to get to work, to feel that I am standing on my own feet, and four years seems an awful time to wait,—for that. What do you think? I do hope you understand just *what* I mean. It is very serious to me, the most serious thing in the world.

I'm glad you're having a good time.

Don't write such nonsense about Miss Dow; you know there's nothing in that direction. Do write and tell me what you think about my plan.

Faithfully yours,
JACK.

P. S. When are you going to send me that new photograph? I have only three of you now, a real one and two kodaks. I'm glad you're having a good time.

No sooner was this letter dispatched and Stover had realized what had been in his mind for weeks than he went to Tough McCarty to inform him of his high resolve.

"But, Dink," said Tough in dismay, "you can't be serious! Why, we were going through college together!"

"That's the hard part of it," said Dink, looking and, indeed, feeling very solemn.

"But you're giving up a wonderful career. Every one says you'll be a star end. You'll make the All-American. Oh, Dink!"

"Don't," said Dink heroically.

"But, I say, what's happened?"

"It's—it's a family matter," said Stover, who on such occasions, it will be perceived, had a strong family feeling.

"Is it decided?" said Tough in consternation.

"Unless stocks take a turn," said Dink.

McCarty was heartbroken, Dink rather pleased, with the new role that, somehow, lifted him from his fellows in dignity and seriousness and seemed to cut down the seven years. All that week he waited hopefully for her answer. She must understand now the inflexibility of his character and the intensity of his devotion. His letter told everything, and yet in such a delicate manner that she must honor him the more for the generous way in which he took everything upon himself, offered everything and asked nothing. He was so confidently happy and elated with the vexed decision of his affairs that he even took the Millionaire Baby over to the Jigger Shop and stood treat, after a few words of paternal advice which went unheeded.

Toward the beginning of the third week in the early days of November, as the squad was returning from practice Tough said casually:

"I say, did you get a letter from Sis?"

"No," said Dink with difficulty.

"You probably have one at the house. She's engaged."

"What?" said Dink faintly. The word seemed to be spoken from another mouth.

"Engaged to that Ver Plank fellow that was hanging around. I think he's a mutt."

"Oh, yes—Ver Plank."

"Gee, it gave me quite a jolt!"

"Oh, I—I rather expected it."

He left Tough, wondering how he had had the strength to answer.

"Look out, you're treading on my toes," said the Gutter Pup next him.

He mumbled something and his teeth closed over his tongue in the effort to bring the sharp sense of pain. He went to his box; the letter was there. He went to his room and laid it on the table, going to the window and staring out. Then he sat down heavily, rested his head in his hands and read:

THE VARMINT

DEAR JACK: I'm writing to you among the first, for I want you particularly to know how happy I am. Mr. Ver Plank——

He put the letter down; indeed, he could not see to read any further. There was nothing more to read—nothing mattered. It was all over, the light was gone, everything was topsy-turvy. He could not understand—but it was over—all over. There was nothing left.

Some time later the Tennessee Shad came loping down the hall, tried the door and, finding it locked, called out:

"What the deuce—open up!"

Dink, in terror, rose from the table where he had remained motionless. He caught up the letter and hastily stuffed it in his desk, saying gruffly:

"In a moment."

Then he dabbed a sponge over his face, pressed his hands to his temples and, steadying himself, unlocked the door.

"For the love of Mike!" said the indignant Tennessee Shad, and then, catching sight of Dink, stopped. "Dink, what is the matter?"

"It's—it's my mother," said Dink desperately.

"She's not dead?"

"No—no——" said Dink, now free to suffocate, "not yet."

XXV

This providential appearance of his mother mercifully allowed Dink an opportunity to suffer without fear of disgrace in the eyes of the unemotional Tennessee Shad.

That very night, as soon as the Shad had departed in search of Beekstein's guiding mathematical hand, Dink sat down heroically to frame his letter of congratulations. He would show her that, though she looked upon him as a boy, there was in him the courage that never cries out. She had played with him, but at least she should look back with admiration.

"Dear Miss McCarty," he wrote—that much he owed to his own dignity, and that should be his only reproach. The rest should be in the tone of levity, the smile that shows no ache.

DEAR MISS MCCARTY: Of course, it was no surprise to me. I saw it coming long ago. Mr. Ver Plank seems to me a most estimable young man. You will be very congenial, I am sure, and very happy. Thank you for letting me know among the first. That was *bully* of you! Give

THE VARMINT

my very best congratulations to Mr. Ver Plank and tell him I think he's a very lucky fellow.

Faithfully yours,
JACK.

He had resolved to sign formally "Cordially yours—John H. Stover." But toward the end his resolution weakened. He would be faithful, even if she were not. Perhaps, when she read it and thought it over she would feel a little remorse, a little acute sorrow. Imbued with the thought, he stood looking at the letter, which somehow brought a little consolation, a little pride into the night of his misery. It was a good letter—a very good letter. He read it over three times and then, going to the washstand, took up the sponge and pressed out a lachrymal drop that fell directly over the "Faithfully yours."

It made a blot that no one could have looked at unmoved.

He hastily sealed the letter and slipping out the house, went over and mailed it with his own hands. It was the farewell—he would never toil out his heart over another. And with it went John Stover, the faithful cavalier. Another John Stover had arisen, the man of heroic sorrows.

For a whole week faithfully he was true to his

grief, keeping his own company, eating out his heart, suffering as only that first deception can inflict sorrow. And he sought nothing else. He hoped—he hoped that he would go on suffering for years and years, saddened and deceived.

But, somehow—though, of course, deep down within him nothing would ever change—the gloom gradually lifted. The call of his fellows began to be heard again. The glances of the under formers that followed his public appearances with adoring worship began to please him once more.

Finally, one afternoon, he stopped in at Appleby's to inspect a new supply of dazzling cravats.

"You've got the first choice, Mr. Stover," said Appleby in his caressing way. "No one's had a look at them before you."

"Well, let's look 'em over," said Stover, with a beginning of interest.

"Look at them," said Appleby; "you're a judge, Mr. Stover. You know how to dress in a tasty way. Now, really, have you ever seen anything genteeler than them?"

Stover fingered them and his eye lit up. They certainly were exceptional and just the style that was becoming to his blond advantages. He selected six, then added two more and, finally, went to his room with a dozen, where he tried them, one after the other, before his mirror, smiling a little at the effect.

Then he went to his bureau and relegated the photograph of the future Mrs. Ver Plank to the rear and promoted Miss Dow to the place of honor.

"That's over," he said; "but she nearly ruined my life!"

In which he was wrong, for if Miss McCarty had not arrived Appleby, purveyor of Gents' Fancies, would never have sold him a dozen most becoming neckties.

When the Tennessee Shad came in, he looked in surprise.

"Hello, better news to-day?" he said sympathetically.

"News?" said Dink in a moment of abstraction.

"Why, your mother."

"Oh, yes—yes, she's better," said Dink hastily, and to make it convincing he added in a reverent voice, "thank God!"

The next day he informed McCarty that he had changed his mind. He was going to college; they would have four glorious years together.

"What's happened?" said Tough mystified. "Better news from home?"

"Yes," said Dink, "stocks have gone up."

But the tragedy of his life had one result that

came near wrecking his career and the school's hope for victory in the Andover game. During the early weeks of the term Dink had been too engrossed with his new responsibilities to study, and during the later weeks too overwhelmed by the real burden of life to think of such technicalities as lessons. Having studied the preferences and dislikes of his tyrants he succeeded, however, in bluffing through most of his recitations with the loyal support of Beekstein. But The Roman was not thus to be circumvented, and as Dink, in the Byronic period or grief, had no heart for florid improvisations of the applause of the multitude he contented himself, whenever annoyed by his implacable persecutor, The Roman, by rising and saying with great dignity:

"Not prepared, sir."

The blow fell one week before the Andover game, when such blows always fall. The Roman called him up after class and informed him that, owing to the paucity of evidence in his daily appearances, he would have to put him to a special examination to determine whether he had a passing knowledge.

The school was in dismay. A failure, of course, meant disbarment from the Andover game—the loss of Stover, who was the strength of the whole left side.

To Dink, of course, this extraordinary decree

THE VARMINT

was the crowning evidence of the determined hatred of The Roman. And all because he had, years before, mistaken him for a commercial traveler and called him "Old Cocky-wax!"

He would be flunked—of course he would be flunked if The Roman had made up his mind to do it. He might have waited another week—after the Andover game. But no, his plan was to keep him out the game, which of course, meant the loss of the captaincy, which every one accorded him.

These opinions, needless to say, were shared by all well-wishers of the eleven. There was even talk, in the first moments of excitement, of arraigning The Roman before the Board of Trustees.

The examination was to be held in The Roman's study that night. Beekstein and Gumbo hurried to Dink's assistance. But what could that avail with six weeks' work to cover!

In this desperate state desperate means were suggested by desperate characters. Stover should go the examination padded with interlinear, friendly aids to translation. A committee from outside should then convey the gigantic water cooler that stood in the hall to the upper landing. There it should be nicely balanced on the topmost step and a string thrown out the window, which, at the right time, should be pulled by three patriots from other Houses. The water cooler would descend with a hideous clatter, The Roman would rush from his study, and Stover would be given time to refresh his memory.

Now, Stover did not like this plan. He had never done much direct cribbing, as that species of deception made him uncomfortable and seemed devoid of the high qualities of dignity that should attend the warfare against the Natural Enemy.

At first he refused to enter this conspiracy, but finally yielded in a half-hearted way when it was dinned in his ears that he was only meeting The Roman at his own game, that he was being persecuted, that the school was being sacrificed for a private spite—in a word, that the end must be looked at and not the means and that the end was moral and noble.

Thus partly won over, Dink entered The Roman's study that night with portions of interlinear translations distributed about his person and whipped up into a rage against The Roman that made him forget all else.

The study was on the ground floor—the conspirators were to wait at the window until Stover should have received the examination paper and given the signal.

The Roman nodded as Stover entered and,

motioning him to a seat, gave him the questions, saying:

"I sincerely hope, John, you are able to answer these."

"Thank you, sir," said Stover with great sarcasm.

He went to the desk by the window and sat down, taking out his pencil.

There was a shuffling of feet and the scraping of a chair across the room. Stover looked up in surprise.

"Take your time, John," said The Roman, who had risen. Then, without another word, he turned and left the room.

Stover smiled to himself. He knew that trick. He waited for the sudden reopening of the door, but no noise came. He frowned and, mechanically looking at the questions, opened his book at the place designated. Then he raised his head and listened again.

All at once he became very angry. The Roman was putting him on his honor—he had no right to do any such thing! It changed all their preparations. It was a low-down, malignant trick. It took away all the elements of danger that glorified the conspiracy. It made it easy and, therefore, mean.

At the window came a timid scratching. Stover shook his head. The Roman would return. Then he would give the signal willingly. So he folded his arms sternly and waited—but no footsteps slipped along outside the door. The Roman had indeed left him to his honor.

A great, angry lump came in his throat, angry tears blurred his eyes. He hated The Roman, he despised him; it was unfair, it was malicious, but he could not do what he would have done. There *was* a difference.

All at once the bowels of the House seemed rent asunder, as down the stairs, bumping and smashing, went the liberated water cooler. Instantly a chorus of shrieks arose, steps rushing to and fro, and then quiet.

Still The Roman did not come. Stover glanced at the paragraphs selected, and oh, mockery and bitterness, two out of three happened to be passages he had read with Beekstein not an hour before. His eye went over them, he remembered them perfectly.

"If that ain't the limit!" he said, choking. "To know 'em after all. Of course, now I can't do 'em. Of course, now if I hand 'em in the old rhinoceros will think I cribbed 'em. Of all the original Jobs I am the worst! This is the last straw!"

When half an hour later The Roman returned Stover was sitting erect, with folded arms and lips compressed.

THE VARMINT

"Ah, Stover, all through?" said The Roman, as though the House had not just been blown asunder. "Hand in your paper."

Stover stiffly arose and handed him the foolscap. The Roman took it with a frowning little glance. At the top was written in big, defiant letters: "John H. Stover."

Below there was nothing at all.

Stover stood, swaying from heel to heel, watching The Roman.

"What the deuce is he looking at?" he thought in wonder, as The Roman sat silently staring at the blank sheet.

Finally he turned over the page, as though carefully perusing it, poised a pencil, and said in a low voice, without glancing up:

"Well, John, I think this will just about pass."

XXVI

The football season had ended victoriously. The next week brought the captaincy for the following year to Stover by unanimous approval. But the outlook for the next season was of the weakest; only four men would remain. The charge that he would have to lead would be a desperate one. This sense of responsibility was, perhaps, more acute in Stover than even the pleasure-giving sense of the attendant admiration of the school whenever he appeared among them.

Other thoughts, too, were working within him. Ever since the extraordinary outcome of his examination at the hands of The Roman Stover had been in a ferment of confusion. The Roman's action amazed, then perplexed, then doubly confounded him.

If The Roman was not his enemy, had not been all this time his persistent, malignant foe, what then? What was left to him to cling to? If he admitted this, then his whole career would have to be reconstructed. Could it be that, after all, month in and month out, it had been The Roman himself who had stood as his friend in all the hundred and one scrapes in which he had tempted Fate? And pondering on this gravely, Dink Stover, in the portion of his soul that was consecrated to fair play, was mightily exercised.

He consulted Tough McCarty, as he consulted him now on everything that lay deeper than the lip currency of his fellows. They were returning from a long walk over the early December roads in the grays and drabs of the approaching twilight. Stover had been unusually silent, and the mood settled on him, as, turning the hill, they saw the clustered skyline of the school through the bared branches.

"What the deuce makes you so solemncholy?" said Tough.

"I was thinking," said Dink with dignity.

"Excuse me."

"I was thinking," said Dink, rousing himself, "that I've been all wrong."

"I don't get that."

"I mean The Roman."

"How so?"

"Tough, you know down at the bottom I have a sneaking suspicion that he's been for me right along. It's a rotten feeling, but I'm afraid it's so."

"Shouldn't wonder. Have you spoken to him?"

THE VARMINT

"No."

"Why not?"

"I'm not sure. And then, I don't know just how to get to it."

"Jump right in and tackle him around the knees," said Tough.

"I think I will," said Dink, who understood the metaphor.

They went up swinging briskly, watching in silence the never stale spectacle of the panorama of the school.

"I say, Dink," said Tough suddenly, "Sis is going to put the clamps on that T. Willyboy, Ver Plank."

"Really—when?" said Dink, surprised that the news brought him no emotion.

"Next month."

Stover laughed a little laugh.

"You know," he said with a bit of confusion, "I fancied I was terribly in love with Josephine myself—for a little while."

"Sure," said Tough without surprise. "Jo would flirt with anything that had long pants on."

"Yes, she's a flirt," said Stover, and the judgment sounded like the swish of shears cutting away angels' wings.

They separated at the campus and Stover went toward the Kennedy. Half-way there an excited little urchin came rushing up, pulling off his cap.

"Well, what is it, youngster?" said Stover, who didn't recognize him.

"Please, sir," said the young hero worshiper, producing a photograph of the team from under his jacket, "would you mind putting your name on this? I should be awfully obliged."

Stover took it and wrote his name.

"Who is this?"

"Williams, Jigs Williams, sir, over in the Cleve."

"Well, Jigs, there you are."

"Oh, thank you. Say——"

"Well?"

"Aren't you going to have an individual photograph?"

"No, of course not," said Stover with only outward gruffness.

"All the fellows are crazy for one, sir."

"Run along, now," said Stover with a pleased laugh. He stood on the steps, watching the elated Jigs go scudding across the Circle, and then went into the Kennedy. In his box was a letter of congratulation from Miss Dow. He read it smiling, and then took up the photograph and examined it more critically.

"She's a dear little girl," he said. "Devilish smart figure."

THE VARMINT

Miss Dow, of course, was very young. She was only twenty.

That night, after an hour's brown meditation, he suddenly rose and, descending the stairs, knocked at the sanctum sanctorum.

"Come in," said the low, musical voice.

Stover entered solemnly.

"Ah, it's you, John," said The Roman with a smile.

"Yes, sir, it's me," said Stover, leaning up against the door.

The Roman glanced up quickly and, seeing what was coming, took up the paper-cutter and began to twist it through his fingers. There was a silence, long and painful.

"Well?" said The Roman in a queer voice.

"Mr. Hopkins," said Dink, advancing a step. "I guess I've been all wrong. I haven't come to you before, as I suppose I ought, because I've had to sort of think it over. But now, sir, I've come in to have it out."

"I'm glad you have, John."

"I want to ask you one question."

"Yes?"

"Have you, all this time, really been standing by me, yanking me out of all the messes I got in?"

"Well, that expresses it, perhaps."

"Then I've been way off," said Stover solemnly. "Why, sir, all this time I thought you were down on me, had it in for me, right from the first."

"From our first meeting?" said The Roman, with a little chuckle. "Perhaps, John, you didn't give me credit—shall I say, for a sense of humor?"

"Yes, sir." Stover looked a moment at his polished boot and then resolutely at The Roman. "Mr. Hopkins, I've been all wrong. I've been unfair, sir; I want to apologize to you."

"Thank you," said The Roman, and then because they were Anglo-Saxons they shook hands and instantly dropped them.

"Mr. Hopkins," said Stover after a moment, "I must have given you some pretty hard times?"

"You were always full of energy, John."

"I don't see what made you stand by me, sir."

"John," said The Roman, leaning back and caging his fingers, "it is a truth which it is, perhaps, unwise to publish abroad, and I shall have to swear you to the secret. It is the boy whose energy must explode periodically and often disastrously, it is the boy who gives us the most trouble, who wears down our patience and tries our souls, who is really the most worth while."

"Not the high markers and the gospel

sharks?" said Stover, too amazed to choose the classic line.

"Sh!" said the Roman, laying his finger on his lips.

Stover felt as though he held the secret of kings.

"And now, John," said The Roman in a matter-of-fact tone, "since you are behind the scenes, one thing more. The real teacher, the real instructor, is not I, it is you. We of the Faculty can only paint the memory with facts that are like the writing in the sand. The real things that are learned are learned from you. Now, forgive me for being a little serious. You are a leader. It is a great responsibility. They're all looking up at you, copying you. You set the standard; set a manly one."

"I think, sir, I've tried to do that—lately," said Stover, nodding.

"And now, in the House—bring out some of the younger fellows."

"Yes, sir."

"There's Norris. Perhaps a little serious talk—only a word dropped."

"You're right, sir; I understand what you mean."

"Then there's Berbecker."

"He's only a little fresh, sir; there's good stuff in him."

THE VARMINT

"And then, John, there's a boy who's been under early disadvantages, but a bright boy, full of energy, good mind, but needs to be taken in hand, with a little kindness."

"Who, sir?"

"Bellefont."

"Bellefont!" said Stover, exploding. "I beg your pardon, sir. You're wrong there. That kid is hopeless. Nothing will do him any good. He's a perfect little nuisance. He's a thoroughgoing, out-and-out little varmint!"

The Roman tapped the table and, looking far out through the darkened window, smiled the gentle smile of one who has watched the ever-recurrent miracle of humanity, the struggling birth of the man out of the dirtied, hopeless cocoon of the boy.

And Stover, suddenly beholding that smile, all at once stopped, blushed and understood!

THE END

www.ingramcontent.com/pod-product-compliance
Lightning Source LLC
Chambersburg PA
CBHW030214170426
43201CB00006B/85